MICROWAVE EXPERIMENT:

A STORY OF

GOVERNMENT TESTING

ON A

UNITED STATES CUSTOMS OFFICER

Mary Efrosini Gregory

Published by:
Credos Books
An imprint of:
Trine Day LLC
PO Box 577
Walterville, OR 97489
1-800-556-2012
www.CredosBooks.com

Library of Congress Control Number: 2011934072

Gregory, Mary Efrosini
Microwave Experiment: A True Story Of Government Testing On A United States Customs Office—1st ed.
p. cm.

Print (ISBN-13) 978-1-936296-24-8 (ISBN-10)   1-936296-24-1

FIRST EDITION
10 9 8 7 6 5 4 3 2 1

Printed in the USA
Distribution to the Trade by:
Independent Publishers Group (IPG)
814 North Franklin Street
Chicago, Illinois 60610
312.337.0747
www.ipgbook.com

Publisher's Foreword

When I get to the bottom
I go back to the top of the slide
Where I stop and turn
and I go for a ride
Till I get to the bottom
and I see you again
Yeah, yeah, yeah

— Paul McCartney, *Helter Skelter*

Welcome to America, 2011, home of the free, brave and downright strange. This is our second book under our Credos imprint, where we serve up beliefs rather than the usual fare of begats, facts and alternative viewpoints.

Microwave Experiment enters a world beyond nightmares, one of madness and uncertainity, where discernment can drop away, leaving distress and paranoia questing for answers, validation and survival.

The study of covert behavior modification (mind control) is fraught with much mis- and disinformation, and one begins inquiries with skeptic trepidation. Having delved into the subject and having found, yes, some spooks and kooks, one also finds many sincere individuals with very compelling accounts of abuse, plus scholarly inquiries validating the reality of this sordid phenomena.

Within in this milieu, microwave harassment is one of the most pernicious. A slight amount of covert provocation is quite enough to drive folks, literally, right out of their minds.

I was personally acquainted with a case where an officer-of-the-court stumbled upon the spoor of a covert narcotics operation, and though this person, initially, wasn't connecting any dots – strange incidents began befalling. Once the assault starts, a familiar pattern develops: educating oneself about microwave harassment, paranoia, and desire to tell the world. We tried to bring that story to press, but time's toll was steep and every attempt got snarled in the disturbance brought on by the harassment. It is a very vicious cycle – once bitten, twice shy.

Several times we thought we were close to a publishing agreement, but the downward spiral of the person's life stopped any publication.

With *Microwave Experiment*, we may finally enter the nightmare. Throughout this horror Mary Gregory successfully served in US Customs for thirty years and has published three books on the French Enlightenment and two on Orthodox Christianity, since her retirement in 2008.

This is her story. I was not there to experience it. The technology is available and anecdotal evidence says that women, especially Federal workers have been the main targets. Gregory says that the Pentagon sent an electromagnetic pulse through the brick wall of her building and broke a piece of her cranium, burned a hole through her lower left eyelid, punctured her skin, riddled aluminum tarpaulins with thousands of pinholes, decimated walls and ceilings; she submitted 2,000 hi-def photographs to me. The mainstream media provides only a whisper of this: through-the-wall imaging has been reported in Boston; roving vans that view into homes patrol our cities; Nevada DMV is drawing up rules for driverless cars. Gregory says that her way to fight back is to inform us of the military's domestic occupation.

Gregory at the end of a protracted process rejected our's editng suggestions, and asks her tale told as she has written it, taking the reader directly into her world.

At least we are simply visiting and are not trapped within her ordeal. The officer-of-the court, mentioned earlier, also after much work would not allow her manuscript changed in any way.

So, we are left to simply presenting Gregory's words and pictures – letting the reader decide.

Onwards to the Utmost of Futures

Peace,
Kris Millegan
Publisher
TrineDay
June 21, 2011

Contents

Preface 1

Introduction 3

A Summary of the Untimely Deaths in the U.S. Customs Service
1978–200 37

The Carter Years (1977–1980) 41

The Reagan Years (1981–1988) 57

The Reign of King George I (1989–1992) 77

The Clinton Years (1993–2000) 93

The Reign of Terror of King George II: The First Year (2001) 111

The Reign of Terror of King George II: The Second and Third Years
(2002–2003) 141

The Reign of Terror of King George II: The Fourth Year (2004) 157

The Reign of Terror of King George II: The Fifth Year (2005) 181

The Reign of Terror of King George II: The Sixth Year (2006) 211

The Reign of Terror of King George II: The Seventh Year (2007) .275

The Reign of Terror of King George II: The Eighth Year (2008) 297

Conclusion 299

Timeline 307

Preface

The military seeks to create the perfect warrior: one who accepts adversity and aggravation with complacency and docility; one who remains focused and composed in the midst of confusion; one who becomes energized and aggressive in battle. Electromagnetic waves, proven to cause chemical changes in the brain, can deliver all of this and much more. As you read my narrative, pay attention to the multiple threads that run throughout: my coworkers and I are continually dosed, as is evidenced by the electromagnetic phenomena that reverberate around us, deaths, and obsessive-compulsive disorders; we remain docile and indifferent even as targets act out and create distractions around us; we are focused and composed despite chatter and metallic noises; we can be depended upon to perform our tasks with obsessive care, scouring the minutiae of invoices to collect the maximum duty for the government, and arrive and depart on time like finely tuned Swiss watches.

I switch the lens of magnification from the microcosm (my office, home, neighbors) to the macrocosm (international events) and back again to show how microwave war is being exploited at every level and is being used against sovereign nations. Pay attention to world events as they unfold during my 30-year career: the US continually imposes its will abroad and commits atrocities to promote Empire. As RF science advances, the Pentagon begins to commit new kinds of slaughter using electromagnetic pulse attacks. Hence forth, you will view earthquakes, cyclones, volcanoes, roof collapses, subterranean pipe explosions, train signal fires, and brushfires with new eyes as you discover that in 1996 the Air Force published a compendium of papers in which it brags that by 2025 the US will "own the weather" and that this can be effected via the electromagnetic disruption of the ionosphere. Pay attention to the warnings of Senator Claiborne Pell in 1975 and Secretary of Defense William Cohen in 1997 about eco-terrorism, altering the climate, creating earthquakes and setting off volcanoes with EMs.

Thus, the experiments to which the federal employees in this book have been subjected are intimately intertwined with politics, current events, and natural disasters carefully crafted to bully, intimidate, enslave, and exploit. Today's experimentation on Americans will guarantee military superiority tomorrow.

I did not get paid to write this book, nor will I accept any royalty or financial remuneration. I just want to public to know the criminal ways that our intelligence agencies are using their funding and technology.

Pseudonyms have been used to protect the privacy of the survivors and families of the deceased.

One might think that perhaps this narrative is a vociferous call to initiate congressional investigations. Unfortunately, any investigation would merely be a dog and pony show. Moreover, such proceedings would not be covered by the media. The way to stop this is to vote incumbents out and support only those candidates who promise to cut all funding to the military and intelligence agencies. The upper echelons of the Pentagon cannot be trusted to use their technology in an ethical manner.

—Mary Efrosini Gregory, Rego Park, February 14, 2011

Introduction

I may not have a scepter, but I have a pen.[1]
—François-Marie Arouet de Voltaire, *Letter to Madame Denis* (October 15, 1752)

America has a long sordid history of experimenting on its citizens, most often with neither their consent, nor knowledge. This fact has been well documented and there exists a large body of literature on the subject. Read Michael Christopher Carroll, *Lab 257: The Disturbing Story of the Government's Secret Plum Island Germ Laboratory*, to learn how we were infected with Lyme disease and West Nile virus, courtesy of the USDA on Plum Island. Carroll uncovers the fact that the Nazi germ warfare scientist, Erich Traub, emigrated here after WW II under Operation Paperclip and was affiliated with both Fort Detrick and Plum Island.

The titles of other books also betray the nefarious government experiments recounted therein: Andrew Goliszek, *In the Name of Science: A History of Secret Programs, Medical Research, and Human Experimentation*; Allen M. Hornblum, *Acres of Skin: Human Experiments at Holmesburg Prison: A Story of Abuse and Exploitation in the Name of Medical Science*; James H. Jones, *Bad Blood: The Tuskegee Syphilis Experiment*; Jack Kevorkian, "A Brief History of Experimentation on Condemned and Executed Humans" in the *Journal of the American Medical Association*; Jonathan D. Moreno, *Undue Risk: Secret State Experiments on Humans*; Eileen Welsome's Pulitzer Prize winning book, *The Plutonium Files: America's Secret Medical Experiments in the Cold War*. These are just a few examples—to cite a complete bibliography of the multitudinous disclosures of the Nazi-style experiments that the Pentagon has conducted on Americans would fill a volume in itself.

Moreover, these experiments were not always conducted on Americans: sometimes they were performed in Canada. Naomi Klein, in *The Shock Doctrine: The Rise of Disaster Capitalism*, describes the Nazi-style electroshock experiments that Ewen Cameron of McGill University conducted on his victim, Gail Kastner, under the auspices of the CIA.[2] Delivering 150–200 shocks to her body 63 times, he succeeded in annihilating her memory "while her body convulsed violently on the table, causing fractures, sprains, bloody lips, broken teeth;"[3] drugs were administered; other results were radical personality change, baby talk, and incontinence. These experiments were funded in Canada from 1957 until 1961 through money laundering because "if word got out that the CIA was testing dangerous drugs on American soil, the entire program could be shut down."[4]

The hubris with which the United States military conducts recklessly dangerous experiments on its soldiers is a proven fact: there is a Supreme Court case on this subject. In *United States v. Stanley* an army sergeant sued the government for putting LSD in his food during the Vietnam War to ascertain the effect that it would have on him. The majority of the Supreme Court justices ruled against the plaintiff: the majority opinion held that the U.S. military is not compelled to divulge its secrets, thereby defeating the victim and giving the Pentagon blanket authority to conduct any kind of testing it wants, as long as it is kept secret. However, quite significantly, in a dissenting opinion, Justice Sandra Day O'Connor valiantly stated that if this one man is not safe, then no one is safe. Hence, this court case underscores just how critical the choice of who sits on the High Court is to the safety of Americans.

Let us not forget that in 1945 the U.S. gave American citizenship to and recruited thousands of Nazi scientists for secret projects including germ warfare (Project Paperclip). It is also a documented fact that the U.S. government experimented on its Navy when, in 1962–1973, the Pentagon tested chemical and biological weapons on 4,300 Navy personnel (Project Shipboard Hazard or Project SHAD). The government also experimented on prisoners: in 1965 inmates at the Holmesburg State Prison in Philadelphia were exposed to dioxin in order to ascertain whether it causes cancer. Not even unsuspecting New Yorkers commuting to work were immune from such assaults: in 1966 the DoD casts light bulbs containing *Bacillus subtilis* into three New York City subway stations to see if it could theoretically kill a million passengers. The prodigious documentation on the subject indicates that the Pentagon usually preys on single women, the handicapped, hospital patients, prisoners, and military personnel. It prefers to choose single women in particular as test subjects because the Nazis conducting these experiments consider single women to be marginal citizens and also because when people live alone, there are no witnesses present to provide corroborating testimony in court.

Therefore, let us begin with a summary of my ordeal. When I landed a job in the United States Customs Service, I had no idea that one day, as a career woman living alone, I would join the ranks of the countless American citizens who have been subjected to physiologically and psychologically damaging stimuli that would be applied for the purpose of enhancing and perfecting the Pentagon's arsenal of microwave weaponry. I became, what experimenters in the intelligence community call, a targeted individual (TI). This government testing consisted of subjecting federal employees to microwave radiation over the course of 30 years and then carefully gauging changes in behavior and any manifestations of disease that occurred.

Thirty years ago, doors in offices in the World Trade Center were unlocked with skeleton keys at night so that operatives from another agency, most certainly acting on behalf of the Pentagon, could enter and set up experiments with microwave technology and germ warfare. However, more recently, with the advent of electronic doors that require a pass embedded with one or more microchips, sophisticated electronic doors in Customs offices were knocked out with jammers at night so that secret operatives could enter the worksite and set up their experiments.

The first evidence that I found of such experimentation was provided by the loud crackles, pings, and taps that reverberated off the desks, filing cabinets, bookcases, and textile-covered modular walls of the Customhouse at 6 World Trade Center. After 9/11 my division was relocated elsewhere. At the new site, not only did the electrostatic pops and crackles continue, but over the years they increased in intensity until finally, I was receiving deep burn marks in my skin and the sensation of a tiny dagger piercing the top of my head. These physical assaults were always accompanied by thunderous, angry, vociferous electrostatic snapping sounds, evidence that Customs employees were continually bathed in a highly dense microwave environment, a phenomenon that significantly, was never experienced on other floors occupied by private industry.

Concurrently, my coworkers, after having been subjected to these phenomena for 30 years, began to develop exotic diseases, cancers and the strangest obsessive-compulsive disorders I have ever seen. Moreover, single women were usually the victims. An examination of the demographics of the morbidity stats indicates that single women, the handicapped, and Jewish employees were the ones who suddenly died, developed all kinds of cancers and exotic diseases (such as progressive supranuclear palsy or PSP) and OCD.

The next thing that happened was that I noticed that the government had very strategically and methodically placed paintings on the wall, spaced only a few feet apart, so that we were completely surrounded by wall hangings. After 9/11, the Federal Emergency Management Agency (FEMA) donated dozens of paintings to Customs and the supervisors not only displayed them, but they bolted them to the wall so that one could not move the paintings, not even an inch, to look behind them.

Subsequently I purchased a radio-frequency detector (bug detector) and ascertained that of the approximately 60 paintings on the walls of my floor, all but two were bugged. It was after I articulated my concern that such paintings were sold on the Internet as surveillance cameras and my subsequent discovery of outgoing radio signals from the paintings, that my life became a living hell. I decided to write this book after I received a violent shock to the top of my head, so strong in fact, that it chipped a tiny fragment of my cranium.

On August 7, 2006 I was sitting at home, at the foot of my bed, correcting the galleys to my first book, *Diderot and the Metamorphosis of Species*. I was hoping to present the published book to the French Department at Columbia University in fulfillment of the dissertation requirement for the Ph.D degree. As I was seated at the foot of the bed, hunched over a plastic tray containing paperwork, I was struck from overhead by a violent and piercing blow to my crown. Suddenly my consciousness exploded into a miasma of yellow light, my heart momentarily stopped beating for a second or two, and I desperately gasped for air, much like a fish frantically gasps for air as it thrashes about, when it is pulled out of water. When I regained my breath, I was overwhelmed by a throbbing pain in my crown. It felt as if a dagger had pierced my skull and had penetrated my brain. When I touched the top of my head, the contact of my fingertips, as light as it was, caused a wave of pain to course throughout my head. As I lay across the foot of the bed, I was vaguely aware that a huge jumbo jet was flying directly overhead.

I wondered where this electronic assault could have come from. Could it have originated from the apartment upstairs? There was no one was living above me: the woman who rented the apartment directly above lived outside of New York State and used her dwelling in Rego Park to warehouse antiques for her family-owned business. Was there someone else in her apartment doing this through the ceiling?

I arose from the bed, stumbled over to the window, and peered outside. Could this assault have originated from an apartment across the alleyway? I had no idea what kind of electronic devices my neighbors were harboring in their homes.

I gazed up at the TV antennae situated just behind the roof ledges. There were two large antennae pointing at the entire length of my apartment—the kitchen, living room, bedroom, and bathroom. Did a powerful signal emanate from them? Were they transmitting radio waves as well as receiving them?

I staggered into the bathroom. Leaning towards the mirror, I tilted the crown of my head downward and very gently parted my hair. The skin was as red as a beet. Moreover, there was something sharp and hard that was protruding from my skull. A very tiny part of my cranium had been fractured and it was pointing upwards. As I repeatedly brought my fingers back to that one spot, I was certain that something sharp was jutting up.

Today I understand that my skull had been nicked by a powerful laser pulse delivered aerially: on September 29, 2009 (1–2 PM), October 16, 2009 (5:15 AM), October 30, 2009 (8–10 PM), October 31, 2009 (5–9 AM), November 9, 2009 (1:45 AM), and December 19, 2009 (3:15–3:25 AM), aluminum shielding in my apartment was thoroughly rifled with holes by a NORTHCOM aircraft hovering directly above my apartment building. The military has the ability to pierce metal through walls and concrete and today it is attacking persons and their property on domestic soil using technology that was thought to have been developed for the military theater abroad.

The physics involved is like that of decimating kidney stones on the other side of a barrier with a focused beam of ultrasound. In lithotripsy, first the target is imaged from a distance; then an electropulse penetrates barriers such as flesh, ribcage and organs, leaving them intact; then the pulsed beam destroys the target lying at a point beyond them. This procedure has been available since the early 1980s.

It was fortunate that I had already taken a shower that afternoon. The next day when I stepped under the showerhead, the throbbing was so overwhelming that I could not bear to let the stream of water hit the wound. The area on my crown remained bright crimson and the pain lasted for an entire week.

This book will enumerate and describe every kind of electronic assault that I have experienced in my office at my federal worksite, as well as the electronic attacks that dozens of my neighbors residing in Queens and I have suffered inside our apartments, on the streets of Queens and Manhattan, and in subway stations. When I began discussing these microwave onslaughts with my neighbors, I was astounded to hear that many of them have been experiencing them, too. The victims are usually people living alone, the handicapped, and Jews—these demographics are deeply disturbing as they are reminiscent of Nazi Germany. Moreover, it indicates that U.S. government experimentation on American citizens is much more widespread than most people suspect. If these attacks are occurring in New York City, they must be transpiring in other metropoli as well, where people are transient and immigrants are not likely to write letters of complaint to their congressional representatives. Big cities are the best places for the Nazis that infest the Pentagon to conduct their human experiments. They can gather and collate huge amounts of data that can be garnered only from burgeoning populations. Because these residents are immigrant and transient, discovery and exposure to the media is minimized.

Many of my neighbors and I have been getting violent electronic shocks to the body both in our sleep and while fully awake. In my case, the electronic assaults began as pinpricks, tiny burn marks to the skin that occurred at work and at home. Eventually they escalated to electrical shocks to the brain that were so pronounced, they caused my head to involuntarily jerk from left to right. Then I started getting electrical whacks to the back of my head while standing outdoors reading a newspaper. This happens seconds before a commercial airline passes by overhead. That is why I am led to believe that the Pentagon has made an arrangement with commercial carriers to carry microwave/laser pulse technology that permits the military to image and conduct strikes remotely from a distant location, Nevada being one such site. When I question my neighbors and cashiers working in nearby shops, many admit that they are victimized by such electronic attacks on a nightly basis.

It was not until seven years after the electronic assaults began, that I learned how the government generates these phenomena: the U.S. military has laser pulse weapons and high-powered microwave (HPM) technology that can image inside buildings and vehicles and deliver nonlethal blows to the people inside from airplanes that are passing by at a distance. During the 1970s the Russians boasted that they could kill a goat at a distance of one kilometer with radio waves; the Pentagon had been experimenting with this science since the 1960s.[5] The third book of this *Microwave* trilogy, *The Science behind Microwave War*, chronicles the history of the weaponization of electromagnetic waves.

The town of Rego Park is situated in New York City's borough of Queens, roughly midway between LaGuardia and JFK. It lies directly in the descent path of the planes headed for LaGuardia. Gargantuan 767 jumbo jets continually pass over our apartment buildings every few minutes as they fly north, make a swerve, and then make their gradual descent towards the runway. In addition, military aircraft take off from a nearby army base in Brooklyn every night after dark. Military planes and black helicopters are also frequently seen during the day circling around various towns in Queens; my neighbors and I have witnessed a black military helicopter circling our block in the daytime for hours at a clip. They are equipped with microwave/laser pulse technology that permits the Pentagon to image and strike people in their homes and vehicles via a network from a remote location. This is done at night or above artificially created cloud cover during the day. Queens has been the site of continuous weather modification experiments for several years. First we see white streaks across the sky; the next day it rains. The clouds are not naturally occurring clouds, they are white dots or larger wads that recur across the sky with absolute mathematical precision. This betrays the fact that electrically charged particles have been brought together by a spray of aluminum, barium and cadmium crystals and/or ionization of the upper atmosphere. The white chemtrails quickly dissipate into a thick, impenetrable haze that permits military aircraft to remain ever present, unobserved, unphotographed, but heard. I have also witnessed the sky go from black to white in the space of one half hour.

It is significant that many of electronic assaults that my neighbors and I suffer occur at the precise moment that commercial airplanes, not military, are approaching our buildings. All of us can accurately and flawlessly predict when a commercial plane will make an overpass simply by the pinpricks and shocks that we experience: the physical assaults occur within one minute of an overpass. People suffer tiny burn marks to the skin; electrostatic whacks against the back of the head that feel like foam plastic bats striking the body; a tap on the blanket at night; a moving wave that travels either laterally or longitudinally across the top of the blanket; an electrical shock to the heart that causes it to momentarily stop beating and results in the victim gasping for air; an electrical shock to the brain that causes the victim to see yellow light; loud angry snaps and taps reverberating off wooden floors, walls, ovens, sinks, refrigerators; a blast of sound that explodes in midair, inches from the ear; a powerful thud that drops on the blanket from above; an involuntary tremor that lasts for one second in which the entire body shakes from head to toe; a dagger penetrating an organ in the torso or an arm or leg.

The question arises as to whether these phenomena are being caused by 1) electronics aboard commercial carriers and/or 2) military aircraft flying at high altitude, 65,000–70,000 feet above the ground. One must deduce that both choices are true. Since I began researching this issue, I have discovered that military antipersonnel aircraft that is small, the size of a missile, whose electronics are bonded onto its skin, and that is equipped with high-powered microwave weapons, is fully capable of effecting powerful strikes from a high altitude.

The reason that I hold that the origin of the phenomena is often military aircraft is because I have been keeping a log and the assaults to my body continued during the major snowstorm of March 1–2, 2009, when commercial aircraft were grounded at La Guardia, JFK, and Newark Airports. As the heavy snowstorm raged outside my window, local radio stations repeatedly announced that planes had been grounded at all three major airports: nonetheless, the continual and persistent buzzing of an aircraft overhead continued throughout the night. Concurrently, I suffered electrical shocks to my body and heard snaps and taps ricochet off my wooden floors, walls, and kitchen appliances; the following morning there were fresh gashes in my walls and paint and plaster on the floor. The military was imaging for human beings in every room in my apartment. I was not in the bedroom: I had dismantled my bed and moved the mattress to the hallway floor. There, while lying on the floor beneath my blankets, in a very narrow corridor between the front door and the kitchen wall, I heard violent taps and crackles lash against the wooden flooring in every room in the apartment. There were pings reverberating off of every appliance in the kitchen. The paint and plaster was falling in the living room and bedroom. I received burn marks to my skin and electrical shocks to my body. It is highly significant that all of this happened, repeatedly and persistently throughout the night, when it was too dangerous for commercial airplanes to fly. It was a military aircraft, emitting the buzzing of a helicopter, originating from the nearby army base in Brooklyn, conducting imaging and strikes in my home.

There it is: a summary of my ordeal this past decade. In October 2001 I began getting tiny burn marks to my skin when seated in my new Customs office. By 2004 I was getting electrical shocks to my brain in my apartment. Since these electronic attacks began, the violent shocks have very gradually increased in force and in frequency. The shocks to the brain cause my head to involuntarily jerk from left to right; the assaults to my chest cavity cause my heart to momentarily stop beating and I gasp for air; sometimes my whole body involuntarily moves, from head to toe, for one second. These assaults always occur with 60 seconds before a commercial jet flies overhead or at night when a helicopter continually buzzes overhead. The origin is both commercial and military aircraft.

On Saturday, November 1, 2008, at about 10:30 AM I received an electrostatic blow to the back of my head on a sidewalk in Rego Park. I stopped walking, instinctively covered the back of my head with my palm, and looked up. Two seconds later, a small plane appeared over the apartment building behind where I stood. It resembled the dozens of such planes that I have since photographed between 5–7 AM from my roof, on Tuesday and Friday mornings, when cars are most frequently stolen, aerial surveillance is conducted, thieves are nabbed, and electronic shocks to the brain and heart proliferate. Clearly, the overt purpose is crime stopping from the air; this book delves into the covert purpose—causing cancer aerially by repeatedly targeting the lymph nodes in the armpits, groin and around the mouth.

At other times, it is commercial airplanes that emerge over the rooftops seconds after an electronic shock. Hence, I must necessarily extrapolate that commercial carriers have made an agreement with the military, under the rubric of "homeland security," to be outfitted with black ops technology that permits the military to image and strike people from a remote location, in real time, via a network. It is probable that the people in the commercial airline industry who agreed to carry the equipment have no idea what the Nazis in the Pentagon are doing with it. It is also highly probable that in addition, the military is conducting strikes via unmanned drones flying at an altitude of 65,000–70,000 feet and that it is using commercial planes as a distraction.

The notion of fighting a war from a distant site is nothing new. By inserting the phrase "air force 2025" in your search engine, you will be able to read the Air Force training document entitled, *Air Force 2025*. This book was written in 1996 as an instruction tool to train Air Force personnel at the Air Force's Air University, located at Maxwell-Gunter Air Force Base, Alabama. The document explicitly states that in the future, wars will be waged from a remote location using unmanned aircraft in the military theater. Therefore, all any aircraft needs is laser pulse high-powered microwave (HPM) weapons and the ability to receive and transmit data to a remote location where the decision to strike is made in real time.

The technology that was anticipated in that 1996 Air Force document is here now and has become ubiquitous. David A. Fulghum, in an article entitled, "Wonder Weapons; U.S. Army Plans Computer-Attack Devices, Directed-

Energy Weapons for the Front Line," published in *Aviation Week & Space Technology*, on October 10, 2005, discusses two items that the US government was developing as the article was going to press. The first weapon generates high-powered microwave pulses that can skew the electronics in cars, planes, radio and television stations, and power plants. The second weapon is a laser that generates a plasma that permits the user to look inside a building or vehicle and identify everyone and everything inside.[6] This technology is so sophisticated and the imaging is so precise, that the user is able to discern an armed individual from an unarmed one. Keep in mind that the imaging is performed from the equipment on an airplane flying at a distance; the decision to strike is made from a remote location in real time. The Pentagon acknowledges that since this article was written in 2005, these weapons have been developed, tested, and are currently being used in the military theaters of Iraq and Afghanistan. What the Pentagon will not admit, but my experience and that of my neighbors in Queens indicates, is that this weaponry is being used against unsuspecting, non-consenting American citizens on domestic soil.

Laser pulse weapons can do much more than generate pictures to a site at a remote location. They can deliver a stunning blow long distance to a target on the other side of a barrier such as a brick wall. They can strike the cranium and nick a piece from it; this feels like one has been stabbed in the crown with a dagger. In other attacks, the victim feels as if he has been struck with a heavy blanket. A particularly vicious form of assault is that which delivers a powerful electrical shock to the brain that causes the head and/or the entire body to involuntarily move for one second. I have received many such electronic shocks, both asleep and awake, that cause my head to involuntarily jerk from left to right or my entire body to shudder for one second. When directed at the heart, the laser pulse wave causes the heart to momentarily stop beating and the victim gasps for air.

This has happened to me many times, always as an aircraft approached my building. Because HPM and laser pulse technology has existed and has been used domestically for a number of years now, innumerable Queens residents can corroborate that they have been victimized by it as they sit or sleep in their homes.

The U.S. government prefers to conduct its experiments on women living alone because there are no witnesses present to testify in court. Furthermore, it is believed that women make ideal test subjects because they have been hardwired over millennia of evolution to stay at home and be submissive; their brains are hardwired to be sensitive to the verbal messages of another (ie: the cries of their babies). Conversely, men have spent millions of years banding together, going out, hunting for food, killing animals, dragging them home, and using teamwork to accomplish their tasks; it is now known that risk taking is associated with testosterone levels. In short, human males are hardwired to get the job done. In the event of an electronic assault, taking action would entail writing to congressmen, hiring lawyers to sue, and notifying the media to get maximum publicity. Female test subjects are believed to be less likely to go out into the world, assemble with others, take action, sue, and expose the culprits. They are considered to be ideal experimental mice. Moreover, the Nazis conducting these experiments consider single women to be marginal citizens, as they do the handicapped, mental patients, hospital patients, prisoners, those in veterans' hospitals, and military personnel.

The government selected me to be a lab mouse because federal employees make ideal test subjects: they can be relied upon to work in the same place for 30 years and thus they can be observed long term; federal employees rarely quit their jobs; they are much less likely to relocate to another city than are people working for private industry. Furthermore, my psychological profile is such that I am too good an opportunity to pass up: I am afraid of change, I resist moving out of my apartment, and so I can be watched, even after I retire, for the rest of my life. Risk-taking during my youth culminated in disaster and that was how I learned to resist change at all costs: my brief stint at the Bronx High School of Science was a disaster; I could not do anything with my M. Phil in French from Columbia; I could not garner a teaching appointment in French because there was no demand for French teachers; the only way that I could support myself and be independent was to become a paper-pushing bureaucrat.

I briefly worked as a Customs Aide at JFK Airport and then procured a transfer to the World Trade Center. Even as early as January 1978 I heard violent snaps and lashes emanating from empty rooms at the JFK site. My coworkers explained that the steam pipes housed inside the metal frames in the windowsills could be noisy at times. The sounds always originated in an empty room when I was seated alone in an adjacent office; they did not sound like typical steam pipe grumbling. The sounds that I heard were deafening, violent strikes against glass windows and metal filing cabinets. Furthermore, I was certain that they had descended down from the ceiling, not arose up from a steam pipe concealed beneath a windowsill.

After my transfer to the World Trade Center, I encountered more violent sounds emanating from empty rooms—distinctive snaps against metal filing cabinets, the sides of metal desks, and acrylic-covered modular walls. Back then I was not yet aware that these thunderous crackles provided evidence of a highly charged, extremely dense electromagnetic environment and that my coworkers and I were virtually getting our brains fried in a microwave oven. Eventually I connected the EMs to the proliferation of deaths, serious debilitating diseases, and psychological aberrations that became manifest among the employees.

There were plenty of psyops in the Customhouse during the Carter years: lights were found turned on in offices in the morning when employees were certain that they had snapped them off the night before. Ashes were found strewn across the floor in offices in which no employee smoked. One morning a room had been found locked and a huge desk was pulled up just behind it: the intruder had exited the room from the vents in the ceiling during the night.

Employees were just beginning to exhibit psychological and physical disorders: two employees continually talked to themselves all day long and could not stop; they had lost their impulse control and constantly articulated their stream of consciousness as they performed their work; one woman chain-smoked from morning until night. One woman who lived alone developed lupus, an autoimmune disorder, and almost died; she retired on a disability at an early age. She was merely the first in a long line such as herself: in the years ahead I met dozens more single women who acquired debilitating autoimmune diseases, died suddenly, died at a young age after a short term illness, or developed serious obsessive-compulsive disorders, some of which led to death.

During the Reagan years, I first met many single people in the Customhouse who would one day die suddenly and mysteriously. Edmund lived with his mother; after 9/11 his mother suddenly died and he, too, soon after that. Karlton lived with his mother; she died and he did, too, soon thereafter. Jeanne had a heart attack and placed a hot iron on her chest to make the pain go away; her body was discovered with the iron still on her chest. Sahara incessantly talked to herself and exhibited multiple personality disorder: many different kinds of voices came out of her, both male and female. I learned about this when one of my coworkers disclosed that one day, he had heard many people arguing in the hallway; when he turned the corner in the hall, he discovered this woman standing there all by herself. After 9/11 she suddenly and mysteriously dropped dead. Christine, another single woman, went home after work, walked directly to her bed, and dropped dead over it. Ilana, a handicapped woman, suddenly dropped dead after 9/11.

What I have in common with all of these people is that I, too, live alone. In 1987 my life took a sharp turn for the bizarre: several times a week a steam pipe cracked in my building and my landlord was forced to shut off the boiler to make repairs. This occurred on an average of three times per week and it lasted for two entire decades. It created stress and anxiety endlessly: I could not take a shower when I came home in order to prepare for the next work day. Today I surmise that the Pentagon was imaging inside my building and delivering strikes to the steam pipes with EMs from passing aircraft in order to test its weapons and to create stress and anxiety.

NORTHCOM can image and then riddle aluminum and plaster with thousands of pinholes on the other side of a barrier such as a brick wall. I have taken 3,000 hi-def photographs to prove it. On six occasions NORTHCOM perforated several 9 x 12 foot aluminum tarpaulins in my apartment. First I heard an aircraft overhead; then the aluminum shook violently; afterwards, when I held the tarpaulins up to the light, I was stunned to discover that they had been thoroughly rifled with thousands of tiny pinholes! Eventually I, too, was physically struck with EMs as were the walls and floors in my apartment; my walls became pock marked with tiny depressions like golf balls, broken plaster and paint chips fell all over the floor every night, and then deep and incisive cracks started to appear across all of my walls. Today there are deep fissures in every wall in my apartment and in those of many of my neighbors. We leave them there as evidence of the nightly electromagnetic assaults.

Moreover, something else new and different took place immediately after my promotion and move to a new floor: I decided to go on a crash diet, lose weight, and try to look gorgeous. This was unnecessary because I was 5'8" and I weighed 140 lb. It is significant that weight loss suddenly became the new preoccupation of all of the employees on my floor; we all became concerned about our weight at the same time and obsessed endlessly over it.

By the time that George Herbert Walker Bush took office, I had suffered a loss of impulse control and I began searching for food in garbage cans. I also became obsessive-compulsive about saving money. Indeed, I did end up saving $1.1 million—I had metamorphosed into someone who got the job done.

During a couple of details, I met a woman who was the top executive in her division. A single woman, she, too, suddenly developed cancer and died soon after 9/11. How much EM radiation did the government douse her with?

I also met a youthful looking man during that detail. He was about 28, but he had the appearance of a 20-year old. I was horrified to meet him in an elevator 11 years later: he had the appearance of a senior citizen in his 80s. Moreover, he behaved in a doddering manner, shook his head from side to side, had a high pitched voice, and used expressions like "when I was your age."

There is a proven scientific way to get people to age rapidly: lab experiments have shown that recurring sleep deprivation, night after night, causes accelerated aging. Now this is happening to me: every night my sleep is disrupted, first by a thud that drops over the comforter directly over my ankles, and then by a moving wave that travels longitudinally over the bed directly over my body from my ankles up to my shoulders. The EMs disrupt the body's natural Circadian rhythm and after this occurs, it is impossible to return to sleep. Over time, one's appearance radically changes and accelerated aging sets in. My appearance has significantly changed since this began and I now look twenty years older than I actually am.

During the Clinton administration four people suddenly died who had worked on the same floor of the Customhouse; three of them were young; they all died around the same time. One was a Chinese woman in her thirties who had contracted cancer; one was a young black man in his early thirties who suddenly fell sick and died; one was a white woman in her early thirties who died suddenly over the weekend; one was a black male, much older, perhaps in his 50s, who died of cancer.

The Clinton years were characterized by the following phenomena: electronically generated snaps and cracks angrily lashing off the metal filing cabinets, desks, and acrylic-covered modular walls; the deaths of single women due to strange diseases and obsessive-compulsive disorders; and more and continued psyops. One of my colleagues, Nelson, could not sit still for one moment, but was compelled to prance about his office, continually opening and slamming shut the drawers of metal filing cabinets; one woman sat at her desk and ripped paper all day long when there was a paper shredder in a large office around the corner; I was retrieving unsold packages of food from the garbage bags of restaurants, collecting soda cans and beer bottles for a nickel, and checking every telephone coin return and Metrocard vending machine for change, well on my way to saving my first million. Meanwhile, we were all surrounded by loud cacophonic snaps from morning until night that betrayed a dense electrically charged atmosphere.

Two single women working in this environment developed debilitating diseases that ultimately resulted in death: Andrea started eating compulsively and became so obese that she had to be lifted out of her bathtub. Helena developed progressive supranuclear palsy (PSP), a neurological disorder that caused her to fall backwards; she was forced to retire and subsequently died in a nursing home. Moreover, Raymond, who worked in that immediate area, developed colon cancer and required a colostomy. Their office space was the site of loud, violent, perpetually electronically generated cracks and snaps lashing off the walls. I am certain that Andrea and Helena's deaths and Raymond's colon cancer were directly related to the densely charged, electro-magnetic environment.

The psyops continued: I arrived at work one morning to discover a gaping hole in the wall, just above my chair, at the precise spot where my head would have been if I had been sitting behind my desk. It looked as if someone had thrust a screwdriver or a pair of scissors into the sheetrock. More-over, there were ugly black stains on the rug all around my desk and "X" marks dabbed all over my modular walls with a dirty finger that had been dipped in black liquid.

On September 11, 2001 at 8:46 AM my coworkers and I evacuated 6 World Trade Center and splintered off into many directions. I raced through the footbridge that spanned Vesey Street that connected Six to Seven. It was in 7 WTC that I learned that a federal secretary who had come in early that morning had said that the CIA, which had offices on the 25th floor of Seven, had arrived at 6 AM and had moved out its filing cabinets. When I asked a secu-rity guard for confirmation of this, he replied that it was not at 6 AM, but shortly before 7:30 AM, say 7:20 or 7:25 AM that the CIA had arrived and moved out its filing cabinets. One security guard said that the CIA was "LONG gone" and he emphasized "long" by increasing the pitch and volume of his voice. The CIA was long gone by the time that the first plane had hit One at 8:46:40! This is significant because the CIA leaked a false story to CBS News and said that the Agency had lost its files. It had not: it came in early and moved them out.

By the middle of October 2001 my division had set up temporary office furniture in our new lodging. That marked the beginning of vicious electronic phenomena and the mass loss of impulse control. It was during 2002 and 2003 that I suffered violent, electronically generated assaults both at home and at the office. I had the habit of arriving early at work and it was then, at 6 AM, as I sat alone in my office, that a fierce, vehement snap would lash across a metal cabinet, just feet away from me. It sounded as if a loose wire on a telephone pole had delivered a 40,000 volt strike to a tree. This betrays the fact that the atmosphere was so densely charged, it must certainly have been unhealthy to work there. Soon I started getting pinpricks to my skin as I was sitting at my desk behind the computer. Upon close examination, I discovered that tiny saucer-shaped craters were being burned into my skin. The small holes rapidly filled with blood; then the blood hardened and left a permanent brown dot on my skin. Today my arms and legs are covered with these burn marks. Then I discovered that I felt the pinpricks whenever people pointed their cellphones in my direction and turned them on. It happened on the street and in the subway.

Concurrently, when employees arrived in the morning they discovered that various items that they had left on their desks had been deliberately misplaced: a woman's name plate was placed on the floor beneath her desk; another woman's monthly report was turned upside down and stuffed into a pencil box. Individuals started hearing sounds in bathrooms when they knew that they were alone there: one morning I heard the distinctive sound of keys drop on the ceramic floor tiles just outside my bathroom stall; when I came out I discovered that I was alone in the bathroom. Another employee heard the sound of a woman's high heel shows clicking across the floor outside of his shower stall; he was the only one there. It was psyops: our experimenters were gauging our responses at that time so that they could compare them to future reactions after we had been subjected to more EMs.

Then people began to exhibit strange behavior and the loss of impulse control. One man walked through the hall making very low pitch sounds that sounded like water gurgling down the bathtub drain. Days later he violently and uncontrollably pushed open the door to his office so hard, the door would have gone through the sheetrock if there had not been a metal door guard screwed to the floor. On another occasion, he forcefully hurled a wheeled office chair across the room and narrowly missed hurting one of his co-workers. This caused me to stop and reflect on my own loss of impulse control and the fixed ideas that I had: all I cared about was saving money.

After we acquired permanent office furniture and moved into newly built permanent offices, FEMA donated a great number of paintings to Customs. I found it significant that they had been carefully placed, only a few feet apart from each other, in every hallway and facing every exit. Everywhere we looked, we were within eyeshot of a picture.

I thought that I had detected a tiny pinhole camera in the texture of one of the paintings facing an exit door. It resembled a fisheye. I was very vocal about my suspicions and made sure that everyone was aware of the fact that paintings such as these were sold on the Internet to bosses who wished to spy on their employees.

It was precisely when I raised questions about the wall paintings that things took a sharp turn for the worse. I was awakened from my sleep that night by the sensation of a powerful wind vehemently blowing against my face and hair. As I slept, I felt my hair blowing wildly in the gusty squall; I woke up abruptly. Subsequently I learned that such a sensation can be electronically generated.

I walked through the hallways at work and leisurely articulated my view that America was the greatest terrorist nation on earth and that it had found a way skew the electronics in aircraft, trains, and cars from a distance, crack steam pipes from afar, and create earthquakes on demand. One day in the future I would purchase an RF detector and discover that almost all of the paintings hanging in the hallways were bugged. Were the electronic assaults that I was suffering a government exercise in behavior modification or attitude change?

In 2004 I moved down the hall to occupy the cubicle of a man who had recently died of liver cancer at the age of 54;

originally he had suffered from pancreatic cancer and was operated on for that. However, the cancer metastasized to his liver. I was suspicious of the fact that a blackout occurred every morning in my new office space as unknown electrical work was being done in and around my new location: the morning that I moved into my new cubicle, there was no electricity until 10 AM. This continued for more than a week. I wondered why this was the second time that this had happened: there was no electricity in my old cubicle either when I first moved in, but there was in all of the other work spaces on the floor.

Beginning around 2004 there were an inordinate number of deaths that occurred. Andrea, a woman with whom I had worked in 1980, had developed an eating compulsion and could not stop eating; she became so heavy that she had to walk with a cane and be helped out of her bathtub; her legs became infected with sores; she died of obesity. Then there was Freeman, a man who had had a kidney transplant: he was doing well at first and returned to work, but then he became very ill and died at the age of 52. I wonder whether his ability to accept a foreign organ had been substantially impeded by high doses of microwave radiation that we were all getting. Customs had seen two cases of pancreatic cancer over the years: the woman survived because it was caught early; the man did not, as the cancer had metastasized to his liver.

Then the cigarette poisoning began. Every morning at 6:30 AM a thick stream of cigarette smoke wafted into my cubicle from the air vent directly over my head. It happened every morning from 2004 until I retired on January 3, 2008. The smoke made me gag and once it began, I had to keep a cup of water on my desk and intermittently take sips from it. My supervisor did not care about my plight and when I called him over to my office to witness the situation, he denied that he smelled cigarette smoke. My coworkers smelled it, but because it was directed into my cubicle and not their own, they were not concerned enough to complain about it. It is highly significant that neither I, nor my co-workers, complained about the cigarette smoke or caused a commotion about it: lab experiments have shown that over time, electromagnetic waves cause docility in test subjects. It was certainly true that we had become an extremely docile group.

After I relocated to the new office down the hall I discovered that Nelson, my neighbor in the cubicle behind mine, had developed an OCD that involved feeding his coworkers. Every morning he arrived at work with shopping bags filled with expensive exotic treats. He laid out a spread on a hallway table and drew attention to every passerby that there was food there. I moved into this area in April 2004 and worked there until I retired in January 2008. During that interim, there was not one day when Nelson did not bring a shopping bag filled with deserts from the deli.

One night during the summer of 2004 I received an electrical shock to my brain that was so powerful, my head involuntarily jerked from left to right. The next day I moved my bed out of the bedroom and into the living room. That night it happened in the living room, as well. Concurrently there were taps and snaps that resonated off the walls in every room. In the morning I discovered broken plaster and paint chips on the floor in the corner of every room. Invariably, the debris would always fall from the ceiling in a corner of the room where two walls and the ceiling meet; and always by a wall that also served as a façade to the building. I hypothesized that the electromagnetic waves were directed at my apartment building at an angle and that was why the paint and plaster always fell on the floor by an exterior wall. Then I started to notice pock marks in the walls. Very soon my white walls were covered with little saucer-shaped craters like those on the surfaces of golf balls.

In the summer of 2004 I made a new friend who lived across the street from me. Soon we became good friends and she divulged that she, too, experienced electronic phenomena in her apartment. She had inserted a metal bar in her window to keep the window open. A powerful force, of unknown origin, had whacked the metal bar out of its place and caused it to fly across the room. Moreover, she was sitting in bed watching the news at about 6:30 PM when she felt something drop on her blanket. After first she thought that it was the cat that had jumped onto the bed; however, when she looked around she discovered that the cat was in another room.

My neighbor's pets were being troubled by the electronic phenomena, as well. Something was making her dog so uncomfortable that it could not sleep on one side of the living room; the dog would get up and go over to the other side of the room to lie down and sleep. The cat would get up in the middle of the night and leap up into midair in an effort to grasp something invisible.

Another neighbor who lived across the street, a woman my age, was being assaulted with pinpricks in her home: her entire abdominal area was covered with tiny red dots, the diameter of a pin. This was a relatively recent occurrence—she never had them before.

It is also significant that a third neighbor, one who also lived across the street and was a very successful real estate agent, was suddenly carried out of her apartment in a straitjacket one day. This was surprising because she was highly intelligent, very introspective, and had given me priceless advice throughout the years. Note that all four of us are single women living alone. Moreover, the real estate agent died of pancreatic cancer the same month as five other tenants in her building succumbed to cancer.

In 2005 I developed the compulsion to announce to the world the stunning news that I had just learned from my colleagues. Customs had looked in the diplomatic mailbags at the JFK Mail Branch and had found monetary certificates with swastikas at the top, underwritten by a major financial institution. I surmised that this was evidence that an ancestor of George Bush had traded with Hitler. The story is all over the Internet and books have been written about it. However, what is not on the Internet is what my colleagues discovered in the diplomatic mailbags. The financial instruments were unmistakable: a flying eagle at the top and across the bottom, the inscription that it was underwritten by a corporation. The monetary certificates were going out of the country 50 years after they had been purchased. It did not matter that Germany had lost the war: they were guaranteed by the underwriter.

The first thing I did was to ask my supervisor whether federal rules permitted me to call radio talk shows and discuss my opinions over the air. He vehemently shook his head no and informed me that such activity was not allowed. I decided then to start screaming public service announcements in the streets, at subway stations, and in subway cars. And scream I did, for three years.

Every morning I was seized by the uncontrollable urge to tell everyone what I knew. I shouted my message on silent Queens streets at 5 AM; I made proclamations in subway cars to passengers as they read their morning papers. The broadcasts went like this: "Ladies and gentlemen, my colleagues in the United States Customs Service have opened the diplomatic mailbags at JFK Airport and have discovered Nazi monetary certificates inside. These financial instruments have swastikas across the top and are underwritten by..." I articulated the name of the corporation, but will not name it in this book because if it sues me, I will have to haul my coworkers into court to testify and they will not appreciate the disruption to their lives. Federal employees are not permitted to talk to the public; once retired, we can sing like a canary.

It was after I started proclaiming my message in the streets and trains of New York City, that several dangerous and potentially deadly events transpired. One morning I was sitting on a folding chair in front of my house when a car abruptly jumped the curb and stopped short just an inch from me. The driver quickly threw the car in reverse, then in forward, swerved, and sped away. The following morning I had another close call: as I was taking a leisurely stroll on the sidewalk, a taxicab crashed into a parked car inches from where I stood on the street. Then the taxicab backed up and sped away. The side of the car that had been parked was completed destroyed. A few days later, just as I was crossing the street at a corner, a car abruptly turned at 40 mph and I jumped back just in the nick of time to avoid it. The only reason I missed getting hit was because I saw it coming and was prepared to jump back. When I looked at the vehicle as it was speeding away, I noticed that its rear license plate bore the name of the corporation that had underwritten the Nazi monetary certificates. Were these events were purely coincidental?

It was also significant that the expensive high-tech electronic doors on our floor were perpetually broken. Were our experimenters jamming the electronics in the doors so that they could come in at night and set up their experiments? After years of malfunction, the doors were finally repaired and they worked the few weeks preceding my retirement.

There is additional evidence of the Pentagon's experimentation with microwave electronics in my town. In August 2005 I saw the first driverless cars in Rego Park—not just one or two, but eventually a couple dozen. At first the windows were clear and it was easy for pedestrians to identify the driverless vehicles. However, very soon the Pentagon figured out that blackened windows would preserve its anonymity better. The cars carry $200,000 worth of electronic equipment aboard and the Pentagon does not want them pilfered. However, these vehicles are not safe: one of the driverless cars struck and killed a man on Queens Boulevard. When the police opened the car, they discovered that there was no one inside. From this I deduce that Rego Park is the test site of a DARPA experiment. When one considers the electronic imaging perpetually conducted from overhead and the surveillance by driverless cars at street level, one must necessarily extrapolate that my town has been chosen to be the test site for a Pentagon ring-of-steel project. If our streets are flooded with driverless cars, may we logically conclude that the planes delivering the electronic strikes from above are also drones, operated in real time, from a remote location?

By 2006 I was subject to sleep deprivation night after night—there was a tap on the comforter over my ankles and that was succeeded by a moving wave traveling longitudinally up my bed to my shoulders. Seconds later a strong puff of air blasted against my face.

Then I started hearing electronic sounds in my sleep; the moment I awoke they disappeared. They were a rhythmic "ping, ping, ping." Or else they were a "tap, tap, tap" against the window glass. The military has had the technology to throw sounds at a distance for decades. In 1958 Dr. G. Patrick Flanagan invented a device that permits people to hear sounds without the benefit of the human ear.[7] Instead, hearing is accomplished through the bone, skin, and body liquid. When the sound is transmitted at the precise extra low frequency (ELF) on which the brain operates when the person is asleep, the test subject will hear the sound only when asleep, not when awake. Moreover, my neighbors and I have been awakened from sleep in the middle of the night by a burst of sound that suddenly erupts in midair near the ear. It is significant that the people in my neighborhood who are experiencing this harassment are single women living alone.

As time elapsed, the electronic phenomena changed: a sound exploded just an inch from my ear that was only a phoneme in length—ah! or oh!; sometimes I heard a recording of the hubbub of a room full of people. When I was walking through the halls at work early in the morning, the printers that I passed would suddenly start to whirr and then stop just as I passed them. Then when I sat down in my cubicle my day would be a living hell. First the cigarette smoke would start to filter into my cubicle and cause me to cough. Then I would get assaulted with pinpricks that left my arms and legs covered with permanent brown dots. Violent snaps and cracks viciously resonated off metal cabinets and modular walls just inches from my body. The angry lashes that whipped off the furniture occurred several times a minute and recurred throughout the day. The electronic assault had been stepped up considerably.

Then I met a young man on Queens Boulevard who said that he had felt that a bug on his back—it was as if something had gripped his skin and would not let go. Passengers riding the subway to work in the morning have also related that they have experienced taps on their blankets and moving waves traveling laterally and longitudinally across their beds at night. These people reside in various towns in Queens: Astoria, Jackson Heights, Corona, Jamaica. That was how I discovered that these phenomena are widespread.

Finally I decided to purchase a radio frequency (RF) detector and find out whether the numerous pictures on the wall in our Customs office were indeed really bugged. I went to one of the spy stores in Manhattan and I purchased a bug detector for $150. The next morning, of the sixty or so pictures on the floor, I got a positive reading from all but two. Now I had all the information that I needed to ascertain that the government was watching our every move. The problem was that I did not know what to do with the information. Ultimately, I did the only thing that I could do: I retired on my thirtieth year to the exact day and I wrote a book about it to warn others who may be entertaining the notion of landing a federal civil service job.

Soon after I made my discovery with my bug detector, I picked up a bug of a very different variety: one morning, the whites of my eyes turned crimson and blood started to run out of both nostrils. I looked like I had Ebola. When I saw myself in the bathroom mirror, it looked as if I were hemorrhaging out of my facial orifices, much as Ebola victims do in Africa. I immediately started taking a 1,000 mg capsule of vitamin C every hour and fortunately, the condition cleared up by the next day. Where did this bug come from? Was it something that the Pentagon had cooked up in Fort Detrick, MD? Or was it electromagnetic in origin? When the Russians assaulted the U.S. ambassador in Moscow with EMs, his eyes began to bleed (Project Pandora). Did this malady have anything to do with my discovery? Or was it coincidental?

Concurrently, Nelson, who occupied the cubicle behind mine, lost all of his impulse control. He came to work one morning and angrily opened and then slammed shut the door to his metal clothing closet. His temper tantrums took place more and more frequently and with greater and greater vehemence. It got to the point that people started leaving their cubicles and took breaks when he arrived in the morning. By the end of the year, I could not take it anymore. I had put in my 30 years and I decided to retire.

There exists a proliferation of scientific data that indicates that electromagnetic waves destroy the brain and other parts of the body in test animals and humans. For example, cellphone radiation breaks up the single- and double-strands of DNA in the brains of rats;[8] mobile phone radiation destroys the neurons in the brains of rats;[9] the use of mobile phones for more than 10 years is associated with an increased risk of brain tumors;[10] cellphone users run a greater risk of contracting brain tumors in rural areas than they do in urban settings because in the rural environment, the towers are farther apart and therefore, the signal is stronger;[11] laptops can cause sterility in males because it raises body temperature.[12]

What This Book Offers That Is New

Customs found Nazi monetary certificates with a swastika across the top in the diplomatic mailbags at JFK. They were underwritten by a major financial institution.

On the morning of 9/11 the CIA moved it filing cabinets out of its office at 7 World Trade Center at 6 AM.

The pictures at one particular Customs site are bugged and electronic snaps and crackles vehemently ricochet off of metal and sheetrock.

The demographics of deaths in the federal government are reminiscent of Nazi Germany—the victims are single women, Jews and the handicapped.

NORTHCOM aircraft not only images through the apartment buildings in Queens every night, it delivered pulses that rifled aluminum sheeting in my apartment with thousands of pinholes on multiple occasions. It delivers a moving wave targeted at the lymph nodes of women living alone and these people develop cancer of the lymph nodes soon after.

Regarding experiments that use Customs employees as test subjects: 56 employees have died, become seriously ill, developed OCDs, exhibited signs of loss of memory and inability to focus, or have been victimized by accelerated aging. Many of these people fall into several categories, i.e., they developed compulsions that eventually killed them. Of these 56 individuals, there were 30 males, 26 females, 18 single females who never married, 6 single males who never married, 34 Christians, 21 Jewish, 8 handicapped, and 6 minorities (5 black and 1 Chinese).

These numbers have great statistical significance: out of 56 victims, 18 are single women never married and 6 are single men who never married. $18 + 6 = 24$. In other words, the government preys on single people, since they constitute 42% of the total number of victims. Statistically, 42% is too significant to ignore. Moreover, 37.5% of the victims are Jews, a startling figure; 14% are handicapped. Now let us include the divorced and widowed among the single people. Let us also add the singles, Jews, and handicapped and make them one group. There are people who fall into more than one group, for example, one woman was single, Jewish, and handicapped. Of the 56 victims, 40 fall into one or more of the following categories: single, Jewish, or handicapped. This is an incredible statistic! 71.4% of the victims are single, Jewish, or handicapped! 71.4%! Is this reminiscent of Nazi Germany, whose experimenters preyed on single people, Jews, and handicapped because the Nazis considered them to be marginal citizens? This statistic alone demands a Congressional inquiry

(Endnotes)

1   "Je n'ai point de sceptre, mais j'ai une plume." François-Marie Arouet de Voltaire, *Lettre à Madame Denis*, October 15, 1752, in *Œuvres de Voltaire avec prefaces, avertissements, notes, etc.*, 70 vols., edited by M. Beuchot (Paris: Lefèvre, 1829–1840), 56:206.

2   Naomi Klein, *The Shock Doctrine: The Rise of Disaster Capitalism* (New York: Picador, 2007), 29–48, 56–58.

3   Ibid., 30–31.

4   Ibid., 42, 45.

5   Douglas Pasternak, "Wonder Weapons," *U.S. News & World Report*, July 7, 1997, 38–46.

6   David A. Fulghum, "Wonder Weapons; U.S. Army Plans Computer-Attack Devices, Directed-Energy Weapons for the Front Line," *Aviation Week & Space Technology* 163, no. 14 (October 10, 2005): 28.

7   William Moeser, "Whiz Kid, Hands Down," *Life* 53, no. 11 (September 14, 1962): 69f.

8   Henry Lai and Narenda P. Singh, "Acute Low-intensity Microwave Exposure Increases DNA Single-strand Breaks in Rat Brain Cells," *Bioelectromagnetics* 16, no. 3 (October 1995): 207–10; Henry Lai and Narenda P. Singh, "Single- and Double-strand DNA Breaks in Rat Brain Cells after Acute Exposure to Low-level Radio Frequency Electromagnetic Radiation," *International Journal of Radiation Biology* 69, no. 4 (April 1996): 513–21; Henry Lai and Narenda P. Singh, "Magnetic-field-induced DNA Strand Breaks in Brain Cells of the Rat," *Environmental Health Perspectives* 112, no. 6 (May 2004): 687–94; "Exposure to Low-level Magnetic Fields Causes DNA Damage in Rat Brain Cells, Researchers Find," *Science Daily*, February 19, 2004, http://www.sciencedaily.com/releases/2004/02/040219075606.htm (August 14, 2008).

9   Leif G. Salford, *et al.*, "Nerve Cell Damage in Mammalian Brain after Exposure to Microwaves from GSM Mobile Phones," *Environmental Health Perspectives* 111, no. 7 (June 2003): 881–83.

10   Stefan Lönn, *et al*, "Mobile Phone Use and the Risk of Acoustic Neuroma," *Epidemiology* 15, no. 6 (November 2004): 653–59.

11   Lennart Hardell, *et al.*, "Use of Cellular Telephones and Brain Tumour Risk in Urban and Rural Areas," *Occupational and Environmental Medicine* 62, no. 6 (June 2005): 390–94; Stephan Lönn, *et al*, "Output Power Levels from Mobile Phones in Different Geographical Areas; Implications for Exposure Assessment." *Occupational and Environmental Medicine* 61, no. 9 (September 2004):769–72; Lennart Hardell, *et al.*, "Further Aspects on Cellular and Cordless Telephones and Brain Tumours," *International Journal of Oncology* 22, no. 2 (February 2003): 399–407; Mild K. Hansson, *et al.*, "Mobile Telephones and Cancer: Is There Really No Evidence of an Association?" *International Journal of Molecular Medicine* 12, no. 1 (July 2003): 67–72.

12   Yefim Sheynkin, *et al.*, "Increase in Scrotal Temperature in Laptop Computer Users," *Human Reproduction* 20, no. 2 (February 2005): 452–55 (August 13, 2008).

The main New York office of US Customs at Building Six of the World Trade Center, where Mary Gregory worked from 1978 until the building was destroyed on September 11, 2001.

Chapter One

A Summary of the Untimely Deaths in the U.S. Customs Service 1978–2008

But what do you mean by prolonged experiments?[1]
        —Denis Diderot, *Sequel to the Conversation*, 1769

The voluntary consent of the human subject is absolutely essential. This means that the person involved should have legal capacity to give consent; should be so situated as to be able to exercise free power of choice, without the intervention of any element of force, fraud, deceit, duress, overreaching, or other ulterior form of constraint or coercion; and should have sufficient knowledge and comprehension of the elements of the subject matter involved, as to enable him to make an understanding and enlightened decision. This latter element requires that, before the acceptance of an affirmative decision by the experimental subject, there should be made known to him the nature, duration, and purpose of the experiment; the method and means by which it is to be conducted; all inconveniences and hazards reasonable to be expected; and the effects upon his health or person, which may possibly come from his participation in the experiment.[2]
—*The Nuremberg Code*, 1947

•   A male died of diabetes. He went into shock at work, had to be carried out of the Customhouse on a stretcher, and subsequently died.

- A male died of diabetes after we relocated to a new building.
- A female died of ovarian cancer in 1991.
- A female who could not stop eating died of obesity.
- A female developed progressive supranuclear palsy (PSP), a rare degenerative disease that impairs movements and balance and died in 2001.
- A male died of liver cancer in 2004.
- A male died of kidney failure after he had received a kidney transplant.
- A female died of cancer soon after she retired.
- A female developed a blot clot in her leg; was operated on; retired; died soon after.
- A male in his 50s fell to the ground of a heart attack; died.
- A male suddenly became ill and dropped dead soon thereafter under mysterious circumstances.
- A female suddenly became ill and dropped dead over the weekend.
- A female developed cancer and died.
- A male died of cancer.
- A woman went home, entered through her front door, walked into the bedroom, and collapsed dead on the bed.
- A female suffered a heart attack; her chest pain was so excruciating that she put a hot iron on her chest in an effort to make the pain stop; she died and was discovered with the iron still on her chest.
- A male suddenly dropped dead soon after his mother died.
- A female suddenly dropped dead right after 9/11.
- A handicapped female suddenly dropped dead right after 9/11.
- Another handicapped female suddenly dropped dead right after 9/11.
- A male suddenly dropped dead right after 9/11.

- A female developed breast cancer and died after 9/11.

22 people died. Of these, there were 9 males, 13 females, 13 singles (10 single females and 3 single males), 8 married, 1 divorced or widowed, 17 Christian, 4 Jewish, 4 handicapped (3 single handicapped females and 1 single handicapped male). The fact that 10 out of 22 were single females (45%) and 4 out of 22 were handicapped (18%), is stunning and reveals a lot about the preferences of the experimenters.

(Endnotes)

1   Denis Diderot, *Sequel to the Conversation* in *Rameau's Nephew and D'Alembert's Dream*, translated and introduced by Leonard Tancock (New York: Penguin Books, 1966), 232. "Mais qu'entendez-vous par des tentatives suivies?" Denis Diderot, *Suite de l'Entretien* in *Œuvres philosophiques*, edited by Paul Vernière (Paris: Garnier, 1998), 382.

2   *The Nuremberg Code* in *Trials of War Criminals before the Nuremberg Military Tribunals under Control Council Law No. 10* (Washington, DC: US Government Printing Office, 1949), 2:181–182.

As I sat at the foot of my bed, I received a powerful blow to the top of my head. Second
later I heard a plane roar by overhead. Afterwards I discovered that they had broken a piec
of my cranium: a tiny sliver jutted up like a toothpick. 3 ½ years later I shaved my head an
photographed my crown. A scar remains.

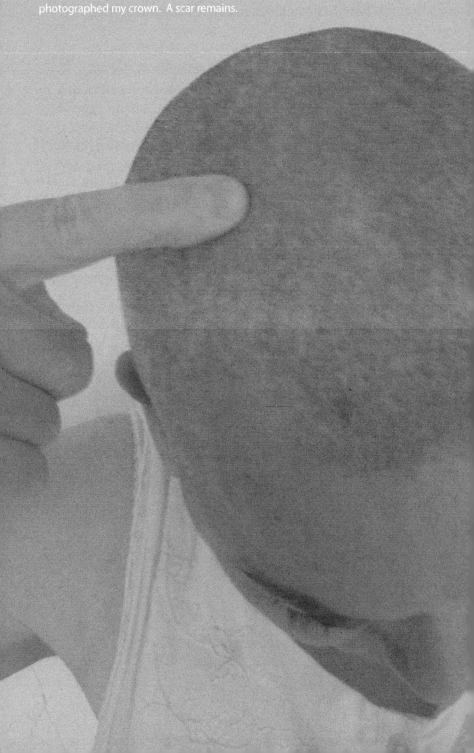

Chapter Two

The Carter Years (1977–1980)

I warn every animal on this farm to keep his eyes very wide open.[1]

—Squealer, in George Orwell's *Animal Farm* (1945)

There was evidence of a highly charged electronic environment in all three buildings in which I worked: at JFK Airport, the U.S. Customhouse at 6 World Trade Center, and our post 9/11 worksite. In the case of JFK, it was when I worked alone in the office at lunchtime, when most people had driven to a nearby diner for lunch, that I heard thunderous metallic clatter emanating from nearby unoccupied offices. It sounded like an electrical bolt had hit a metal filing cabinet. This happened a few dozen times. When I arose from my desk to investigate, I always discovered that the room from which the noise originated was empty. When I asked my colleagues about this, I was told that it must have been the boiler kicking on. I did not accept this explanation: it did not sound like a boiler, but rather, like something electrical snapping angrily off metal furniture. After a transfer to Manhattan, I heard identical sounds again in the WTC and the new building, significantly, in rooms that had no pipes leading to any boiler. By 2002 the sounds were accompanied by the sensation of a dagger to the skull and internal organs.

JFK

I was sitting alone in the office at lunch time. The other employees all had cars and had driven to a nearby location to dine. Because I was a loner by nature, I preferred to spend lunch hour by myself working. Looking back on it now, I realize that it was precisely this personality, that of the loner, that made me the ideal lab mouse for the government.

I opened an entry and unfolded a long packing list. The packing specifications were in kilograms and therefore, it was necessary to convert the kilos to pounds. I clicked on the calculator and multiplied the number of kilos by 2.2046…SSSSST! Suddenly a deafening hiss exploded in the room next room. It sounded as if an invisible lash had snapped viciously against something metal—or as if a bolt of thunder had just delivered 40,000 sizzling volts to a steel plate. Greatly startled by the violent thrash, I looked up and gazed at the doorframe leading to the other room. Mystified, I arose from my desk and walked in to see what had happened.

Everything was utterly still. I gazed at the metal windowsill: it was covered with Customs documents, law books, back issues of *U.S. Customs Today*, and daily currency conversion sheets affixed to clipboards. Then I stared at the metal filing cabinet. I wondered where the vehement crackle had come from. Did it originate from above? Did it emanate from the metal windowsill? Could it have been the boiler kicking on? Perhaps. Or maybe not. I did not know enough about the terrain of my new environment. I never thought to ask my boss when she returned from lunch. Because I had nothing to relate it to, I promptly forgot about it.

A week later an importer wandered into my office and asked to see a supervisor. He was missing the documents required to get release of his goods and he was told to confer with a supervisor. I arose from my chair and led the importer out into the hallway. Because I knew that there was a manager in the corner office next door, I decided to look for him and ask for assistance. Just as I was approaching the doorframe of his office, I heard a violent snap burst forth from the room. When I entered inside, the supervisor was not there. I gazed fixedly at the windowsill with great curiosity and then up at the ceiling. It sounded like something had violently lashed down from the ceiling onto the metal windowsill. What could have caused the fierce clatter? I was left wondering. Perhaps it might be the plumbing, electrical wiring, or the boiler system. I decided that whatever it was that had caused the thunderous sound, it must have been all right. Again, the continual business activity that was going on caused me to promptly forget about it.

The next day I spent lunch hour alone scanning entries for requisite documents. Once again a violent, deafening CRACK! burst forth from the door frame leading to the next room. It sounded as if the glass window had just been smashed. I bolted up from my chair and rushed into the empty office.

All was still. The window was in one piece. I looked up at the ceiling. Then back at the window. Finally my gaze remained on the metal window sill because it was the only metal fixture in the room and I thought that the clatter must have surely emanated from there. I made a mental note to ask my colleague, as soon as she returned from lunch, what that sound might have been.

"Perhaps you heard the boiler kicking on," she suggested. "It can sound pretty scary if you don't know what it is." I accepted that as a rational explanation and put it out of my mind.

Although I loved my new job, I had great difficulty commuting to JFK without a car. I decided to ask for a transfer to the Customhouse so that I could take the subway to work. I called the personnel office and requested a transfer to the city. The personnel officer advised me that under federal regulations, I had to be in grade for 90 days before I could procure a transfer. As a new employee, I was on probation and I was required to obtain a rating from my supervisor after 90 days on the job. After that, I could be moved.

I obtained a transfer to the World Trade Center in April 1978, on my 91st day on the job. Little did I suspect then that I was about to enter a highly controlled environment, one that provided an excellent laboratory for psyops, germ warfare, and the altering of the human brain via a continued barrage of electromagnetic waves. This was the price that I about to pay for having majored in French and taking the road less travelled by. It made all the difference.

THE BIG CITY

In my new office I was assigned to sit between a man who incessantly and uncontrollably talked to himself as he was performing arithmetical calculations and a woman who obsessively chain smoked. The former felt the compulsion to articulate every mathematical operation that he performed from morning until night.

"8400 times 32 ½ % plus 25¢ a pound. Now let's see, how many pounds?" He rustled the pages as he turned to the packing specifications. "Ah, yes, there are 1500 pounds in this shipment. Now let's see. Oh, the invoice is in Deutschmarks. Now where is my currency conversions chart? Hey, does anyone know where the currency conversion chart is?"

"Will you please shut up, all ready, you are driving me crazy," Tina, seated on my left, shouted across my desk to Jack.

Moreover, Jack was obsessive-compulsive about requiring a purchase order for every single shipment in order to ascertain the price paid or payable on the date of export. Customs assessed duty on the value of goods on or about the date of export. Since, due to currency fluctuation, the price usually went up between the time of purchase (shown on the invoice) and the date of export (shown on the purchase order), it was the obsessive-compulsive employee who was the government's most valued worker. He was the one who tirelessly scrutinized every detail on the paperwork to squeeze the most duty of importers.

Consider this: if the Pentagon can find a way to make someone obsessive-compulsive via a barrage of electromagnetic waves, it can produce a super soldier, one who is far more efficient, and who does not mind overextending himself in his efforts. Now, thirty years later, as I am looking back on this, I surmise that if anyone was bombarding us with electromagnetic waves and was surveilling the results via hidden pinhole cameras, he would readily ascertain that the experiment was a stunning success: my coworkers and I arrived early each morning, headed straight to our desks, obsessively scrutinized every piece of paper in the office, and made sure that Customs had collected every last penny in duty. We never complained, arrived punctually in the morning, went to lunch at the exact same time every day, returned promptly, and continued to work feverishly until closing time. Like my coworkers, I was exceptionally punctual both in my departures and returns.

In 1978 it did not occur to me that perhaps Jack read the purchase orders aloud, vocalized every thought, and disturbed everyone in the room because he was brain damaged. As I reflect back on this now, I conclude that something was indeed wrong with him. It is not normal for someone to articulate every thought he has from morning until night. Moreover, as time elapsed, more and more employees started talking and muttering to themselves obsessively, ad infinitum, from morning until night.

That same year I encountered Allison, seated in another office, next to a window, who also articulated every written word that she read all day long. Because I was a fast worker, my boss assigned me to sit in front of her for one day to clean up a backlog of work that had accumulated. Much to my surprise, Allison read every word aloud until it was time to go home. Back then I thought that perhaps she was merely struggling to make sense of what she was reading. Now I suppose that she was. However, the human brain is wired to read quietly. Something changed that in her. There was something wrong with her. It would not be until thirty years later, when I would be writing a book on 21st century science, that I would learn about the damage that electro-magnetic waves can do to the human brain.

Furthermore, Tina was a nervous wreck. She smoked incessantly and became frantic when messengers, working for Customs brokers, brought us work to do. She jumped up from her desk, groaned quite loudly, and glanced worriedly through the new folders. She was perpetually overwhelmed by the arrival of more work and because she chain smoked from anxiety, she had to empty her ashtray every little while.

Now that I think back, I distinctly remember hearing, on several occasions, a violent metallic CRACK! emanate from the back room in that office. The adjoining rear office was where the GS-13 sat.

One rainy day when all of my colleagues had gone to lunch, I found myself seated alone at my desk trying to process a backlog. Suddenly a violent and distinctive metallic SNAP! emanated from the other side of the doorframe leading to the GS-13's office. It sounded as if someone had struck a whiplash hard against a sheet of metal. I jumped up from my chair and rushed into the empty office: everything was now rock still. I looked all around the room. It was an inner office without a window and so, because there was no window sill, there were no pipes leading upstairs from the boiler to the heater in a windowsill. However, there was an array of metal filing cabinets alongside a desk; the front and sides of the desk were also constructed of metal. I had heard something snapping off of metal, but I did not know what to make of it. Since I was new in the city, I had no idea what the plumbing was like inside the walls. Looking back on it, it was identical to all of the violent snaps that would haunt the Customhouse, later our new building, and ultimately, my apartment.

There were a few unusual occurrences at our worksite and gradually, the incidents became spookier. I discovered all the lights turned on in the office in the morning even before we unlocked the door: light emanated from beneath the door. Back then, we did not find this to be significant: someone must have forgotten to turn them off. The last person to leave the night before was thought to have been the culprit. This caused arguments to begin: "You forgot to turn off the lights, last night!" "I did not! It was you!" Today I understand that the three of them were right when they said that it wasn't any of them.

This did not happen only in my office. Employees working across the hall, around the corner, and down adjacent hallways, also arrived in the morning to find the lights turned on in their offices even before they had unlocked their doors. There was always someone in every office who would holler argumentatively that he distinctly remembered having snapped the lights off the night before. Soon it became a game. People deliberately made a note of closing the lights before departure and yet, the lights were always found turned on in the morning upon arrival. Employees concluded that Customs agents must have been looking for evidence of wrongdoing and that they were probably visiting the offices and rifling through filing cabinets.

Today it is evident that another government intelligence agency had used 6 WTC as early as 1978 to conduct psyops. Many of the incidents that occurred were malicious and therefore, evidence of psyops, not the gathering of import information. People were subjected to pranks— heavy desks were pulled behind locked doors and the perpetrators exited the rooms through ceiling vents, rugs were soiled with semen, swastikas were drawn in dust around desks, long trails of cigarette ashes were left on rugs, walls were stabbed behind desks with sharp instruments right where the heart would be if the person had been seated there, Xs were drawn with dirty liquid all over office walls, money was stolen from safes. The psyops continued for the entire duration of my 30 years of employment, and judging from stories about mental illness in previous employees, most probably earlier than that.

Very soon my colleagues and I became very comfortable with one another and we became one big happy family, putting up with one another's eccentricities, as family members do. My coworkers frequently talked about the employee that I had replaced, and how badly she had hurt their feelings. My predecessor had utterly devastated them: one day, after thirty years on the job, she quietly picked up her purse, went upstairs to the personnel office, and handed in her retirement papers. Then she walked out of the building and was never heard from again. What a dastardly crime, everyone thought. How could anyone do that? Why would anyone want to? We were all like family. In fact, because we spent more waking hours together than we did at home, we were family carried to an exponential power.

Back in 1978, I had no idea that one day, in the distant future, I, too, would choose to retire in utmost secrecy and quietly slip out of the building; that I would opt to escape as soon as I legally could, exactly thirty years from the day I started, right down to the day.

THE BIG PROMOTION

In April 1979 the branch chief summoned me to his office and congratulated me. Not only was I promoted, but I also would be seated next to a sunny window overlooking Alvin J. Tobin Plaza. Tobin Plaza was a 5-acre public plaza, larger than St. Peter's Square in Rome, serving the 40,000 workers in the 7-building World Trade Center complex.

My new boss, an elderly man, was brilliant with money. He was one of the first people in New York to purchase a co-operative apartment at Lincoln Center on Columbus Circle. Since then his property has become worth millions.

"What is your salary?" he asked. I told him that I was a grade 7, step 1, that I made $13,014 a year, and added that I had paid off my New York State education loan in full before I graduated and so the interest was forgiven. I had managed to save money working as a substitute teacher in junior high.

"Listen, now, and listen carefully. In order to make money in this world, you need money. Therefore, it behooves you to save as much money as quickly as you can. That way you can put it to work. This is what you are going to do: the first year, you are going to save $5,000. The second year you are going to save another $5,000. Exactly two years from now you are going to purchase your first Treasury bill for $10,000. You will take it out for one year and you will get a year's interest up front, immediately, the Thursday after the auction. You will purchase this Treasury bill directly from the Federal Reserve Bank, right down here on Liberty Street. There is no state or city tax. These are the advantages to purchasing a T-bill directly from the Federal Reserve Bank: first, you get the interest immediately and you can invest it and draw interest on the interest; secondly, there is no state or city tax. Meanwhile, you will save another $5,000. In three years, your $10,000 T-bill will come due. You will take out a new one, this time for $15,000. You will get a year's interest immediately and you can begin to collect interest on the interest again. In four years, you will take one out for $20,000, and so on. Eventually, you will get so much interest up front that you will purchase a $10,000 T-bill with your interest. By the time that you retire, you will have a nice nest egg."

My new boss was absolutely right and I am very glad that I listened to him and did everything that he advised me to do. Today I am a millionaire.

I sat down and calculated how much money I could save by the time I reached 40, 50, 60, 70, 80, 90, and 100 years of age. The numbers became so large at retirement age, I wondered how I was going to pay federal income tax on all the interest. Clearly, this was a case of diminishing returns. Two hours later I knocked on the GS-13's door with urgency and asked for a solution.

"The answer is simple. The day will come when you will purchase triple exempt, triple tax free municipal bonds.

That way you will not have to pay any federal, state, or city tax on the interest." I was in awe of his genius.

What I did not suspect back then was that I was on the road to becoming obsessive-compulsive about saving money. In fact, 15 years later, I visited Alvin J. Tobin Plaza, concealed beneath a black hooded anorak, and fished out all of the pennies, nickels, dimes, and quarters that tourists had thrown into the fountain. I managed to retrieve every last coin from the water and my little caché added up to $60. This required a lot of nerve because not only did I have to avoid attracting the attention of the security guards, but also, because the fountain was situated right in front of the Customhouse, I had to make sure that anyone looking out of the window would not see my face. As time progressed I became more obsessive about saving money, and as I did, I became less concerned about who saw me.

TIME FOR A TRANSFER

A common phenomenon continually recurred in Customs: because of personality clashes and too many hours spent together, people made their rounds getting transferred from office to office. Our branch chief once quipped that his job was to put out brush fires. As it turned out, one of the employees in my new office talked incessantly and was unable to stop. My mind was continually invaded by his Proustian flow of consciousness. Not only did he make it hard to concentrate, but even worse, his Proustian stream always focused on the shortcomings of women and it appeared that he was oblivious to the fact that the new hire seated in front of him was a woman who might take his remarks personally. Someone explained to me that he was angry at women because his wife had recently divorced him. I wondered which came first, the chicken or the egg.

A vacant spot opened up down the hall and my supervisor permitted me to fill it. My new coworker, Andrea, was a very professional and kindly woman. She was slightly stout, but not much. She certainly did not have an eating disorder back then. This is significant because 25 years later she would die of obesity, which is a horrible way to die. When we first worked together in 1980 she was not obsessive-compulsive. She did not keep food on her desk to munch all day long. She did not talk to herself. She had hobbies and interests and kept herself busy. She belonged to an acting troupe in her town and regularly participated in productions with her friends, including Shakespearean plays, in local church basements. She was a very talented actress, had a lot of friends, and had a healthy life. She had majored in education in college, but because there was a glut of teachers in the 1970s, she found a job working in a Five and Ten. She was glad to be able to finally land a job in Customs because like all the rest of us, she discovered that she could not use her college diploma to find a job in her chosen field. Andrea appeared to be healthy and sound, in body and in mind. Her spare time was filled learning her lines and doing dress rehearsals with her theater ensemble.

CUSTOMS CROOKS

During the period 1980–1981 Customs was featured on the front pages of newspapers with recurrent regularity. The stories were not flattering: a number of high grade Customs officials were being indicted for all kinds of crimes, not the least of which were fraud, extortion, theft, kickbacks, conspiracy, bribery, and perjury.

The *Boston Globe* reported:

> Federal officials have cracked a $1-million-a-year kick-backs-for-favors ring in the New York region of the US Customs Service...Customs officials took kickbacks in exchange for helping foreign manufacturers who were bringing goods into this country.
>
> ...the officials would use their discretion to help the foreign interests—for example, labeling blue jeans as

work clothes instead of as fashion clothing, thus assessing duties of 10 percent instead of 20 percent.[2]

The *New York Times* reported:

> Nine present and former employees of the United States Customs Service in Manhattan were charged yesterday with a variety of crimes relating to the service's monthly auctions of confiscated and unclaimed merchandise.
>
> A Federal grand jury in Manhattan alleged conspiracy, bribery, theft and perjury...The defendants...either took part in or lied under oath about a scheme to sell information and provide samples to certain prospective purchasers in advance of the auctions at the World Trade Center.[3]

The United States Department of Justice reported the following to Congress:

> New York, Southern District: In another continuing investigation of corruption in the Customs Service, in New York nine Customs employees were convicted of a variety of crimes including conspiracy to defraud the United States, perjury committed during their appearance before the grand jury, bribery and theft of goods from the United States Customs warehouse.[4]

STRANGE HAPPENINGS IN THE CUSTOMHOUSE

It was around this time, 1980–1981, that strange events began to transpire and they became the object of conversation on a daily basis.

One morning when we opened the door to our office, the lights were on and there was a trail of cigarette ashes across the floor leading from the front door to the metal cabinets in the back of the room. Cabinet drawers were open and file folders were resting on top of open files. The light was on in the sample closet and wearing apparel samples were strewn about the floor. We all looked at each other in astonishment.

However, the strangest occurrence by far, was what happened in one of the other offices. One morning Kyle arrived at work and was unable to open the door. He pushed and pushed, but was unable to force the door to budge an inch. A muscular employee gave the door a forceful shove and it moved just enough to permit Kyle, who was very slim, to slither through.

A huge desk that must have weighed a ton was right behind the door. Several ceiling panels just behind the door were missing. It was apparent that someone had moved the desk behind the door and had exited from the vents overhead. Kyle was extremely distraught. He thought that he was the subject of a probe and that the agents were investigating him.

No one was examining his work. If they were, they would not pull the desk behind the door and exit from the ceiling. It was a psyop, pure and simple, designed to intimidate. And the victim? Significantly, a single Jewish male, the typical lab mouse of the Nazi. Kyle became distraught and smoked one cigarette after the next. Soon all of the neighbors were getting crazy. The entire floor thought that they were under surveillance for theft and graft.

No doubt that the table-behind-the-door caper was a psychological operation (psyop) performed by a military intelligence agency. This incident and similar happenings continued to occur throughout the years and they were designed to intimidate and raise stress levels. Our reactions to stress at that time were being documented so that they could be compared to responses at a future date after more EMs had been administered. Significantly, by the time I retired in January 2007, my coworkers were highly passive and oblivious to strange events at the worksite: name plates were placed beneath desks overnight and it was passively accepted; in my case, very thick and heavy cigarette smoke was continually wafting into my cubicle from 6:30 AM making it impossible for me to sit and work, and I did nothing about it; I was getting electrical shocks to my brain while working at my computer and I accepted it; several people were contracting cancer, many were dying, and no questions were asked; loud and obvious taps and snaps were vociferously crackling and ricocheting off of metal furniture and not one word was mentioned about it. The experiment was a stunning success: after 30 years of exposure to EMs, betrayed by the cancer rate and loud electronic taps reverberating throughout the offices, Customs employees were dumbed down, passive, and uninterested in anything except eating, drinking, and working. What stunning data with military applications!

DEIRDRE: THE SECRETARY WITH LUPUS

In 1980 I made an acquaintance whom I sometimes saw in the hallway or elevator. One day we met on the sidewalk in front of Alexanders (4 WTC). It was a balmy June day and all of the employees who worked in the WTC complex had come downstairs to eat, shop, or sunbathe in Alvin J. Tobin Plaza. Men were seated in the park on Church and Liberty, playing chess for money, as they did every day at lunch, weather permitting.

Deirdre worked on another floor. She was single, living alone, and had recently acquired lupus, a debilitating auto-immune disease. She was in continual agony and confessed that she was in discomfort even as she spoke to me. She was only 40 years old, and yet she had become so crippled and immobilized, she was forced to retire on a disability. The day that I met her on the sidewalk at lunchtime, she was just about to retire. She described her hospital stay and all the gruesome details of her illness. And yet, she had to engage in a fierce battle with the government in order to be permitted to retire: the government did not want to give her a disability check and its argument had been that she was too young, that she had not worked long enough, and that she was not sick enough. I was very surprised that someone who was only 40 had become so sick. I never saw her again after that day.

Deirdre was the first in a long list of single women living alone who died (sometimes suddenly under mysterious circumstances), contracted serious autoimmune diseases or developed obsessive-compulsive disorders. The general overall statistics reveal that 71.4% of the victims were single, Jewish, and/or handicapped.

(Endnotes)

1   George Orwell, *Animal Farm*, prefaced by Russell Baker, introduced by C.M. Wodehouse (New York: Signet Classics, 1996), 82.

2   "Probers Reportedly Crack Customs Service Fraud Ring," *Boston Globe*, February 18, 1980, 1.

3   "THE CITY; 9 Customs Workers Indicted on Auctions," *New York Times*, April 14, 1981, B8.

4   *Report to Congress on the Activities and Operations of the Public Integrity Section for 1981* (Washington, DC: Department of Justice, April 1982), 13.

They punctured the living room wall with three circular holes just inches above the spot where I stored a huge roll of homemade aluminum tarpaulin. Not only did they perforate the aluminum with thousands of pinholes, they knocked it down to its side and I discovered it several feet away from its original spot.

Chapter Three

The Reagan Years (1981–1988)

Proper preparations should be made and adequate facili-ties provided to protect the experimental subject against even remote possibilities of injury, disability, or death.[1]
—*The Nuremberg Code*, 1947

1981

The Branch Chief GS-15 made his rounds from office to office, asking whether anyone wanted to volunteer for a detail on another floor to work on a special project. I accepted the offer because I wanted a promotion.

"Oh, you! You would go to the moon!" he chortled.

Alas, if that were only true! But no, travel was out of the question. I was one among the many solitary homebodies in the Customs Service who would not allow any change in their lives. This personality trait made me the ideal lab mouse for a military intelligence agency that required a pool of single people who could be depended upon to work in the same location for thirty years.

The next day my new branch chief escorted me around the vast floor introducing me to people who sat behind desks, hidden behind stacks of work piled 2–3 feet high.

EDMUND

Edmund was sitting behind his desk sporting a colorful Hawaiian shirt. His shirt featured a teddy bear resting in a beach chair, wearing sun glasses, hands comfortably folded behind his neck; a radio was on one side, suntan lotion on the other, and the surf was up in front of him. After I complemented him on his cheerful attire, he mentioned that he had a number of such shirts. Just how many, I would eventually find out.

Edmund was a mama's boy, about 30, very pleasant and courteous. He did his quota of work for the day and then some. Afterwards, he felt free to relax and visit with the other employees. Whenever I ascended to his floor on business, I often saw him wandering through the hallway, sporting a different Hawaiian shirt. He always waved hello. I thought that he must have really hated his rotten job. I quickly understood that his only escape from a mundane and predictable existence was to traverse the long hallways. That was all that he had to look forward to.

The sedentary people in Customs' goldfish bowl consciousness murmured about him behind his back: he lived with his mother; he was afraid of women; he will never get married; he wears loud shirts to get attention.

Thirty years later, right after 9/11, Edmund was one of a dozen people living alone who mysteriously dropped dead. First his mother suddenly died and left him to live alone in the apartment. Soon afterwards he was discovered dead, as well.

More than a dozen people, mostly single, Jewish, and living alone, suddenly met their demise after 9/11. One day I would ask why so many single people had suddenly collapsed and died; why an inordinate number of people living alone contracted autoimmune diseases or significant obsessive-compulsive disorders (leading to death in the case of two single women). I am certain that if someone were to compare the death statistics in Customs with those of the general population, specifically the number of deaths of people living alone as compared to those of people living with at least one other person, one would find that an inordinately larger percentage of Customs employees living alone died.

Below I enumerate some of the low grade staff that lived alone and suddenly collapsed and died. With the exception of Christine, all were clerks that had been hired under a special program for the handicapped.

KARLTON

Karlton, like Edmund, was a single male who suddenly died immediately after his mother did. He was a very kindly, polite and highly articulate gentleman who pushed a metal wire cart from room to room and delivered new work to employees; he always took the time to greet and briefly converse with each one.

One day, just as Karlton was entering the room, there was an eclipse outside the window and Alvin J. Tobin Plaza disappeared in the pitch of night. As he deposited work in the "in" basket by the door, we all greeted him, the topic turned to the phenomenon outside.

We soon discovered that his hobby was astronomy and that he owned a telescope and camera. He frequently went out at night and searched the heavens for something interesting to capture on film. He was extremely articulate about his hobby and with all of the expertise of a science teacher, he discussed the canals on Mars, the distance and amount of time that it would take NASA to get there, the composition of Saturn's rings, and the storm that constitutes Jupiter's red eye. He had a plethora of photo albums containing snapshots that he had taken of celestial bodies and rare spectacular events.

When Karlton did not come around to deliver new work for several consecutive days, I asked about him. I was surprised to learn that he had suddenly collapsed and died: he had lived with his mother and she had recently departed this world; he succeeded her soon thereafter.

JEANNE: THE WOMAN WHO DIED WITH A HOT IRON ON HER CHEST

Jeanne also pushed a metal wire basket around the building and delivered work to the various offices. She was very short, had distinctive large, brown eyes, was single and lived alone. She was a very diligent worker and always took extra care to sort out her work and make sure that each piece was delivered to the proper office. Then one day she disappeared. I asked what had happened.

It turned out that she had lived alone and had suffered a heart attack. The pain was so overwhelming that she could not stand it and so, she placed a hot iron on her chest to alleviate the throbbing. She was discovered dead in her apartment with the hot iron still on her chest. She had very generously donated her body to science in her will before she died.

SAHARA: THE WOMAN WHO INCESSANTLY TALKED TO HERSELF

Sahara was an African-American, very tall and heavy, who delivered our work to us. Her distinguishing characteristic was that she continually muttered to herself from morning until night, both as she wheeled her wire basket around each floor, and when she sorted her work in her office.

One of my associates informed me that one day, as he was walking down the hallway, he heard several people arguing loudly at the end of the corridor, around the corner and out of view. Two of the voices sounded male. When he turned the corner, he was surprised to see this woman, standing there all by herself, staring vacantly into her metal cart. He deduced that she had multiple personality disorder.

Our clerk suddenly died immediately after 9/11. Had the government finished with its little experiment and tied off loose ends?

ILANA

Customs hires the handicapped to work in the Mail Room and these employees are assigned to deliver the mail that arrives from the post office. The handicapped are extremely reliable and dedicated workers: they are extremely careful when they work and can be relied upon to ensure that each piece of mail reaches its proper destination. They are also sweet, courteous, and open human beings that easily converse with others.

We had an amiable and much-loved mail clerk, Ilana, who sported distinctively frizzy hair. Whenever I entered the mailroom, she always promptly arose from her chair, asked what I required, and took care of all of my requests. I was greatly saddened to hear that she suddenly collapsed and died right after 9/11. Was the government doing something special with the clerks that precipitated their unexpected demise?

CHRISTINE: THE WOMAN WHO COLLAPSED ON HER BED

There were also clerks who had not been hired under a special program, who also victims. Christine, single, African-American, went home after work, opened the front door of her house, walked directly to her bed, and collapsed dead over it. Her sister discovered her body after her phone calls went unanswered. Looking back on this, I find it significant that an inordinate number of people who lived alone did live long enough to retire.

It also bears mention that there was another woman, Randi, white, single and living alone, who worked in the same office as Christine and sat in close proximity to her. Randi developed a serious debilitating autoimmune disease, rheumatoid arthritis, and her illness became so unbearable, she had to have both knees replaced with metal plates. After several years had passed, she required a cane to walk. Eventually she retired on disability because she was too young to retire on a regular pension.

CHASING THE NEXT PROMOTION

It was during the 1980s that I discovered two invaluable books that were worth their weight in gold to me: John T.

Molloy's *The Women's Dress for Success Book* and Kenneth Blanchard and Spencer Johnson's *One Minute Manager*.[2] I had dreams of rising to the top of the Customs pyramid. I purchased a new wardrobe of business attire—Evan Picone blouses and wool skirt suits. I compulsively arranged them in my closet in order of color, from the lightest to the darkest. At the extreme left I arranged the tailored shirts and bow blouses: white, light pink, dark pink, and navy. To the right of these, I added the wool suits: camel, light gray, charcoal gray, dark brown, navy blue, and black. It did not occur to me that I was becoming obsessive-compulsive about arranging things in proper order. Now that I look back on this, there were a bunch of sick women in Customs who, before I retired, were lining up their high heel shoes strictly in order of color. I wondered whether they had always behaved in this manner or whether it was a recent development. Looking back, people were invariably and predictably becoming gradually more compulsive about something: arranging things perfectly, cleaning, eating, talking, feeding their co-workers, repeating the same thing over and over again, or piling up garbage to the ceiling.

I dressed for success every day and followed the advice of *The Women's Dress for Success Book*: wool skirt suits provide presence when a woman enters a room. Presence is everything. So is social class. Therefore, it behooves the professional woman to always be seen in a dark-colored wool skirt suit, preferably navy blue or black, and a white business blouse. However, I loathed shoes with heels and so I did not follow Molloy's advice about wearing small Cuban heels. I matched the suits with leather penny loafers of the same color. Everyone thought that I was destined to become Area Director. What they did not know was that I had an aversion to travelling, that I had never been in an airplane, that I could not even visualize myself boarding a flight to a far away city. This proved to be my Achilles heel: to get promoted past a GS-12 in Customs, one must be willing to travel.

Nevertheless, I applied for promotions and performed some special and unusual tasks to distinguish myself from the herd. I filled out an application in the Public Affairs Office to do outside speaking engagements and included the fact that I spoke French and Greek fluently. Two weeks later I was invited to address a delegation of importers from Montreal that were meeting in One World Trade Center.

The evening was very pleasant: I had the opportunity to speak French and I managed to hold my own in conversation. Topics of discussion included wearing apparel quotas, entry requirements, and foreign trade zones. At that time I had foreign trade zones at my finger tips because I was teaching a class on the subject to Customs personnel. The importers from Montreal were particularly interested in manufacturing in zones. Most of the evening was spent on FTZs.

Another time I addressed an auditorium filled with importers on wearing apparel quotas. I prepared a two hour lesson and the organizers of the event supplied a chalk board and podium.

The course that I taught on foreign trade zones to Customs personnel was particularly challenging. The employees came from diverse disciplines within the Service and their knowledge of foreign trade zone law varied greatly. I had auditors in the room who had actually put corporations out of business: these auditors knew a lot more about the intricacies of foreign trade zone law than I did. However, most of the people in the room knew nothing about zones. We covered manufacturing activities that were permitted in zones, first-in, first-out (FIFO), forms required for admission, manufacture and exit from a zone, and how to determine what is dutiable and what is not.

Therefore, no one was surprised when, in December 1982, I got a temporary promotion to GS-12. They all expected it.

In January 1983 I was returned to the GS-11 position and I had to reapply to get a permanent GS-12. It was then that an event occurred that changed my outlook on life and my goals for the future.

One day a Frenchman walked into the office carrying two suitcases filled wool sweaters from France. He inquired as to the duty rates for wool garments and the requisite documents. The moment I heard his French accent, I started speaking to him in French, and very soon we became friends. As it turned out, his fiancée had just received her Ph.D in French from Columbia. Her dissertation sponsor was the same as mine and he gave her the topic that had once been assigned to me. However, the professor informed her that the woman who had previously had the topic was unable to complete the assignment because the subject matter was too narrow. Therefore, he broadened the topic considerably so that she would have more to write about. She found enough material to fill up 200 typewritten pages and she got her Ph.D. Upon graduation she was hired immediately to teach French at a university and was given tenure sight unseen because after all, they were getting a Ph.D from Columbia.

My jaw dropped open. I was too stunned to speak. So, I thought, it was not me, after all. It was the topic. Maybe I should go back and try it again. Maybe I should call the French Department and talk to the chairman.

THE TORNADO OF OCTOBER 5, 1985

Just as my hand touched the doorknob of the rear entrance to my apartment building, the wind started to blow violently behind me. I hurried inside and went straight upstairs. Seconds after I entered the front door, I discovered that the living room curtains were violently flapping outside the open windows, on the verge of becoming disengaged from their rods. I climbed onto the windowsills, pulled the curtains inside with much effort, and shut the windows. What kind of weather was this, I wondered.

The next morning trees were found strewn across the avenues and streets in Rego Park and Forest Hills. The newspapers reported that it was an F-1 tornado, a rare occurrence in Queens, and that it had injured 6 people. It was localized: it touched down and destroyed the trees and telephone lines in only a few towns and then disappeared as suddenly as it had materialized.

A few weeks before the tornado hit, one of my neighbors had dug a fish pond behind my apartment building and had filled it with very expensive exotic fish. The ichthyophile had engineered the pond with the utmost expertise: he dug a huge crater in the dirt and then lined the bottom with plastic sheeting so that it would retain water. Then he added several fish, a colorful and picturesque, ceramic underwater castle and several human figures, also made of ceramic, to decorate the pond. I purchased a beach chair and every day after work, I brought it downstairs, set it down alongside the fishpond, and read until it got dark.

The day after the tornado hit, I went straight home from work and circled to the back of my building to check on the fish. I was devastated to see that the storm had swept away the fish, the ceramic decorations, and the plastic liners. All that remained was a cavernous abyss. I felt very badly for the poor fish.

This bizarre F-1 tornado that touched down on Queens provides evidence that even back in 1985, five years before HAARP was started, the military was experimenting in weather modification. New York is not situated in any tornado belt and powerful storms can be effected by the generation of electromagnetic waves.

GETTING A PERMANENT GS-12

When I applied for the permanent promotion, I decided to speak to the branch chief upstairs. All of the GS-12 vacancies were in her branch and if I had to impress anyone, it was her. I asked whether travel was required for the job. She informed me that no travel was required and encouraged me to apply for the job. I was promoted permanently soon thereafter.

It was around that time, April 1987, when more and more employees were starting to clean compulsively. I used a very powerful cleaner to spray my telephone receiver each morning. Eventually the corrosive chemical burned through the plastic and one morning when I picked up the receiver, the mouthpiece dropped out. I was terrified that I would get into trouble for destroying government property and frantically searched for another phone. Fortunately, due to Reaganomics, there were empty rooms all over the floor with unused telephones. I switched receivers with another phone, and after that I began using alcohol to clean all of my devices: phone, calculator, and computer monitor. I presumed that it would kill head lice as well as the corrosive sprays did.

One of my coworkers also cleaned with alcohol. Upon arrival in the morning the first thing that he did was to thoroughly saturate everything with alcohol. One day he confided that he, too, had destroyed a black rotary phone with the same corrosive cleaner that I had used. As it turned out, we were both promoted and we ended up working together in the same room. Ours was an immaculate office, needless to say.

Hence, prior to my permanent promotion in April 1987, I was aware of only one victim of autoimmune disease; two people who talked themselves incessantly; one nervous wreck; two people who cleaned compulsively; several offices had been intruded upon in the middle of the night.

LIGHTS ON AND DOORS OPEN

Soon after my promotion there were a few strange occurrences on my new floor: on many occasions when we arrived at work in the morning the lights were on in the offices and the doors were wide open. The employees distinctly remembered that they had locked the doors and shut off the lights the night before. We figured that the agents were coming in at night at looking at the documents in the filing cabinets.

Concurrently another employee who worked in my new office suddenly came down with the flu. She was coughing and blowing her nose all day long. Back then I did not consider the fact that it is highly unusual to contract the flu in April. I do now. Don't these things go around in the winter time? How did she get it in April?

BAD LUCK ON THE FLOOR

On September 30, 1991 there was a death from ovarian cancer across the hall. And that was just the first horrible thing that happened to the people working in that room. Looking back, I believe that at least three of my coworkers across the hall were casualties of microwave radiation.

First, Alexis, a very lovely lady who was married to another employee on the floor, suddenly got sick and died of ovarian cancer. It happened very fast. She felt fine and then she died soon thereafter. She was a young woman, only 41. The problem with this disease is that it is a silent killer: it is undetectable until it has metastasized elsewhere in the body.

The woman who succeeded her in the office contracted pancreatic cancer and had to have her pancreas removed. Many years later, after I began asking questions, someone confirmed that she had undergone surgery for pancreatic cancer, and that fortunately, the surgeons had removed it all. Such would not be the case for another Customs pancreatic cancer victim, a man who would die at the age of 54: one day, in the distant future, I would move into his cubicle after he had died of liver cancer that had metastasized from his pancreas. He would die on January 12, 2004; I would move into his cubicle in April 2004.

There was also a man who worked in that office who had transferred to a Customs office in San Francisco. He died after his transfer. I do not know the cause.

PIPES BURST THREE TIME PER WEEK

It is significant that at that time, the pipes started to burst in my apartment building. Every day when I came home from work there was no hot water coming from the tap. This frustrated me because the only thing that I wanted to do was to take a shower and then proceed to the next chore on the agenda. I remembered Kenneth Blanchard and Spencer Johnson's *One Minute Manager*. I decided to take corrective action then and there. This is significant because as the years elapsed, my response time to problems became more and more protracted until finally, I stopped getting problems solved altogether.

Back in 1987 I would storm out of the apartment and make my descent into the basement to ask the super why the hot water had been shut off. The response that I always received was the same: an emergency had suddenly occurred because a pipe had burst somewhere in the building; there was a flood on one of the floors and the boiler had to be shut off. Back in those days, I did not believe a word of any of it and I surmised that it was harassment, pure and simple: the landlord was in the process of converting the building into a coop and he was turning off the water in order to get people to move out. Or so I thought.

Then one day I learned that it was all true. When I came home from work and was greeted by two rusty drops that sputtered out of the bathroom tap, I angrily stormed downstairs and straight to the cellar to pay the super a visit. There I discovered a thunderous waterfall surging down from a broken pipe in the basement's ceiling. Two plumbers were standing soaked on stepladders, fervently attacking the ceiling above them with axes, in a desperate effort to identify the location of the break. The inundation on the floor had risen to a level of 3". I accepted the idea that there really had been such a thing as a building emergency, after all.

I asked the neighbors whether they thought that it was unusual that pipes should break in our building on an average of three times a week. They responded that it was an old building, what did I expect? This explanation did not seem valid to me. I thought that the statistical probability that a rupture would occur with the frequency of several times a week was so remote that coincidence could be effectively ruled out.

I asked neighbors residing in buildings across the street and elsewhere on the block whether their steam pipes cracked three times a week. They unanimously responded, "What? Are you kidding? Of course not. They rarely burst." I found it significant that all of the buildings in the neighborhood had been built around the same time. Why were the pipes all cracking in my building?

Today I hold fast to the hypothesis that the government was conducting target practice on my residence using high-powered microwave (HPM) and laser pulse technology. U.S. military aircraft in Iraq and Afghanistan are equipped with devices that can deliver a stunning blow from a distance. Moreover, they can pinpoint their targets with the utmost precision: they can image inside a building or vehicle with such a great degree of accuracy, they can discern an armed individual from an unarmed one; they can identify the chemical composition of everything behind a barrier.

We know that the government had the weaponry as far back as April 19, 1993 because it used it in Waco, TX. It is significant that rapid flashes of light were seen moments before the fire erupted inside the Koresh complex. These flashes of light suggest that either the FBI had in its possession state of the art high powered microwave weaponry or that it had gotten such weaponry from the British.

On March 11, 2000 CNN reported:

> Infrared tape shot April 19, 1993, from an airplane over the Branch Davidian complex shows rapid flashes of light. Attorneys for the Davidians contend the flashes represent federal agents shooting at the Davidians.
>
> The FBI has insisted its agents fired no shots. Its experts say the flashes of light are reflections.[3]

Lawyers for the Davidians argue that the FBI's aerial infrared surveillance footage proves that gunfire was directed into the building as it burned. It appears that the FBI used laser pulse weapons to set off an explosion resulting in fire.

What we do know for sure is that the FBI employed forward looking infrared radar (FLIR) to image inside the complex. Infrared radar can penetrate walls and smoke and discern human beings by the heat that their bodies generate. It is used for the surveillance of people, locating people through barriers and walls, and search and rescue operations in wooded areas. FLIRs detect thermal energy to create a picture of a location. Forward looking can be distinguished from sideways tracking infrared radar; they have been made obsolete by FLIR because they cannot image in real time.

The FBI admits that it used FLIR to image inside the compound and create pictures of all the items in each room. What it does not concede is that it used a different device, a laser pulse, to cause a fire in the compound.

Had the U.S. military chosen my apartment building for target practice because my landlord was Egyptian? Or was it done in order to ascertain how I would respond to stress after EMs had been administered? The stress was protracted. The water was turned off and on, continually and obsessively, from 1987 until around 2006, when a plethora of coops were sold and most of the apartments had been converted. The timing of the broken pipes is significant because the following question arises: had the government targeted the pipes in my building, long distance, via manned or unmanned drones, for the purpose of experimentation? Is the compulsive behavior that ensued a direct result of this stress or a result of subjection to EMs?

It is significant that neighbors living directly across the street from me experience phenomena that betray EM bombardment: they may not have broken pipes, but several single women who live alone state that they receive burn marks to their skin that eventually become permanent little red dots; they get taps on their blankets that feel as if something has dropped on the bed; metal rods that they insert beneath open windows to keep them open are knocked out of the window frame and across the room. Moreover, cats jump up into the air and grasp at objects that do not exist and dogs become so uncomfortable on one side of the room that they have to move to the other to sleep. They are awakened in the middle of the night by a sudden scream that erupts in midair just inches from their ears. In addition, there have been an inordinate number of residents on my block who have died of brain cancer.

One of my neighbors who lived alone across the street from me was a real estate agent and a very capable and responsible individual. I spoke to her often on the sidewalk and she was articulate and intuitive. That is why I was surprised to learn from another neighbor that EMS had removed her from her apartment on a stretcher, tied up in a straitjacket, ranting, raving, and thrashing her arms about uncontrollably. Eventually, she was permitted to return to her apartment. Ultimately, she died of pancreatic cancer (it is significant that five other people in her building also died of cancer that same month). Did she have to be placed in a straitjacket as a result of a continual onslaught of microwave radiation? Is that why she contracted pancreatic cancer? She was above average intelligence and had spent a lot of money on therapy; she was a highly respected and very capable professional woman. In fact, she gave me priceless words of wisdom: 1) when disappointments occur or something bad happens, just pick yourself up and keep going and 2) I was just "acting out" when I retrieved things from garbage cans and it behooved me to find out why. It is also disturbing that all four of us are single women living alone; and that three of our group are Jewish. The demographics of the targets in Queens is similar to those among Customs employees—the victimization of my neighbors in Queens is discussed in the second book of this *Mi-*

crowave trilogy entitled, *Microwave War: The Government's Preparation for the Police State and Extension of Empire.* In that book I discuss the plight of two twin brothers, both Jewish, who are also being victimized by electromagnetic phenomena in their home. It is significant that the experimenters find twins useful in their studies: twins can provide significant data as to inherited susceptibility to EMs.

The reason that I hold that my sleepy little street in Rego Park has been chosen to be the site of a DARPA experiment is because of the multitude of driverless cars that I have seen there. Since August of 2005 I have observed more than two dozen vehicles with no driver in the driver's seat. So have my neighbors. One of the postal employees in our local post office advised me that one day someone was struck and killed by a car on Queens Boulevard: when the police opened the door there was no one inside. This tells me that Pentagon experimentation is much more widespread than most people believe and that Rego Park has been selected to be the site of a ring-of-steel DARPA project.

CRACKED STEAM PIPE IN THE BATHROOM AND CRACKED RADIATORS IN THE BEDROOM AND LIVING ROOM

I expected to have hot water when I came home because I was paying rent. Evidently, I figured wrong. I knocked on several neighbors' doors in an effort to rally some support, but I was surprised to find indifference. They were all immigrants from countries where there was no indoor running water. They confessed that they had not even noticed that there was a problem. I decided to confer with my new neighbors downstairs. They had just moved in and I had not met them yet. A woman who appeared to be thirteen months pregnant came to the door. She rolled her R's when she spoke.

"Ameh-ricahns take too mahny bahths," she said. Oh, really? Well, that's the end of that. I decided to take things into my own hands.

I remembered when I was a kid in the Bronx, the neighbors used to take an ashtray and click it against the radiator to let the super know that they wanted heat. I did not have an ashtray, but I did have a hammer. I tapped lightly on the steam pipes and radiators with the hammer. It never occurred to me that I might crack the metal. Looking back on it now, perhaps it was not I who had done the damage to the pipes.

It was 11:30 PM and I was lying in bed listen to my walkman. Suddenly the bedroom lit up with bright orange and red light just as a thunderous POOF! spewed from the steam pipe in the bathroom. I stared at the doorframe leading into the hallway. The bathroom was situated next to the bedroom. That was a violent explosion, I thought. If I had been standing there at that moment, I could have been permanently blinded or worse.

The next day I spoke to the super. He came upstairs and took a look.

"The steam pipe is not cracked. It's all in your mind."

"There was an explosion last night when the boiler kicked on at 11:30. Red and orange light came out of it and there was a violent sound. The whole bedroom lit up. I am afraid that I am going to get hurt in here. Can you change the pipe?"

"No, I can't change the pipe. It runs from the basement up to the top floor. See? I would have to remove the entire pipe. Listen to me when I tell you that there is nothing wrong with the pipe. It's all in your mind, that's all." Then he walked out the door.

Now the ball was in my court. I would have to file a lawsuit to get the pipe replaced. Did I want to do that? Not really. I went down to the basement and looked over the garbage. I found four pieces of metal that I could use to cover up the pipe so that if it explodes again, at least I would not get hit in the face. I also found a wooden board that was six feet high and two feet wide. I brought that upstairs, too, for added protection.

I did not get hit in the face, but I had another problem: every time the boiler kicked on, which was very infrequently, the thick stench of poisonous burning fuel inundated my apartment and made my heart palpitate. First I would hear pssssssssssst emanating from the steam pipe. Then I would smell burning fuel. Then I would feel faint and I would have to open the windows before I passed out. On several occasions I felt faint and had to lie down in a hurry. Through all of these years, I actually dropped to the floor on only one occasion, on March 6, 2008, recounted in *Microwave War*.

A few weeks later the radiator in my bedroom also exploded. It was the middle of the night and I happened to be awake. Bright orange and red light shot across the bedroom, not far from my bed and a thunderous whoosh erupted simultaneously. POOF! The next day I asked the super to remove the radiator and screw a cap over the pipe in the floor.

The radiator in the living room cracked next. Early one morning I was walking back and forth through the apartment, doing my chores, getting ready to go to work. When I was passing through the living room, a burst of light shot out of the radiator accompanied by a loud POOF! I found that if I shut off the valve, I did not get any more bursts of light. Today I am wondering whether I had been the one who cracked these heating devices or if it had been done by laser pulse. The result of all of this is that I have been breathing burning fuel every winter since 1987 and I have not taken any legal action to have the situation corrected.

THE CRASH DIET

Now that I had a permanent GS-12 and I lived alone, I decided that the time had come to do everything that I always wanted to do. The first thing on the agenda was to lose weight. I was 5'8" tall and weighed 140 lb. That is considered to be normal. However, I wanted to be thin and svelte. And so, I started to carefully count my caloric intake. I subsisted on canned tuna and lettuce. Soon I was 118 lb. I did it in three months. I soon found out that I had exercised poor judgment.

The moment I dropped down to 118 lb., my coworkers told me that I looked like a movie star. One importer said, "I'm so proud of you." Another remarked, "You look great! How do you feel? I'm so happy for you!" The compliments never stopped. I bought new Evan Picone suits, having gone from a size 14 to a size 6. My coworkers next door scrutinized my appearance in the hallway and decided that perhaps they should lose some weight, too. Soon they formed a club. They photographed themselves and taped their pictures on the wall beneath a sign that read "Hall of Shame." One woman purchased an electric scale and they all weighed themselves. Very soon everyone was health conscious and weight conscious.

Looking back, I am now wondering why all of the sudden I became obsessed with the way I looked and with losing weight. And why did all of my coworkers on my floor imitate my behavior? Why were we all obsessing about the same thing at the same time? Were our experimenters falling out of their chairs laughing and high-fiving each other?

And what pathogens were being filtered in through the air vents? The woman in my new office had contracted the flu the month that I got promoted and moved to the new floor. She could not shake it. She was sick continually. The people next door were sick. Finally I started to cough and sneeze.

GROUP OBSESSION

After my promotion I decided to lose weight. The question arises as to why everyone on the floor became preoccupied with losing weight at that particular time. When I went next door to visit my coworkers one morning, I found them all pouring over calorie counters and scrutinizing their breakfast items in an effort to double check that they were adhering to the morning's quota allotment of calories.

One woman brought in a scale. They taped their pictures, before and after, on the wall. They discussed caloric intake and nutritional supplements endlessly. How did this confluence come about?

It was during this time, when I was thin and looked like a movie star, that I fell into a trap and remained ensnared there for 20 years. I loved the way I looked. I was perpetually amazed at the stunning stranger with the baby face in the mirror. I wanted to hold on to my svelte physique at all costs. But my body was lacking many nutrients because I was subsisting on tuna fish, lettuce, and black coffee. Something had to give. The evolutionary process took over. Nature grabbed the reigns and all I could do was follow.

(Endnotes)

1   *The Nuremberg Code* in *Trials of War Criminals before the Nuremberg Military Tribunals under Control Council Law No. 10* (Washington, DC: US Government Printing Office, 1949), 2:181–182.

2   John T. Molloy, *The Women's Dress for Success Book* (Chicago: Follet Publishing Company, 1977); Kenneth Blanchard and Spencer Johnson, *One Minute Manager* (New York: William Morrow and Company, 1981).

3   "Space Blankets May Aid Waco Investigators," March 11, 2000, http://archives.cnn.com/2000/US/03/11/waco.probe/ (March 29, 2009).

Chapter Four

The Reign of George I (1989–1992)

But who will guard the guards?[1]
　　　—Juvenal, *Satires* (late 1ˢᵗ-early 2ⁿᵈ century AD)

THE OBSESSION WITH SAVING MONEY

I am standing on the corner of Broadway and Fulton, waiting for the light to change, when my gaze happens to fall upon the top of the garbage can next to me. There I observe a thick roast beef sandwich with lettuce, tomatoes, and toothpicks pressed through it, housed safely in a clear plastic clamshell; little packets of mustard and mayonnaise rest on one side, a bag of pickles and a rolled up paper napkin on the other. I take it.

The garbage can on the next corner is jam packed with loaves of Italian bread. I look for the expiration date. Yesterday. That explains everything. I tuck three loaves under my arm and press on.

I find a large shopping bag. Perfect. I can use this to carry the bread and any other goodies I find. What else is in this can? A white plastic clamshell with Chinese lettering. I try to lift it. It weighs several pounds and is stapled shut in two places. I squeal with delight. Only in America! I place my Chinese dinner at the bottom of the shopping bag and put the Italian bread on top.

Soon it occurs to me that there is something else worth money in all of these garbage cans that I have been ignoring: the empty soda cans. I estimate how many cans I can collect and carry at lunchtime. However, there is nowhere to redeem them in the Business District: I will have to carry them back to Queens.

Every day I make my rounds and collect soda cans, beer cans, and beer bottles. I learn to carry them in plastic shopping bags because paper ones are unreliable: the remnants of soda drip out and the bottoms always get wet and tear open, spilling 120 cans onto the ground, predictably in the middle of a tightly packed subway car.

I am averaging $6 per day in Manhattan. Then I start collecting on weekends on Queens Boulevard. This constitutes another $12 in nontaxable income.

Soon I am checking telephones and Metrocard vending machines to see whether there is any change in their coin returns. I am thoroughly nonplussed by how stupid and careless New Yorkers are with their money. Don't they care? Not a day goes by when I don't find at least two or three $1 coins in Metrocard vending machines. I find another $2 in telephones. This is amazing, I think, I live a charmed life. Soon I discover that I do not have to make withdrawals from the bank. I visit the bank only to withdraw money for rent.

I spend the next 20 years scrounging through garbage cans and frolicking in dumpsters. Since I purchase an unlimited 30-day Metrocard once a month, I can ride the subways all I want at no additional cost. Soon I am diving into the cans on 5th Avenue by St. Patrick's Cathedral. I find extremely expensive garbage in the cans along 5th Avenue between Central Park and 42nd Street, from FAO Schwartz up to the library: brand new designer tote bags with high falootin' signatures; a heavy duty luggage cart with bungee cord that must retail for at least $100; two shopping bags each containing two six-packs of beer; cameras; shoulder bags. My only regret is that I do not know what to do with it all, nor how to get it home.

The soda and beer cans, and tickling the telephone coin returns and Metrocard machines, provide enough cash to pay for toothpaste, bathroom tissue, contact lens solution, and other miscellany. All bank withdrawals cease with the exception of the one required to pay the monthly rent. I call IRS and ask the specialist if I have to report money that I make from collecting empty soda cans on my 1040. She is taken aback by the question, and has to pause and think for a moment, but then recovers and responds, "No, you don't." That satisfies me. If she had said, "Yes," I would.

If anyone had investigated my bank transactions, he might have arrived at the erroneous conclusion that I was procuring additional income via unlawful activities. It never occurred to me that I might attract undercover law enforcement because I stopped making bank withdrawals.

Furthermore, I never thought that I would elicit the interest of the law enforcement community because I did not fit the profile of a homeless person. One day as I was scouring Grand Central Station, I caught the gaze of a Metro North employee who was staring squarely at me. I went up to him and told him that I had the distinct feeling that I was being watched and that I thought that perhaps it was because I took great pleasure in taking things out of the garbage. His laconic response was, "You don't fit the profile." This floored me and I had to collect myself. The disparity in how different people are treated angered me: the homeless are free to roam the streets and collect soda cans, unimpeded, and the cops choose, rather, to harass middleclass citizens who have discovered how to cash in on a good deal and beat the system.

As the years elapsed, I became more and more resentful of undercover cops who were following me around with cellphones. Then I remembered that employees in department stores sometimes steal merchandise and move it out of the building in the store's garbage. They return after closing time and pick it up from the curb. From this I extrapolated that perhaps a popular way to transport drugs in Queens was via garbage bags. Very soon I reached the point when, just as I thought that I had spotted an undercover cop seated in a parked car with an open window, on his cellphone, watching the garbage bags, I would reach up to my ear to adjust my imaginary ear piece, audibly articulate "Psst, psst, psst," to my nonexistent accomplice on the other end of my fictive line, and then clearly and robustly enunciate, "There's a big drop today." This hostility stemmed from a growing hatred for both the law enforcement community and the electronic technology that facilitates following people around like criminals.

I have since concluded that because of the nexus of law enforcement systems and databases, it is evident that local police are unwittingly being used by the Pentagon to report on the location and behavior of people with which the military is experimenting. The police have a computer data base that alerts them to watch someone; the information that they gather, store online, and communicate via their radios, is then intercepted and used in Nazi experiments by the feds. For example, if the Pentagon wants to drop the new dust-sized RFID chips in food and administer it to someone who eats from the garbage, it can put a message in the data base that local police use so that the cops will ascertain that this particular individual should be followed through the streets. Hence, the cops unwittingly report the direction in which the person is walking and the feds use the information to drop a pastrami sandwich imbedded with RFID particles in a garbage can along the test subject's path.

MY FIRST AIRPLANE TRIP

My branch chief was required to sign up a certain number of GS-13s to attend a computer class in Leesburg, VA. However, because it was a frigid snowy February and many were out with the flu, she had to resort to recruiting GS-12s to fill the requisite quota. As a favor to her, I agreed to go. However, I hated every minute of it. Both planes, going and returning were propeller driven, not jets and the rides took hours; I got lost on the Leesburg campus; I hated the shower facilities as very little water came out of the shower head; the immediate area outside my room was a student lounge replete with a 27" TV, and it blasted all night long. I was miserable. Moreover, I was fortunate to be able to return home Friday morning because a snow storm hit and my prop was the last plane permitted to leave Dulles that Friday. If the storm had hit any sooner, I would have been stuck in DC all weekend. To make matters worse, my supervisor did not allow me to add my $5 tip to the cabbie on my travel voucher because I did not have a receipt. This amazed me as he had been sitting in the cab right next to me! However, I got another supervisor to sign off for me and I got my $5 back.

After I returned, the GS-13s, GS-14s, and GS-15s that had not attended were curious and inquired as to how it went. I told them that I had spent four days and three nights in hell and that I did not intend to travel ever again for the rest of my life. As it turned out, this negative experience travelling made me an even more valuable lab mouse, as I could be relied upon to stay in the same place the rest of my life.

ANOTHER DETAIL, MORE CASULATIES

In 1991 a supervisor made his rounds and asked whether anyone would be interested in spending 90 days working on another floor. I volunteered, and because management wanted to fill up a room with thirty volunteers, everyone who applied was chosen.

I made a lot of lovely friends during that detail. However, some very unfortunate things happened to some of these people that now convinces me that the Pentagon was experimenting with them all along.

DANIELLE

I met Danielle, a classy and charming executive who was the highest ranking officer in her division. One day in the distant future I would be greatly saddened to learn that this lovely person suddenly contracted cancer and died after 9/11. How much radiation did the Pentagon douse her with?

CHARLES: THE MAN WHO AGED RAPIDLY

The scariest fate of all of them was what happened to the young man who sat at the desk in front of me during the 90-day detail. We were working on different projects. He was considered to be a fair haired boy: he was a white male, college graduate, married with children, and very quiet. He had a meteoric rise up the GS pay schedule. He was very quiet, kept an ultra low profile, and rarely spoke. He had learned early in his career to show the managers exactly what they wanted to see: someone who maintained a low profile to the extent that he disappeared into the wallpaper. Therefore, he spent the entire 90-day detail with his eyes focused down on the paper in front of him. He never looked up or to the side. He never complained about the noise level when his neighbors blasted the radios on their desks. That was the sort of person that the managers promoted.

In 1991 he had a very youthful appearance. The skin on his face was moist and supple; there were no bags under his eyes; there was not a wrinkle anywhere on his face or neck. I surmised that he was about 28, but he resembled a 20-year old.

That is why I was shocked to see him in the elevator 11 years later. By 2002 he looked like an 80-year old man. Deep creases lined his forehead, cheeks and neck. His skin was dry and flaky. Crows' feet had plowed deep treads alongside his eyes. When he listened to those speaking to him, he held his head tilted to one side and facing down and he regarded the floor; his head was shaking from side to side with tremor.

His personality had drastically changed, too: he was no longer silent, distant and unapproachable, sporting the façade of someone who aspired to be a tough manager; he no longer pretended to be Mr. Ice in order to impress bosses who tended to promote unapproachable individuals because they thought that they could command the respect of others; he was no longer afraid to be seen by his superiors conversing with fellow workers. He smiled and grinned and used the language of a senior citizen: oh, dear me; did you, now; have a safe trip home and take care of yourself; when I was young; now when I was your age. When was he my age? He couldn't be more than 40!

At that time I wondered how the Pentagon did it. Now I know: there is ample scientific literature that indicates that electromagnetic waves disrupt the sleep patterns of human beings; lack of sleep causes accelerated aging. It is a scientific fact. Apparently, the U.S. military has found a way to eliminate its enemies by making them grow old fast.

The thing that scares me is that since the year that I have retired, my aging has accelerated as well. Today I look vastly different from the way that I did just one year ago. I look like an old woman. And I know why.

My sleep is interrupted every night with electrical shocks to my brain; deep stabbing daggers to my stomach, liver, and pancreas; deep sharp pinpricks to my arms, legs and torso that first draw blood and then leave little brown dots; taps on the blanket; the moving wave rippling across my blanket all by itself when I lie perfectly still in the solitude of the night; the Nazis maliciously focus the wave on the groin area to harass their victims even more. When my body is assaulted with EMs, my entire metabolism is disrupted; the EMs energize me and I cannot return to sleep. This physiological response has already been demonstrated in university labs: EMs transmitted at the precise frequency that the brain uses when the body is active cause people to become energized. EMs can wake someone up or put him to sleep by projecting those that the brain naturally uses in the waking or sleeping states: this is called brain entrainment. The government can wake someone up or put him to sleep on demand. This has military applications: a war can be won by causing enemy soldiers to become drowsy; or by accelerating the aging process of vast populations.

These days the assaults from overhead are more frequent and more pronounced. They seem to have increased in intensity soon after I started sending out prolific email messages to publishers, to every large newspaper in the country, to producers of radio stations, and an Ivy League university website, discussing my experiences and my intentions to publicize them. Now I am down to getting a mere four hours of sleep each night. That is not enough. An adult, even one in her fifties, requires eight. Because there is a direct correlation between sleep deprivation and accelerated aging, I must necessarily extrapolate that a causality exists among the increased electromagnetically-induced shocks from aircraft, the subsequent loss of sleep, and the fact that I have aged very rapidly in the past year. This is what they must have done to the young man who sat in front of me during my detail: they took a man who looked 20 in 1992, inundated him with EMs either at work, at home, or both, and made him look 80 by 2006.

MICHELLE

There is someone else who has deteriorated, as well. During my detail I became friends with a colleague, one who is highly educated. At that time she was alert and had a good memory.

However, when I worked with her 15 years later, I was troubled to discover that she was experiencing difficulty remembering things. She would search for the right word, a name, and place, and could not find it. The funny thing is that when I worked near her, I could no longer remember things either. Whenever we visited one another we spent much of our time trying to remember a detail that we wanted to include in our comments. We both had trouble completing our sentences because we always sought a word that eluded us. *The Science behind Microwave War* cites numerous scientific papers in which EMs are proven, under laboratory conditions, to cause confusion, disorientation and temporary loss of memory in human subjects. The purpose is preparation for war in the 21st century.

ANOTHER PSYOP

A particularly bizarre event transpired during my 1991 detail when one day, someone stole money from a safe in the office. Everyone assumed that it must have been one of permanently assigned employees in the division, someone who was privy to the combination of the safe, someone high on the pyramid. Security was tightened up. People had to sign in and out upon leaving in order to keep records of who was there and who was not. Every time people got up to go to the bathroom, others got up and watched where they went. People on a detail hoped that the supervisors there did not suspect that it was one of them. I asked one of them if they did. He assured me that they did not—we did not know the combination to the lock.

Looking back on this occurrence, I believe that it was a psyop performed by a military intelligence agency: raise stress levels, get them all looking at one another with suspicion, increase anxiety, and then make a record of people's responses to stress. The data can be compared to responses to stress at a future date. The variable: doses of electromagnetic radiation. I do not for one millisecond believe that any Customs employee ever stole any money: they are too healthy, their self-esteem is too high, and they already make a good salary. Why would they risk their pensions to perpetrate a stupidity? No, it was surely a Pentagon psyop.

I loved my 90-day detail and one year later, when the boss came around again and asked if anyone wanted to apply for another detail, I volunteered and was accepted.

ENCORE!

During my second stint, the faces and assignments changed. I was not assigned to the same group anymore. I was in a different room and had different chores.

Every day at lunch time I retrieved the plastic shopping bags that I had hidden beneath my desk and ventured outdoors on a safari. I had a lot of spare time, people were coming and going on assignments, and because I was not in my regular office, my supervisor was not around to watch me. I hit the streets of Lower Manhattan and returned an hour later with my $6 daily allotment of soda cans. No one noticed, no one cared, and I stashed my treasure beneath my desk.

On one particular day I had a special chore to take care of. I glanced at my watch. It was lunchtime and everyone was out of the office. Now was the time to quickly do what I needed to do. What I was about to do was very embarrassing and I did not want anyone to witness this: I called the Consolidated Edison Company of NY, Inc., and terminated my account. It did not want to have to pay the electric bill anymore. I had found another way to beat the system.

MY BRANCH CHIEF PUTS ME UP FOR ADOPTION

Word got around that I had been seen bending over and reaching into garbage cans. The buzzer on my black rotary phone heaved a deep animal sound. That meant that it was the front office. My branch chief wanted to see me.

She invited me to sit down. Then she hemmed and hawed and hesitated.

"Frankly, dear, I do not know how to broach the subject," she said in an icy tone. I decided that I would help her along.

"Does it have anything to do with the fact that I eat out of the garbage?" I asked meekly.

Her eyes welled up with tears and she stared at me. Her face was red and the tears dropped down her cheeks.

"I want you to see someone who can help you." She gave me the name of a licensed psychotherapist who had a contract with Customs. She had an office in the building and had office hours during the week. I processed the information rapidly as if I were calculating all of the possible permutations in a chess game. With lightning precision, I made my decision.

"I don't want anything kept in a government file. Everyone knows that the government has two files: the one that they show you and the one that they don't." She remained silent as she gave it some thought. I asked whether this were mandatory. She thought some more.

"No," she finally replied.

"I will take a pass because I have my whole life ahead of me and don't want anything in a government file." She understood the logic and rationality of my point. She dismissed me and began to consider what she might do next. A few days later she called me back to inform me that I would be happier working on another floor in another branch.

THE PSYOPS BECOME OBVIOUS – 1992

It was after I moved to a new location that strange happenings started to occur. Looking back on it, I am convinced that a military intelligence agency was experimenting with us, mostly on single women living alone. We were the object of psyops, germ warfare resulting in death, and a barrage of electromagnetic waves that would eventually cause obsessive-compulsive behavior, autoimmune disease, difficulty focusing, the inability to concentrate, and the loss of memory.

Customs was undergoing reorganization and my office move had to be negotiated with the union. The two sides reached an agreement that Mary Gregory would be transferred to another floor and that she would have her own office. My new quarters would be a certain walk-in clothing/sample closet, big enough for a GS-12, but much too small for a GS-14's ego. The managers decided to reward me for all of my efforts and they agreed that I could have the closet. It had a door with a lock on it.

I had brand new, royal blue, deep pile carpeting. Because I was resourceful and inventive, I took the freight elevator to the subterranean B-2 level and inspected the Customs trash for furniture that the government was throwing away. I promptly found the Regional Commissioner's desk. It was huge and it sported a chipped edge at the top right hand corner. It also weighed a ton. One morning I arrived at work at 5:30 AM, headed straight to the basement, and slowly pushed the heavy monster into the freight elevator. Then I slowly pushed it down the hallway to my office. Fortunately, the new pile rug made it glide like an air train. By 7 AM I found two muscular GS-14s to turn it right side up in my new office. My new office was my castle.

It was fortunate that I had a lock on my door: I very soon discovered that Nelson, my next door neighbor, was obsessive-compulsive. He arrived at 9:30 AM every morning and demanded attention. He swept through the door like a hurricane and switched on his stereo sky high. Then he opened and slammed the metal cabinet drawers loudly and continually. He needed attention and he acted spontaneously to get it. He had no impulse control at all, absolutely none.

Nelson continually collected garbage. Old newspapers were stashed to the ceiling and squeezed to the limits beneath desks and chairs. Boxes and boxes of rusty pen refills whose ink had long dried, coins covered with mold, rusty scissors, rusty paperclips, Customs documents from World

War II, were crammed into drawers that were falling off their hinges.

He was a compulsive talker: he could not stop if someone were pointing a gun to his head. I quickly surmised that his was the rubber room and that the supervisor had put him there so that he could bounce off the walls away from the other employees. Everyone knew that he was compulsive and hyper, but it did not matter because they did not have to sit next door to him. I did. Even with the door closed, I heard the metal cabinets that were situated along the wall that we shared, open and slam shut perpetually. The heavy metallic sound reverberated in my office as if I were situated in a sardine can and the wall between us shook with a muffled thud. I heard the stereo blare. He got on the phone and conversed as if the person on the other end were deaf. Looking back on it, I now question whether there even was anyone on the other end of the line. Who would want to talk to him? My castle may have been paradise, but on the other side of the wall there lurked a snake.

SEMEN ON THE FLOOR – 1992, Customhouse

One morning when I arrived at 6 AM and snapped on the lights in my office, I discovered that there was some white material on the rug next to my office chair. It looked like a long drawn out chalk mark. I wondered what was on the bottom of my soles. Had I done that? I looked beneath my shoes, but there was nothing stuck to my soles.

I sat down in my chair, leaned down towards the floor, and scrutinized the white mark on the rug. This was not a solid line at all. It was a series of tiny spots that ran in a perfectly straight line. Furthermore, the farther away that the spots extended from the chair, the smaller they became until they disappeared into the distance. It was semen, designed to intimidate and aggravate. The victim? I was a single white woman, living alone. The lab mouse of choice for the Nazi mind.

SWASTIKAS AROUND THE DESK – 1992

A few months later. I unlocked my door at 6 AM and turned on the light. I was stunned at what I saw: there were swastikas formed in dust all around my desk. Someone had brushed the tip of an index finger and had drawn them in dust. Interspersed among the swastikas were smile faces across the front of the desk and on each side. Furthermore, a sticker of an American flag had been stuck to the side of the desk. I knew that that flag was not there before: the day that I had rescued the desk from the garbage I had removed all decals, from the insides of the drawers and on the exterior, and thoroughly scoured every square inch of surface, on the top, front and sides, with alcohol because I did not want to pick up any lice.

I told a supervisor that someone had drawn swastikas around my desk. Five minutes later a fire alarm siren went off and we had to evacuate the floor for a fire drill. I surmised that the supervisor must have called the agents and that they were checking the floor for a bomb.

Swastikas drawn in soot around the desk. Semen on the rug. This was psyops.

An analogy can be made between these two events and the one that had occurred back in 1980 when Kyle's desk had been pushed behind the door and the perpetrator had exited via the ceiling. All three betray a juvenile and malicious mentality at work; all three were carried out unobserved, in the solitude of the night; all three sought to aggravate and create anxiety in its victims.

As the years elapsed, especially with the advent of Bush II, it became obvious that the targets of these psyops were usually single women living alone and the handicapped: they are considered to be marginal members of society. The experimenters choose as subjects people who live alone for a very important reason: when psyops are conducted at the person's residence, there are no witnesses present to testify in court or provide corroborating testimony. The Pentagon selectively chooses situations where there are no witnesses.

One might argue, "But this was done at work where there are plenty of witnesses!—after the fact, not during the commission of the crime." Yes, but the rest is done at the person's residence where there are none. If any readers have civil service jobs and suspect that they are the non-consenting subjects of government experimentation, keep a log, take pictures, tell people so that they know and may one day testify in court that this has been going on for a long time. Ask your neighbors, at work and at home, whether they are experiencing similar phenomena. You may discover that the people residing on your block are experiencing the same. I did. Government experimentation on unsuspecting, non-consenting American citizens is much more widespread than is commonly thought, especially in metropoli where people are transient and immigrants are not likely to catch on or sue.

(Endnotes)

1   "sed quis custodiet ipsos custodes?" Juvenal, *D. Junii Juvenalis Saturarum libri V*, Mit erklärenden Anmerkungen von Ludwig Friedlaender, Erster Band (Leipzig: Verlag von S. Hirzel, 1895), book II, satire 6, 347–48, p. 325.

Every day an "X" is projected on the façade of the building next to mine in multiple locations. It also appears on the ground outside my window.

Chapter Five

The Clinton Years (1993–2000)

Informed Consent. Respect for persons requires that subjects, to the degree that they are capable be given the opportunity to choose what shall or shall not happen to them. This opportunity is provided when adequate standards for informed consent are satisfied.[1]
> —*The Belmont Report*, Department of Health, Education, and Welfare, April 18, 1979

The Clinton years were marked by an unrelenting march forward in the development of microwave weaponry. The first inkling of this became evident when a laser pulse weapon aboard an aircraft was used to set fire to the Koresh compound in Waco, TX. A cogent argument can be made that the U.S. government has used laser pulse weaponry to attack its own citizens on at least two occasions—its attack on the Koresh compound and the downing of Flight 93 on 9/11. Moreover, I can personally testify that it was used on me, to shock my brain and heart continuously between 2002–2009, and to eviscerate aluminum shielding in my apartment on six occasions on September 29, October 16, October 30, October 31, November 9, 2009 and December 19 (see *Microwave War*).

DAVID KORESH

Let us revisit the showdown between Janet Reno's Department of Justice and Branch Davidian leader David Koresh in Waco, TX on April 19, 1993. The crisis began on February 28 with an ATF raid on the complex prompted by reports that Koresh was stockpiling illegal weapons inside the compound; 4 ATF agents were killed by cult members. A standoff ensued for 51 days and finally, on April 19, Koresh and more than 80 followers, including at least 17 children, died when flames erupted in his sprawling L-shaped Mt. Carmel complex.

It is significant that rapid flashes of light were seen moments before the fire erupted inside the complex. These flashes of light suggest that either the FBI had in its possession state of the art high powered microwave weaponry or that it had gotten such weaponry from the British.

On March 11, 2000 CNN reported:

> Infrared tape shot April 19, 1993, from an airplane over the Branch Davidian complex shows rapid flashes of light. Attorneys for the Davidians contend the flashes represent federal agents shooting at the Davidians.
>
> The FBI has insisted its agents fired no shots. Its experts say the flashes of light are reflections.[2]

Lawyers for the Davidians argue that the FBI's aerial infrared surveillance footage proves that gunfire was directed into the building as it burned. It appears that the FBI used laser pulse weapons to set off an explosion resulting in fire.

What we do know for sure is that the FBI employed forward looking infrared radar (FLIR) to image inside the complex. Infrared radar can penetrate walls and smoke and discern human beings by the heat that their bodies generate. It is used for the surveillance of people, locating people through barriers and walls, and search and rescue operations in wooded areas. FLIRs detect thermal energy to create a picture of a location. Forward looking can be distinguished from sideways tracking infrared radar; they have been made obsolete by FLIR because they cannot image in real time.

The FBI admits that it used FLIR to image inside the compound and create pictures of all the items in each room. What it does not concede is that it used a different device, a laser pulse, to cause a fire in the compound.

Similarly, on 9/11, Flight 93 crashed in Shanksville, PA. Just before it crashed, someone on a cellphone declared that he had just seen a flash of light outside the plane. Then the cellphone went dead and the plane crashed.

The U.S. government has been exploring this technology since WW II. In 1949 Guy Obelensky, an American inventor, was able to duplicate a Nazi device that delivered a shock wave from a distance using radio waves (see *The Science behind Microwave War*). The Pentagon has been pursuing this technology since WW II, it admits that it has laser pulse weapons in its arsenal and that it is using them in Iraq and Afghanistan, but what it does not concede is that it is using them domestically.

LEFTY, THE GUNMAN

Victor sat back in his plush swivel chair and related the legendary tale of Lefty, the Gunman. Lefty was a Customs employee who had suddenly become insane one day, for no apparent reason. He would approach people in the hallway and engage them in conversation. Then, quite unexpectedly, Lefty would lift his right hand and cover both eyes, and extend his left hand out in front of himself and point it as if he were holding a gun. "Bang!" he would cry loudly, and then follow it up with "Boo, hoo, hoo!" as he continued to cover his eyes with his right hand. Real tears fell from his eyes and he was genuinely sorry that he had shot the other person. Victor laughed heartily.

"Well, what do you think of that?" he asked.

"Did he really have a gun?"

"No! That's the whole point! He didn't! It was all make believe. But he was so sick up here," Victor explained as he pointed his index finger to his temple, "he thought that he had really killed the other person and he was afraid to look. Don't you remember him?"

"No, I can't say that I do. What year was this?"

"Not so long ago. You must have just missed each other. He must have left just before you came in." I am grateful that my colleague shared the story of Lefty, the Gunman with me. It leads me to suspect that Customs employees were the subjects of early primitive experiments with EMs just prior to my arrival.

FOUR DEATHS ON THE SAME FLOOR

The managers wanted us to learn fraud investigative techniques and so, they assigned us the task of taking turns, spending one month at a time on another floor where specialists would teach us. I was eager to see if I could detect any fraud from perusing the computer. It was a challenge to try to make a discovery that resulted in millions of dollars in additional revenue. I had already done it once during one of my details. Perhaps I could do it again in the privacy of my office if I knew how.

It was then that my cleaning compulsion surfaced. I did not want to pick up any lice from the furniture upstairs: therefore, on the first day of the detail, yellow legal pad tucked squarely beneath an arm and pen in a breast pocket, I wheeled my office chair into the elevator and to the other floor. Then I came back for a bottle of alcohol and some paper napkins. The time had arrived to scour the tabletop where I would be working. It did not want any lice on my shirt sleeves or suit.

An employee was assigned to escort me around the cubicles and introduce me to everyone. Soon I met them all, including Nia, a Chinese-American, 32; Leyla, white, about 30, a college graduate; Johnson, an African-American man in his 50s, divorced, who assisted people in navigating the myriad functions of the Customs computer; Monty, a young African-American man in his 30s, who worked in a different office, just a few yards away, across a narrow hallway. I met them all and grew to love and respect them. They were always eager to help and set their work aside to instruct those needing help. They were great teachers and equally important, they made me feel that I was welcome in their division.

That is why I was devastated when they all died, one by one, all around the same time, all in the same year. They all worked on the same floor: three were seated in the vast office on one side of the hallway, the fourth, across the hall.

Leyla died suddenly over the weekend. She attended work on Friday and we got the news Monday. Someone said that she had suddenly contracted polio. Monty also collapsed unexpectedly. Everyone was surprised that someone young and in excellent health would suddenly fall ill and die. Nia contracted cancer and died; Johnson also died of cancer. It is significant that one was a Chinese female, two were black males, and one was a white female. Whatever it was that was being tested, it covered a broad racial spectrum and both sexes.

The deaths became the subject of endless speculation. One of the supervisors on my floor declared that their floor was a microwave oven because there was a computer on every desk. He believed that the people's immune systems had been compromised by computer radiation.

Their supervisor suspected that there might be Legionnaire's disease in the air vents. She had samples taken from the vents, but the results were negative

It could have been experimentation with germ warfare. As far back as November 1970 the *Military Review* disclosed that it was the government's intention to develop ethnic weapons that are designed to kill certain races.[3] The *Military Review* is an official publication of the U.S. Army Command and General Staff College. The United States government has a long, sordid, and protracted history of experimenting with its citizens, both civilian and military. Such are the black ops projects that the Pentagon is funding by trafficking narcotics into the country.

However, I would not rule out an assault of electromagnetic waves. EMs do alter human physiology: they cause cancer; disrupt sleep patterns and prevent people from sleeping; continual loss of sleep causes accelerated aging. The military has the capability of assaulting a person with EMs from an airplane at a distance, a truck parked across the street, a nearby apartment, or by putting devices in the walls. In fact, even after the U.S. government made the discovery in 1962 that its embassy in Moscow was being bombarded with EMs, and even after three ambassadors died and many other embassy employees became ill, the government kept its personnel there to glean data and profit from the Russian experiment as late as 1992 (see *The Science behind Microwave War*, Chapter One, Project Pandora). This is indicative of the fact that U.S. government intelligence agencies conducting experiments do not value the lives of Americans.

ALEXANDRA – 1995

Alexandra was a single woman who was sometimes seen dining in the cafeteria with a coworker. She died from cancer the moment that she retired from her job. Now that I look back on this, why is it that I cannot think of one married employee, not one, who suddenly dropped dead the moment he retired? With the exception of Nia, who, most likely, was the subject of an experiment, I cannot think of one married woman who dropped dead.

TAPS ON THE WALLS, DEATHS, CANCER, OCD, AND MORE PSYOPS

I had to move to another office and give up my little room with a lock on it. My next door neighbor continually demanded attention and the noise that he generated by slamming the metal cabinets made it impossible to concentrate. Therefore, my boss did what any effective boss would do: she moved me out of there as soon as there was a vacant spot somewhere on the vast expanse of the fourth floor. I continued to work for the same GS-14s. During the remainder of the 1990s and right up until 9/11, I tried out four more worksites. As it turned out, it was fortunate that I did: I noticed and made a note of unusual electronic phenomena in all four locations and of the people who got sick there.

The four subsequent offices were cubicles enclosed in woven acrylic-covered modular walls. In all four of them there was a continual crackling sound that was bouncing off the textile walls, the metal filing cabinets, and the metal bookcases. BZZZT! FSSST! It was interminable and unceasing from morning 'til night. Looking back on it, I believe that we were being dowsed with heavy doses of electromagnetic radiation. What else could cause a violent metallic snap to crackle off a metal bookcase? The strikes were forceful and quite loud. What else could cause shocks, pings, and ZZZTs to spring off of acrylic wall coverings?

MADELEINE

When my boss yanked me away from my next door neighbor, she assigned me to sit next to Madeleine, a very bright and intelligent woman. As I sat in my cubicle on the other side of divider separating us, there was a continuum of squeaks, bursts of static electricity, and pops ricocheting off the textile-covered walls. Occasionally I heard a violent SNAP! against the metal windowsill coming from her GS-14's office in the back. I was lost in my work, however, and although I heard the noise, I did not focus on it. Engrossed in our work, the two of us perpetually and interminably pounded on our keyboards. As we did, the tapping on keyboards was dramatically punctuated by the electromagnetic waves continually ricocheting off the metal cabinets and acrylic walls: SNAP! BZZZT! FSSST! SNAP! BZZZT! FSSST!

Very soon my neighbor on the other side of the divider began to exhibit obsessive-compulsive behavior. Whenever I pounded on my keyboard, Madeleine began to rip up paper. This constituted a new instrument in our orchestra. I went tap, tap, tap, tap. My printer went hum, mm, mm, mm, mm, mm. She went RIP! RIP! RIP! RIP!

Madeleine's paper ripping continued uncontrollably from morning until night, and after a month of listening to it, I was forced to look for new office space. As it turned out, my new location proved to be a highly charged electronic environment, the site of cancer, progressive supranuclear palsy, and obsessive eating to the point of death.

The new office space was a spot on a vast, mostly unoccupied floor. I rapidly assembled several modular walls around me, plugged my computer into a floor outlet, and started to work. I had barely sat down and signed on in the new location when the electrostatic crackling began. One hour later violent bursts of electrical energy snapped across acrylic covering on the modular walls. BZZZT! SSSSST! SNAP! LASH! Startled I looked up and stared at the walls surrounding me. They seemed to have acquired a life of their own; an invisible force, an energy had materialized from somewhere and was moving across them.

Furthermore, loud crackles and explosions could be heard emanating from the few other cubicles on the far end of the sparsely populated floor. The sound carried loudly across the mostly empty room. The other people had metal filing cabinets in their cubicles. The symphony of bursts and crackles from the acrylic was dramatically underscored by the violent metallic lashes off the filing cabinets. LASH! BOOM! CRACK!

Suddenly BZZZT! FSSST! vengefully exploded just a few inches from my right shoulder. It sounded like two gunshots next to my ear and caused my adrenalin to skyrocket and heart to pound. An invisible force was lashing across the textile-covered walls and it had a life of its own. The place was a lightning chamber. I considered the possibility that the activity resulted from static buildup from the computers. It most certainly had to be electronic in origin.

The death toll that occurred in that immediate area is too significant to ignore: it must be pointed out that two single women working in and around that site developed debilitating diseases that lead to their death, and that a Jewish male supervisor developed colon cancer and required a colostomy.

Andrea, single and living alone, worked there. When I shared an office with her back in 1980, she had no eating disorder. By 1993 she had started eating obsessively; became so heavy that she needed to be lifted out of the bathtub; developed sores on her legs; fell asleep at her desk. Her boss used to spy on her with binoculars from a glass window that faced her office at a 90° angle to see if she was working or asleep. Her OCD was a recent phenomenon in her Customs career. Project Pandora has proven that EMs destroy the normal functioning of the body; laboratory experiments have shown that they radically alter behavior in test animals.

Timothy, white, divorced, also developed glandular obesity, although not at that location. When I first met him at JFK in January 1978 he was slim; after spending 20 years working at JFK, he was unrecognizable.

It is also significant that Helena, who sat directly opposite me in this vast open area, suddenly became disabled by progressive supranuclear palsy (PSP); she kept falling backwards. She was single and in her 60s. She had always appeared to be in good health before. When I first moved into that area, I often stopped by her office to chat for a little while. She was always alert and attentive; she never mentioned dizziness. Our desks were separated by her dividers and mine; both hers and mine were perpetually squeaking and snapping as electrically charged bursts of energy violent lashed off the textile covering, loudly, forcefully, and continually, from morning until night.

Her illness surfaced suddenly. She started losing her balance and kept falling backwards. Shortly thereafter it became evident that she could not continue to come to work. She retired and subsequently died at the age of 67 in a nursing home.

Progressive supranuclear palsy is a rare degenerative disease of the brain: it impairs movements, balance, mood, behavior, personality, and the cognitive processes (thinking, memory, attention, and speech). Researchers know that it is caused by neurofibrillary tangles (NFTs), comprised of abnormal forms of the protein tau, and they are investigating mutations in the tau gene. Normally, tau protein molecules form part of an intracellular transport system that neurons use to move needed molecules in and waste products out. However, in PSP victims, the tau protein gets corrupted and twists together to form fibers or clumps; these anomalies are called taupathies.

Other researchers are investigating mutations in mitochondrial DNA: they are using mitochondrially transformed cells generated from PSP patients to investigate neuronal degeneration resulting from disturbances in calcium homeostasis. Calcium-ion efflux! Dr. William Ross Adey has demonstrated in the lab that subjecting a test animal to electromagnetic waves causes physiological changes in the brain, including changes in the binding of calcium—and this leads to changes in perception and behavior.[4] See *The Science behind Microwave War*, Chapter One, section entitled, "The Pioneering Work of Dr. Adey in the 1960s and 1970s."

Moreover, there exists a substantial number of studies that show a correlation between EMs emanating from our cellphones and DNA damage in the brain: cellphone radiation destroys the single-strand DNA in the brains of rats;[5] cellphone radiation destroys both the single- and double-strand DNA in the brains of rats;[6] mobile phone radiation destroys the DNA in the brains of rats;[7] the use of mobile phones for more than ten years is associated with an increased risk of brain tumors;[8] the use of cellphones is associated with a greater risk of brain tumors in rural areas, rather than in urban (the reason for this is that cellphone towers are farther apart in rural areas than they are in urban, and the signal has to be stronger).[9] These studies are collated and summarized in the forthcoming *Christianity and 21st Century Science*.[10] Since EMs cause DNA mutation, they can cause the body to produce abnormal forms of proteins; they can cause damage to mitochondrial DNA via disturbances in calcium-ion efflux.

It is also significant that Raymond, white, Jewish, married, worked in that same environment and became seriously ill. He had an office next to the PSP victim. This man was professional, courteous, and a very caring individual. He developed colon cancer and had to have a colostomy. Fortunately, the surgery was successful and hopefully, he is enjoying his retirement these days. Project Pandora has proven that EMs cause all kinds of cancer.

Three months later my boss announced that she had found a vacant office for me and that I was required to move again. She assigned me to work in an office occupied by two bullies. Daryl had deteriorated into a very angry, bitter, self-centered, nasty and obnoxious person; no one could have a conversation with him because he had lost his ability to listen. The other bully, Brandon, had also become increasingly more repugnant and despicable in recent years. One day in the not too distant future, he would thrash a door against the wall and swing his chair across a room with the intention of hurting a coworker; one day I would hear him utter a very low pitch gurgle that sounds like water swishing down the bathtub drain, or the low sound that a Tibetan monk makes when he meditates and delves into his consciousness. He would lose his impulse control. Did he have multiple personality disorder, as well?

After I moved into that office it became evident that their minds had deteriorated even more than I had imagined: they were more spiteful and malicious now than ever. Furthermore, something invisible was vehemently snapping off the metal cabinets, the metal fronts and sides of the desks, and the acrylic covering on the modular walls in their offices. On more than one occasion I heard a violent metallic thud drop into one bully's office in the back room. When I arose to see what it was, I discovered that its occupant was not at his desk. I stared at the metal windowsill and then up at the ceiling. Back then I considered only two possibilities: the violent snap had either emanated from the heating pipes concealed in the windowsill or it was static caused by the computer. Looking back, I now deem that it was the result of a high concentration of EMs. I am certain that if I had interrogated employees working for private industry elsewhere in the massive 7-building WTC complex, and asked them if they ever experienced these phenomena, I would have gotten a negative reply each time. One day, in the not too distant future, I would find myself asking that question to people working for corporations in our new building and their response would invariably be "No, never. Are you kidding?"

An interesting case of vandalism occurred in that office. I was the victim. One morning I snapped on the lights and sat down at my desk. I inserted my 3 ½" floppy disk into the computer and discovered that the disk no longer worked properly. All of my Customs work was on that disk. I brought the disk to an IT specialist who examined it: he advised that the disk did not work because I had two FAT files on it. He deleted one of the FAT files and then the disk worked fine. I asked him how that could have happened. He replied that perhaps I had put a metal object, such as a stapler, on the disk and had magnetized it. I assured him that I had never put the disk anywhere near a stapler because I knew not to do that; I asked how else an extra FAT file could be generated. He insisted that it was the result of carelessly touching the disk with a metal object.

At that time, I thought that one of the two bullies might have deliberately sabotaged my disk. However, looking back, I believe that it was a psyop. I never touched my disk with a stapler because I knew that diskettes are comprised of electromagnetic film; someone must have reproduced the FAT file at night to test my response to stress.

Because I was extremely unhappy in that office, I kept watch for the appearance of another empty cubicle. As soon as one materialized, I requested it, and my boss agreed to move me. I moved down the hall, several offices away, and it turned out that that was the perfect office for me: the other two occupants in that room were very thoughtful and sensitive people. It was a pleasure to come to work each day.

Soon after I set up my modular walls, the electrical bursts began with a vengeance. SNAP! LASH! CRACK! The unruly electrons vaulted off the acrylic covering. CRASH! CRACK! BAM! They stabbed the metal filing cabinets in the two offices next to me.

Every day at noontime, after the GS-14 had left to go to lunch, an invisible leather whip would strike the metalwork in his empty office with exceeding ferocity. Every day I would arise from my chair and stand in his doorway wondering what that might have been.

I was the first to arrive in the morning. I snapped on the lights at 6 AM and sat down. Minutes later a vehement CRASH! vengefully struck the metal filing cabinet in the cubicle next to mine. I stepped around the divider and gazed into the empty cubicle. I thought that perhaps it might be a buildup of static electricity emanating from the computer screens.

There was another instance of psyops during this time before 9/11. This time I was the victim. Let us begin by visualizing the following scenario: my cubicle occupies half a room. I have arranged the desk and chair so that I can sit with my back against the rear wall. One morning at 6 AM I enter the room and snap on the light: there I discover a gaping hole in the wall just above the chair at the precise spot where my head would be if I were sitting in the chair. It looks as if someone has thrust a dagger, a screwdriver or a scissors into the wall and opened a hole in the plaster. If I had been sitting in the chair it would have penetrated my nose.

What was being studied here is the human response to stress after the subject has been exposed to specific levels of electromagnetic waves. My cubicle was a microwave oven. The electronic snaps and crackles off the furniture never stopped. The strikes were powerful and continual. How would I react to the mock violence on the wall? The symbolism was obvious. They aimed at my head. Was I stressed out by the discovery?

The GS-14 down the hall advised that on several occasions he arrived to work in the morning only to discover a trail of cigarette ashes on rug around his desk. He did not smoke. Several other GS-14s who worked on that hallway also remarked that when they opened their office doors in the morning, they found that the lights were on: they insisted that they distinctly remembered snapping them off the night before. Apparently psyops were occurring throughout the floor.

A few other things were going on in my cubicle, too. I would arrive in the morning to find a stain of dark brown liquid on the rug next to my office chair. This happened often, and eventually my rug was filthy. I knew that it was not my coffee because I always took care not to spill any coffee on the floor: I was compulsively clean. I would also find "X" marks dabbed on my modular walls with a dirty finger. The first thing that came to mind was that this was the result of an occult ritual. It appeared that someone on the floor was a closet practitioner of the occult. Looking back, I still do, but I keep an open mind: it could have been a psyop that was designed to ascertain my response to stress after EMs had been administered.

The Xs that had been dabbed on the modular walls were reminiscent of the swastikas and smile faces that had been brushed in dust on the front and sides of my desk in 1992. There were some Xs inscribed in the dusty table back then, as well. Could it have been the work of the same hands?

Whoever it was that liked to pour black water on the rug and dab Xs across the walls, he continued this practice throughout the remainder of my career in Customs: it transpired after our move to our new building, as well. There, I also discovered dirty, smudgy Xs applied on the textile-covered modular walls of my cubicle.

Basically, these are my recollections of the Clinton years: violent electromagnetic phenomena ricocheting off the walls, cabinets, windowsills, and desks; and concurrently, a continued and unending litany of deaths including two sudden deaths over the weekend, neurological disorders, cancer, serious glandular disorders, obsessive-compulsive disorders, loss of impulse control, and the inability to restrain one's aggressive instincts. One day in the not too distant future, after our relocation from the World Trade Center, the following would be added to the list: metastatic cancer, inability to retain an organ transplant, accelerated aging to the point of being scary, serious loss of memory, inability to focus and concentrate, and the tendency to be easily distracted.

(Endnotes)

1   "Ethical Principles and Guidelines for the Protection of Human Subjects of Research" in *The Belmont Report*, Office of the Secretary, Department of Health, Education, and Welfare, April 18, 1979, http://www. hhs.gov/ohrp/humansubjects/guidance/belmont.htm (December 2, 2009).

2   "Space Blankets may Aid Waco Investigators," March 11, 2000, http://archives.cnn.com/2000/US/03/11/waco.probe/ (March 29, 2009).

3   Carl A. Larson, "Ethnic Weapons," *Military Review*, November 1970, 3–11.

4   There is voluminous scientific literature that demonstrates that the migration of calcium ions is disturbed by electromagnetic waves. Here are three citations: S.M. Bawin and William Ross Adey, "Sensitivity of Calcium Binding in Cerebral Tissue to Weak Environmental Electric Fields Oscillating at Low Frequency," *Proceedings of the National Academy of Sciences of the United States of America* 73, no. 6 (June 1976): 1999–2003; William Ross Adey, "Neurophysiologic Effects of Radiofrequency and Microwave Radiation," *Bulletin of the New York Academy of Medicine* 55, no. 11 (December 1979): 1079–93; C.F. Blackman, J.A. Elder, C.M. Weil, S.G. Benane, D.C. Eichinger, and D.E. House, "Induction of Calcium-Ion Efflux from Brain Tissue by Radio-Frequency Radiation: Effects of Modulation Frequency and Field Strength," *Radio Science* 14, no. 6S (1979): 93–98.

5   Henry Lai and Narenda P. Singh, "Acute Low-intensity Microwave Exposure Increases DNA Single-strand Breaks in Rat Brain Cells," *Bioelectromagnetics* 16, no. 3 (October 1995): 207–10.

6   Henry Lai and Narenda P. Singh, "Single- and Double-strand DNA Breaks in Rat Brain Cells after Acute Exposure to Low-level Radio Frequency Electromagnetic Radiation," *International Journal of Radiation Biology* 69, no. 4 (April 1996): 513–21.

7   Leif G. Salford, *et al.*, "Nerve Cell Damage in Mammalian Brain after Exposure to Microwaves from GSM Mobile Phones," *Environmental Health Perspectives* 111, no. 7 (June 2003): 881–83.

8   Stefan Lönn, *et al*, "Mobile Phone Use and the Risk of Acoustic Neuroma," *Epidemiology* 15, no. 6 (November 2004): 653–59.

9   Lennart Hardell, *et al.*, "Use of Cellular Telephones and Brain Tumour Risk in Urban and Rural   Areas," *Occupational and Environmental Medicine* 62, no. 6 (June 2005): 390–94.

10   Mary Efrosini Gregory, *Christianity and 21ˢᵗ Century Science*,

Chapter 18, entitled, "The Dangers of UHF Radiation to Humans," currently in the prepublication stage.

The main New York office of US Customs at Building Six of the World Trade Center showing the damage of September 11, 2001.

Chapter Six

The Reign of Terror of King George II: The First Year (2001)

A military operation involves deception. Even though you are competent, appear to be incompetent. Though effective, appear to be ineffective.[1]
— Sun Tzu *The Art of War* (5th century BC)

TUESDAY, SEPTEMBER 11, 2001

I was in the World Trade Center at 5:30 AM. One of the stores on Broadway reliably tossed out loaves of Italian bread each day in the wee hours of the morning and I wanted to pick up a few with yesterday's date. The magazine store opposite the Disney Store, where Casual Corner had once been, was not open. This was unusual because in the past it had always opened between 5–5:30 AM and I liked to be there to observe the movement of furniture and merchandise: candy and newspapers on wooden stands with wheels were rolled around here and there; people used metal handcarts to move new magazines from the closet at the rear of the store over to the aisles where they would be displayed on wooden racks. However, not only had that particular stand not yet opened, all of the newsstands which regularly opened early were closed. It looked like everyone was taking his time.

I decided to stroll over to the park on Liberty Street where men played chess for money at lunchtime. I wondered whether on that day I would once again encounter a herd of tourists congregating on the street in the early morning hours. Yesterday I saw a delegation of 20–30 Pakistanis garbed in their native attire, standing rock still like statues in front of Two, staring up at it. I was annoyed because they were blocking my path and I had to walk out into the street and into traffic in order to skirt around them. I remarked that in recent days, yesterday and last Friday, there were a lot of foreigners on the street over by the Millennium Hotel staring up at One and Two. Last Friday there was a Muslim lying down prostrate on a rug, face down, on Church Street by the Millennium at 5 AM. I wondered whether there would be any more busloads of tourists today. I did not see any.

6 AM. I opened the door to my office and turned on the light. I placed my bank book on top of the desk, and next to it, my statement from the Federal Reserve Bank. I had saved $750,000 in Treasury bills thus far by eating out of the garbage, inserting my index finger in telephone coin returns, and putting my contacts on beneath a flashlight suspending from a string of paperclips on my bathroom mirror. No one in Customs knew that I was so cheap, I had not had an active account with Con Ed since 1992. I dared not mention it to anyone. If they knew, they would talk about me behind my back. However, I was well on my way towards saving my first million and I would have the last laugh.

At 8:42 AM I hit "print" on the keyboard and then walked over to the printer that was situated on the managing clerk's desk. I greeted some of my coworkers who were exchanging pleasantries by the printer. At 8:46:40 AM we heard a muffled metallic thud. We all looked up. It sounded as if someone had thrown over a filing cabinet upstairs. We wondered what they were they doing up there; it appeared that some men were horsing around. We continued talking. I told someone that I was investigating the tax situation in Europe in case the government offered an early retirement. My coworker recommended that I move to Monaco because the citizens of that country do not pay any taxes. Monaco is the second smallest sovereign nation on earth after Vatican City. Suddenly we heard another heavy metallic thud. We looked up at the ceiling again. It did indeed sound like filing cabinets were being overturned. We decided that the people above were doing construction and were moving things around.

Suddenly a GS-14 came running down the hallway with terror in his eyes. "Let's get out of here!" The urgent tone indicated that there was danger. I left my bankbook and Federal Reserve Bank statement on my desk. It never occurred to me that we would not be coming back.

I raced down the steps and exited the Customhouse over the parking garage. As I stood outside, pieces of wooden furniture, parts of chairs and desks, all kinds of debris were falling out of the windows immediately above from One. I deemed that it was not safe to walk outside, but nevertheless, it was urgent that I get out of there as fast as possible. There were steps leading down the side of the World Trade Center to Vesey Street where Borders Books was located on the corner, but falling debris was dropping down all over the steps and sidewalk below. It was not safe to walk down the steps; and if I were to take the chance, the sidewalk was not safe, either. I saw that people were taking the shortest route of escape: the footbridge, enclosed in glass, that traversed Vesey Street, connecting the Customhouse to Seven.

I took shelter near the Customhouse and waited for the torrent of debris to subside. There was a lull in the deluge and, instinctively covering my head, I raced across the footbridge into Seven. One by one, my coworkers started to assemble from various locations. Soon there was a crowd of Customs people standing in front of Seven looking up. One of the floors was on fire. The corner of that floor was bright orange. Suddenly we were stunned to see a man falling 60 stories to his death. His necktie and blazer were blowing upward as he made his rapid descent. He landed in the forty foot asphalt alleyway between the Customhouse and One, out of our view. Soon after that another man fell down the side of One into the alleyway.

Looking around at the startled and incredulous faces that surrounded me, I noticed that my GS-14 was there. I went over to him and stood by his side. He turned and noticed me. I leaned towards him.

"Why are these people jumping?" I asked hoarsely, trembling and disoriented.

"Because it is so hot up there that they can't stand it," he answered very softly and gently. And there we stood, suspended in surreality, as we watched one person after the next jump to his death.

One of the auditors said, after a while, "It's like a train wreck or a car crash. You can't bear to look, but you can't help not to." I turned around and saw a crowd of Customs personnel looking up in horror and nodding assent at his words. That was when I decided that I had had enough of this. Suddenly, I was seized with the urge to get out of there. I turned away and forged a path through the crowds. I had to find an exit right away, but I did not know my way around Seven. I circulated around and around, turning one corner after the next, over and over again, as I navigated tightly packed crowds of people listening intently to their cellphones. I entered rooms only to discover that I had been there before. I recognized the same faces and clothing: I had just seen this woman a few minutes ago, listening fixedly to a handheld device pressed against one ear. I felt uncomfortable about interrupting someone who was on a phone. Then I spied a woman who had just gotten off her cell and was slipping it into her purse. I approached her and smiled.

"Hello, may I ask you, how do you get out of here? Where is the exit?" I asked hurriedly.

"Oh, they're not letting us out," she replied. "They're keeping us here."

"Why?"

"I don't know. They locked all the doors and no one is allowed to leave." Suddenly I thought of the Secret Service. I remembered that there had been a very nice lady who was a Secret Service agent. She used to enter the Customhouse at 6 AM and take the elevator upstairs with me when they worked in Six. Every morning she used to take out her leather wallet and momentarily flash her badge at the security guard at the entrance. She carried herself with authority. I was intrigued by the fact that her badge looked different from mine. One morning she mentioned in the elevator that her agency was relocating to Seven. I never saw her again after that.

"The Secret Service is in here," I volunteered.

"So is the CIA," the lady said. "In fact, the CIA came in here at 6:00 this morning and they moved all of their cabinets out, everything."

"You're kidding!" I gasped.

"No, the CIA is on the 25th floor and it moved out of here at 6:00 this morning. One of the secretaries who works on that floor told me." I was stunned. We were all abandoned and alone and the CIA had left us.

I walked around the floor trying to make eye contact with people so that I could get a confirmation of what I had just heard. I saw a woman putting away her cellphone.

"I heard that the CIA works upstairs."

"They do," she said.

"Someone just told me that they moved out of here at 6:00 this morning. Do you know if that's true?"

"Oh, I don't know, but you know what you can do? Try and find a security guard to ask. They'll know. If you find out, come back and tell me. I would really appreciate that because I'd like to know."

Again I circulated through the tightly packed maze, this time in search of a security guard. Then I spotted several as I approached an exit. The guards were standing squarely in front of the glass doors in order to prevent a mass exodus. I made eye contact with one and smiled cordially.

"Hello. I work for Customs in Six. Are we allowed out of here?"

"No. No one is allowed to leave until we get the word that you can."

"May I ask you another question?" He nodded assent. "Does the CIA work in this building? I know that the Secret Service does because they moved here from Six. But does the CIA work here?"

"Mm, hm," the guard nodded assent once more.

"May I ask you another question?"

"Mm, hm."

"Where is the CIA?" The guard opened his eyes wide and he became animated.

"Oh, they're LONG gone," he replied. He emphasized "long" by increasing the volume and pitch of his voice. I distinctly remember that.

"LONG gone?" I asked.

"Oh, yeah! They're LONG gone!" he laughed.

"And how about the Secret Service. Are they around?"

"No, they evacuated when the plane hit." Suddenly I felt empty inside. I was hoping that we had the CIA and the Secret Service to look after us.

Well, that confirmed it: the CIA was long gone and the Secret Service had left the building, too. I would have liked to know what time the CIA left, but for some reason, I hesitated asking the guard. It was none of my business and I did not want to press him. I thanked him and continued walking around amid the crowds. As I navigated the tightly packed masses, the more and more I became fixated on his words. The longer I dwelt on them, the more I wanted to know how long it had been since the CIA had left. I found the lady who had told me about the secretary upstairs. We made eye contact.

"Hello, you know, I just spoke to a security guard and he said that the CIA was long gone."

"Of course! A secretary on that floor who works for the federal government said that they came in at 6:00 and moved out their filing cabinets!" I resolved then to return to the guard and specifically ask the time they had left. I returned to the hoards standing immobilized, waiting to be released from the building. I found the security guard.

"Hello!"

"Hi!"

"Thank-you for the information that you gave me. You know, uh, I am very embarrassed to ask, but there is something that I would really like to know."

"Yeah, what is it?"

"Uh, I met someone who said that the CIA came in early this morning and moved out its filing cabinets. Is that true?"

"Mm, hm." He nodded assent.

"What time did they arrive? Do you know why I ask? It's because a lady told me that they moved out of here at 6 AM. Is that true?" I stared squarely into his big brown eyes. I thought I saw, in a fleeting instant, abject terror envelope his soul and consume it whole. Then he collected himself and smiled.

"No, they moved out shortly before 7:30 AM. They usually come in at 10:00 AM, that is when they usually come to work, but this morning they arrived early because they are moving to another location. I would say that they got here around 7:20 or 7:25, something like that. Some of them came in early and moved out their filing cabinets. I would say that they came in at 7:20 or 7:25." I was surprised at the disparity in stories.

"Oh, really! 7:20 or 7:25?"

"Yeah."

"They came in at 7:20 or 7:25?

"Yeah."

"Well, thank-you."

"Sure. Is there anything else?"

"No, well, thank-you."

"Right." He made it obvious that the conversation was over and walked away. I stood there perplexed.

For some reason I needed confirmation of this. I needed to hear another security guard tell me the same thing. I resumed navigating the floor in search of another guard. I spotted one standing alone near an exit.

"Hi, excuse me, I work for the Customs Service in Six. May I ask you a question?"

"You may, go ahead."

"Someone said that the CIA moved out of here at 6 AM and someone else said 7:20 or 7:25. Did they move their filing cabinets out of here early this morning?"

"Oh, I don't know!" He looked frightened. I decided to repeat myself, hoping that it would get him to talk.

"You know, a secretary who works upstairs said that they came in a 6 AM and moved out their filing cabinets, but when I asked one of the security guards, he said that it was later, more like 7:20 or 7:25. Is the security guard right?"

"Oh, I don't know! If he says so, it must be." He shrugged his shoulders. I got nothing out of him. The feeling of emptiness and abandonment returned to the pit of my stomach. Misery loves company, but I would not be so fortunate as to find it from these agencies.

Floors 9–10 of 7 WTC were occupied by the U.S. Secret Service; floor 23, New York City's Office of Emergency Management (OEM); floor 24, the Internal Revenue Service (IRS); floor 25 was shared by the IRS, the Department of Defense (DoD) and the Central Intelligence Agency (CIA).[2] Moreover, the *New York Times* reports the following regarding the CIA office: "The agency's New York station was behind the false front of another federal organization, which intelligence officials requested that the *Times* not identify."[3]

The spectacular testimony furnished above is crucial for a very important reason: the security guards' statement that the CIA was "LONG gone," and that it had taken its filing cabinets along with it, is diametrically antithetical to the story that the Agency supplied to the media. Therefore, let us rewrite the story and tell the public the truth: operations were not disrupted because the Agency had already been in the process of relocating to another site for some time. Some of the agency's employees at the site were safely evacuated even before Mohammed Atta's Flight 11 took off from Boston's Logan Airport at 7:59 AM. They were LONG gone.

A CIA official assured CNN that there was "no reason to believe any materials got into the hands of the wrong people."[4] Of course not.

I strongly suspect that the CIA had timed its evacuation with the utmost precision, as it always did, when carrying out a false flag operation.

Something struck me in the BBC's coverage of CIA operations in New York City:

> CIA officers in New York have been forced to share space at the United States Mission to the United Nations, as well as borrow other federal government offices in the city, officials told the newspaper.[5]

Oh, yeah? Does "borrow" mean that they return them the next morning? Do they leave cigarette trails across the rug? Do they leave the lights on? Do they like to pull heavy desks behind doors and exit through the ceiling? Do they like to draw swastikas and smile faces in the dust on people's desks? Do they commit lewd acts while sitting in other people's chairs?

I find another detail to be significant: after the second plane hit Two at 9:03:11 AM, the security guards opened the doors and let us leave. One suspects that the people who were directing them through their walkie-talkies were waiting for the second plane to hit. During the following months, I became embroiled in a heated debate with a colleague over this detail. She staunchly maintained that they did not know that the second plane (UA Flight 175) was going to hit; that they wanted to ascertain whether the crash into One had been a terrorist attack before releasing us. Conversely, I argued that they were waiting for the second plane to hit before letting us go outdoors. For some reason, my position riled my coworker up considerably and she started to scream at me uncontrollably (too much exposure to EMs, perhaps?).

According to *The 9/11 Commission Report*, Flight 175's transponder code was changed twice and air traffic controllers had to guess its position by its near misses with other aircraft. If the controllers could not locate and identify the plane at every moment, how did they know that it was heading towards the World Trade Center?—especially since it passed NYC, continued southwest, and then turned around and returned, heading in a northeasterly direction. Was I correct in arguing that the people who were directing the security guards must have had prior knowledge and were waiting for the second plane to hit before letting us out?

One must also examine my colleague's statement that the people in charge wanted to ascertain whether or not the WTC was under attack before releasing us from Seven. What kind of logic is this? Let us examine both possibilities: if the WTC were, indeed, under attack, why would they keep us locked indoors? Why wouldn't they let us try to escape? They certainly did after 9:03:11 AM, when the second plane hit Two. However, if the WTC were not under attack and the crash into One were an accident, why would they keep us locked indoors? Either way, there was no reason to keep us indoors. There must be a third possibility: they were waiting for the second plane to hit and afterwards, they ascertained that it was over. Dear reader, what do you think?

After I was released from Seven, I looked up at the inferno raging above. My instinct warned me that because all of the floors situated above the fire were comprised of heavy concrete, it was highly possible that the upper floors of One

might crack, break off like a pencil, and fall over at a 90°
degree angle. Therefore, I intentionally avoided running in
a straight line up Church Street or Broadway because they
were in full view of One. I wanted buildings to shield me
from anything that dropped down. I chose to take a diag-
onal path to be out of the way. I ran north one block on
Greenwich Street, east one block on Park Place, north one
block on West Broadway, east one block on Murray Street,
north one block on Church Street. Moving from one block
to the next among the tightly packed crowd proved to be
slow and arduous. I was surrounded by throngs who crept
forward one inch at a time. There was no stepping around
them. I glanced worriedly at my watch. What would happen
if One broke off like a pencil and fell to the ground?

I was still on Church Street when Two collapsed at 9:58:59
AM. It imploded in ten seconds, killing all civilians and
emergency personal inside, as well as people in the Con-
course, the Marriott, and adjacent streets. As it did, a colos-
sal white wave of debris and dust rolled up Broadway: it had
a life of its own. I turned around and saw the white wave of
steel, glass, and dust thundering up behind me, much like a
giant ocean wave rises up high above surfers, curls up over
them, and then buries them in its cavernous hollow. The
thunderous, moving white wave, consuming everything and
everyone in its path, stopped just one block behind me.

Thin, shrill cries rose to the sky from every direction and
resonated across every street and avenue, just like they do
at a rally or a march...except that these screams were those
of terror and panic.

People were on their cellphones. Someone on the street
said that Two had just fallen. I stood in the middle of
Church Street and looked south at the mushroom cloud
of dust and debris. Two had just fallen, I thought. Then I
remembered that of the two towers, Two was the farther
from me—and I realized that if One, the closer of the two,
had fallen first...I am having difficulty typing this...I can-

not bear to imagine...what would have happened...if One had fallen first.

As I stood on Church Street looking at the mushroom cloud of powder and wreckage just one block behind me, another person, holding a cellphone to his ear, hollered that there were two planes. One plane hit One and the other, Two.

A middle aged man was standing on the street shaking his head. I saw that he was expressive and animated so I thought that I would initiate a conversation with him. I would very soon regret that I had made that mistake.

"Two just fell," I said as I stood squarely in front of him.

"It was just an accident, that's all," he replied.

"No," I corrected him, "Someone with a cellphone just announced that there were two planes." Suddenly he became enraged and bugged his eyes out at me.

"And you know what that means," he screamed, "If a second plane hit, then the bridges and tunnels aren't safe! They are going to blow up the bridges and tunnels next!" Hysterical, he looked as if he were about to lunge at me. I backed away from him and continued my journey up Broadway.

When I arrived at the "R" train at City Hall, I discovered that the subway platform was tightly packed with refugees waiting to escape. Rapidly scanning the platform, I recognized an IT person from Customs. Delighted to know someone there, I waved and smiled broadly. He did the same. Then the "R" train pulled into the station and the conductor opened the doors. We all boarded and I squeezed into a space in front of a door leading to the next car. Then the passengers discovered that the conductor intended to wait there a long time before proceeding. As the conductor was listening for instructions on his walkie-talkie, the doors remained opened and even more people rushed inside. The conductor finally did close the doors, but, despite the crowded cars, he insisted on making every local stop.

At 34th Street the conductor surprised everyone with the announcement that the train had arrived at its final stop and that it would go no further. He ordered us off the train. A distinguished looking businessman standing in front of me turned around and nodded to me.

"It must be for security reasons," he explained. "The Empire State Building is right upstairs and this is a high risk location. Moreover, something happened at the Pentagon."

"The Pentagon!"

"Mm, hm," he nodded assent.

When I ascended to the street level, there was a large crowd of people. The story that was circulating on the sidewalk was that if Queens residents wanted to get home, they would have to walk across the 59th Street Bridge. It was time to start marching.

I made friends with a Russian woman who had been taking a computer course in midtown that morning. She lived in Bayside and so we walked together in the direction of 59th Street. The time went by very quickly because I had company and the continual distractions of large crowds.

However, the situation started to get progressively more daunting just as we approached the 59th Street Bridge. The scuttlebutt on the street was that the bridges and tunnels were not safe and that the 59th Street Bridge might get blown up while we were still in the middle of it. People started asking each other whether they could swim.

As I crossed the bridge, I fully expected that I would have to walk all the way home to Rego Park. However, I was pleasantly surprised: just as the throngs of pedestrians were descending the bridge, a caravan of empty buses pulled up to pick up passengers the moment they descended from the bridge. Mayor Rudolph Giuliani was certainly well organized.

A bus stopped in front of me and the driver shouted, "Queens Boulevard!" That sounded like the Q60. "Rego Park?" I asked the driver. He nodded in the affirmative. The moment he opened the doors, hordes of people stormed the bus wildly, both from the front and rear doors. No one bothered to pay the fare and the driver did not care. His assignment that day was to move everyone out of there fast. The bus raced across Queens Boulevard at lightning speed, not stopping once until the Queens Center. I was home at 1 PM.

My behavior that afternoon is very telling of something, I am not sure what. I took a shower; I climbed into bed with my portable CD player and set of Barron's Mastering French compact discs, and I practiced speaking French for three full hours. I went through each disc twice. I wanted to get my Ph.D in French and I wanted to be able to pass a defense in French in case I had to. To say that I was extremely disciplined and focused is to utter an understatement. Prior to 9/11 I would come home from work each day, shower, and then practice French for three full hours. Today, the fact that the World Trade Center had just fallen to the ground a few hours before, did not stop me from accomplishing what I wanted to do. Astute reader, could it be that years of swimming in microwave radiation has made me the ideal employee, the ideal student, the ideal everything? I am oblivious to distractions and I focus on my work. Did it change something in my brain so that, like Albert Einstein, I would obsessively focus on the same problem for twenty years until I solved it?

Finally, I put in my three hours and I turned off the CD player. I switched on my walkman to find out what was going on in the real world. By then it was 5:25 PM. I was stunned to learn that Seven, the great glass fortress in which my coworkers and I had found temporary shelter, had just fallen to the ground, at 5:20 PM. And to think that I had sought shelter in that building just hours before!

Many of the radio stations were not transmitting—they had lost their antennae atop of One. I would later learn that the top of One had fallen down directly into the middle of the Customhouse, giving it a horseshoe appearance. My intuition was right about a piece breaking off like a pencil and falling sideways.

WEDNESDAY, SEPTEMBER 12, 2001

That night as I was listening to the radio, I heard that people were allowed to return to the World Trade Center to retrieve their valuables. Immediately I made plans to visit the Customhouse to retrieve my bankbook and my statement from the Federal Reserve Bank. As it turned out, the news story was a big lie: only financial institutions were authorized to retrieve their gold bullion that was housed in the basement; no one else was permitted past Broadway. I had no way of knowing that in Queens.

THURSDAY, SEPTEMBER 13, 2001

I boarded the subway and visited the site for four hours. Even before I got off the subway I began to inhale crushed glass, toxic chemicals and asbestos. The filthy air was particularly overpowering during the interminable walk through the "A" train's winding subterranean tunnels. After the train had deposited the passengers on the platform and departed from the station, riders discovered that one exit after the next was boarded up and closed. We were forced to breathe the thick stench as we furtively darted about looking for an exit that was open. Many pathways were circular and we entered into spaces only to discover that we had been there before. It took me a half hour to find a way out of there. It was purely accidental; I knew that I could not do it again if I tried.

A police officer advised me that no one was allowed on the site. The finality of his tone indicated that that was the end of that and that the case was closed. As I walked up Broadway I thought about how unjust it was that the banks and investment companies were busy getting their gold out of there, but that I, who was a creditor of U.S. public debt

125

to a great extent, but not as much as China, should not be allowed to get my bankbook and statement. I resented the disparity in rights.

I decided to pay a visit to J & R and get a catalogue if I could, as this might be my last chance to do so for a very long time. The door was open in the lobby and there was a pile of catalogues. They were covered with a thin layer of white powder. I took a handful and exited the lobby. They were my souvenirs of days past. After I got home I wondered if the dust was asbestos from the Towers. Today I am very sorry that I threw them out. I should have sent them to a lab to check for residue of explosives: there is testimony on tape that people heard explosions on multiple floors in the towers.

I struck up a conversation with several people on Park Row. One of them was a tall thin woman in a business suit whose professional attire and perfect haircut suggested that she worked on Wall Street. We conversed for a while and very soon the subject turned to air pollution. She looked at me intensely and asked whether I was aware of the fact that we were all breathing in ground glass: the ground glass would remain in our lungs for the rest of our lives, as there is no way to get it out. The moment that my brain registered what she said, I was taken aback. I thanked her for this information and announced that I had decided to go home.

Unfortunately, I had to return home the way that I arrived: this entailed returning to the "A" train and again navigating its interminable passageways whose air was thickly saturated with filth.

Now that I had ascertained that I could never retrieve my bankbook, I took the subway straight to my local savings bank to explain what had happened. The bank immediately replaced the book that I had lost; my account number was canceled and a new one was opened for me. Then I went to the Queens Center and made a toll free call to the Federal Reserve Bank. The specialist assured me that even if someone were to procure the statement that I had left on my desk, he would not be able to make a withdrawal from my account.

For the first time in my life I realized that having money can be a terrible burden: money is one more thing to worry about and fret over, like a neonate requiring constant care. Moreover, because I was getting a lot of interest on a principal of $750,000, I had to have more and more money withheld from my paycheck for federal income tax. I found myself fine tuning my federal tax withholdings several times a year. And to make matters worse, for all my trouble and effort, I did not have the slightest idea what do to with all of my money. I did not then, and I do not now, as I sit behind my Toshiba, trying to recall these events. Today I am a millionaire. I wish that I could ask my Toshiba what to do with it all.

SATURDAY, SEPTEMBER 15, 2001

I came downstairs and met a neighbor. She always knew what was going on in the neighborhood because a family member had married a police officer in the 112th Precinct. People who had cops in their family knew things that did not appear in the newspapers. I asked her what was new.

"The donut shop on this address and the kiosk at that location packed up and disappeared on September 10. What do you think of that?"

"I'm not surprised. The whole world knew and so I assume that the U.S. did, too, because it planned it."

"Well, I don't know about that, but the donut shop and the kiosk, whose addresses are such and such, boarded up their doors and vanished into thin air."

"Thanks for the information," I said. "You know, I heard several stories on the radio that kids in schools have made remarks to their teachers that indicate that they had prior knowledge."[6]

"Oh, yeah?'

"Yeah. There are a bunch of stories like that. If everyone in the whole world knew, the government knew."

"You think so?"

"Of course! Tuesday morning George Tenet was having breakfast in Washington with former Senator David Boren who had headed the Senate's Intelligence Committee for many years. As soon as the first plane hit One, someone handed Tenet a cellphone, Tenet listened in his cellphone, and then he turned to Boren and told him that the WTC had been attacked by an airplane; Boren was struck by the fact that Tenet had used the word 'attacked'; then Tenet told Boren that it had Bin Laden's fingerprints all over it. I think that the CIA planned the whole thing."

"Why do you think that?"

"Because Tenet used the term 'attacked' right off the bat, like he knew that it was not an accident, and he named Bin Laden right off the bat...What other businesses closed around here?"

"Just those two." I asked her what else she knew. It turned out that that was it.

SUNDAY, SEPTEMBER 16, 2001

I came downstairs to get some air and see what I could find for free. I was walking up 63rd Drive when I spied a man clad in worn out clothing and headphones, holding something in his hand. Just as I passed him, he surprised me with a nasty message.

"Stupid!" he shouted. I was taken aback by the insult. Was he talking to me, I wondered. I continued to walk to the end of the block. The more I thought about it, the more I wanted to get clarification. Was he talking to me? I pirouetted and retraced my steps.

"Hello," I smiled warmly.

"Hello," he said

"My I ask you a question?" He nodded assent. "I just heard you say, 'Stupid.' Were you talking to me? Is it the way

I look?" I noticed that he held a voice recorder in his hands. He looked down and turned some buttons on it.

"No," he smiled, "I wasn't talking to you. It's a nice day, isn't it?"

"Yes, it is."

"This country is going to the dogs. What do you think of what happened last week?"

"Well, I think that the government planned the whole thing."

"You do?"

"Sure. If the whole world knew, you mean to tell me that the government did not know? In fact, you know what?"

"What?"

"The donut shop at such and such an address and the kiosk at that location packed up and disappeared the day before on September 10."

"They did?" he asked with great surprise. Then he adjusted his headphones and reached in his pocket. He took his hand out of his pocket and fiddled with his voice recorder.

"Yeah, the donut shop on such and such a block and the kiosk on such and such a block boarded up their doors and vanished," I repeated. "In fact, I worked at the World Trade Center and I was there at 5 AM and the newsstands did not open."

"Yeah?" We spoke for about 15 minutes. 15 minutes later a car stopped abruptly right in front of us and the driver double parked in the middle of the Drive. She got out and approached the man.

"I got one. It's a lucky day!" he announced gleefully as he removed the tape deck from his device and handed it to her. She abruptly grabbed it, turned, piled into her car, and sped off. I thought that that was interesting, but I did not make anything of it right away. I continued about my walk, checking out the garbage cans.

As time elapsed, the thought occurred to me that perhaps the man in the worn clothing was an undercover cop. NYPD gets a lot of work done with people who look like they are homeless. I wondered if he had taped everything that I told him. I resolved to ask him, the next time I saw him.

MONDAY, SEPTEMBER 17, 2001

I went downstairs hunting for garbage. As I walked along 63rd Drive, I spotted the same man standing on the street. He was still wearing headphones and holding his electronic device. I approached him.

"Hello, it's nice to see you again," I greeted him.

"Hi. Same here."

"May I ask you a question?"

"Sure, go ahead."

"This is embarrassing, but something is bothering me and I just have to know the answer."

"What is it?"

"Yesterday when we were talking, I noticed that you had an electronic device in your hand.

"This?" he asked as he held it up.

"Yeah, uh, in my mind, I had the thought that maybe you might be an undercover cop and that you recorded our conversation."

"Oh, no, this is my music, that's all. I love my music."

"I noticed that you removed the tape and gave it to your girlfriend and she went away in the car. Are you cops?"

"No, we're not cops. We just love our music, that's all. We're not cops." I thanked him and went about my way. I will always wonder what the story really was.

THE DOORBELL AT NIGHT

I was fast asleep when I was rudely awakened by the buzzer downstairs. Someone was trying to get into the building at the main entrance. I resented it when people who forgot their keys would run an index finger across the buzzers on the wall figuring that statistical probability dictated that out of all the tenants in the building, someone was bound to let them in.

I looked at my clock. It was 10 PM. I turned over and lay on one side, pulling the pillow up and over my ear. Then the doorbell rang. Whoever it was, he had managed to find his way upstairs. I tossed the pillow aside and lay still listening. Surely it could not be for me, I thought, because I do not know anyone. And then, even though the bedroom was situated at the extreme end of the apartment, as far away from the front door as the layout permitted, I heard a distinctive cry, "Ms. Gregory? Ms. Gregory?" I put on my sandals and walked hurriedly to the door.

"Who is it?" I asked, bent over slightly with my ear pressed against the door.

"U.S. Customs Office of Investigations." My heart pounded. Now I was in for it. But what had I done? I opened the door wide. A young Chinaman in a suit held out the palm of his hand. It was bearing a leather wallet housing a Customs badge. "Are you Ms. Mary Gregory?" he asked.

"Yes, I am," I replied.

"Ms. Gregory, have you tried to contact your boss?"

"No," I said. "I don't have a telephone. I am notoriously cheap. However, I am expecting the supervisors to send me an official letter telling me where to report like they did when the Vista Hotel was bombed."

"No, Ms. Gregory. They are all very worried about you. I advise that you give your boss a call. No one knows what happened to you. You never called. I advise that you contact your boss right away."

"All right," I agreed. He produced a sheet of paper from his wallet.

"I have a list of employees here that live in your area and that no one has heard from. I have to visit every one of these addresses and make sure that everyone is all right."

"OK, I'll call my boss," I assured him.

At 10 AM the next morning I perused the telephone directories at the Rego Park Library and found the telephone numbers of several Customs managers. I found my supervisor's telephone number and gave her a call.

After a month had elapsed, I was informed that the government was dispersing its various units and hundreds of employees to locations at multiple sites. Construction for our accommodations was underway in one of them. We moved into our new quarters in mid-October 2001.

Dear reader, please take heed that now things are going to get progressively scary and increasingly ugly. The pinpricks to my skin began in 2001; they were followed by electrical shocks to my body.

VICIOUS ELECTRONIC PHENOMENA AND THE MASS LOSS OF IMPULSE CONTROL

Mid-October 2001. I sat in my new cubicle. The government had rented some temporary modular furniture and we would be using that until permanent new furniture arrived. The floor was perpetually under construction: first the electrical wiring needed to be installed; then the lights; the rugs had to be laid down; a door here; a wall cabinet there; each of us was given a computer for his desk; printers and scanners were set up; the photocopy machines arrived.

Workmen in denim coveralls walked around toting ladders and toolboxes as we sat in our cubicles behind our computers. We wondered when the work would start arriving. The managers notified the public that we would be open for business shortly.

The ceiling lights were often out of order when we arrived in the morning and they remained that way for most of the morning. We frequently sat in dimly lit surroundings, having only the small lighting fixtures within the metal cabinetry that housed our tabletops. A man in blue denim overalls was regularly seen standing on a ladder, doing something way up in the ceiling, as his hands disappeared beyond the ceiling tiles. No one paid any attention to him and neither did I...yet. The day would come when I would regard him as a covert intelligence operative from another agency who was setting things up so that some of us, the experimental group, would be assaulted with microwaves, while others, the control group, would not be.

We were given new computers and our IT personnel worked diligently to develop a new local area network and to provide Internet access. Among the first things that we saw on the new computers were pictures of the devastated Customhouse still valiantly standing amid the fallen towers and collapsed Seven. As we stared at the aerial photographs in stunned disbelief, we saw that our feisty little Customhouse had not fallen, but that it was now in the shape of a horseshoe: the top of One had dropped squarely into the middle of it, obliterating a considerable portion, and now it was no longer a rectangular solid, but a "U."

Since we were not yet open for business, we signed on to the Internet and learned how to navigate the new screens and banners. That was when I learned the truth about 9/11. I triangulated the terms "September 11" and "skull and bones" in my search engine. In microseconds I had a list of key events in U.S. history that occurred on 9/11. The events, taken as a whole, point towards the occult obsession of their actors:

- On September 11, 1973 the CIA overthrew the government of Chile.

- On September 11, 1990 at precisely 9:09 PM George Herbert Walker Bush began speaking before a joint session of Congress about the Persian Gulf War. He announced that the war presented an opportunity to usher in a new world order: "Out of these troubled times, our fifth objective—a new world order—can emerge: a new era—freer from the threat of terror, stronger in the pursuit of justice, and more secure in the quest for peace."[7]

- On September 11, 2001 the U.S. government staged a false flag operation that is evidenced by the telltale signs enumerated below.

In July 2000 Mohammed Atta, soon after he arrived in the U.S. from Hamburg, Germany, stayed in the Florida house of Iran-Contra pilot Charlie Voss.[8] Voss worked as a bookkeeper at Huffman Aviation in Venice, FL; Atta and Marwan Al-Shehhi took flying lessons at Huffman Aviation for five months. After 9/11, Florida Governor Jeb Bush confiscated all the filing cabinets of the Huffman Aviation flight school, thereby removing critical documents that listed Atta's U.S. military training, his addresses at U.S. military installations, and the length of time that he lived in Voss' house. Hence, there is no accountability.

The *Washington Post* reported that six of the 19 hijackers lived on U.S. military bases: Mohammed Atta graduated from the U.S. International Officers School at Maxwell Air Force Base in Alabama and Abdulaziz Alomari graduated from the Aerospace Medical School at Brooks Air Force Base in San Antonio; Saeed Alghamdi, a former Saudi fighter pilot, graduated from the Defense Language Institute at Lackland Air Force Base in San Antonio; Saeed Alghamdi and Ahmed Alghamdi lived at a housing facility for foreign military trainees at Pensacola; Hamza Alghamdi and Ahmed Alnami also lived inside the base.[9]

When asked why Saudis had been allowed to come here to study aviation, the State Department glibly replied that foreigners were encouraged to come here and that Saudi Arabia was the "flavor of the month."

Two of the hijackers, Khalid Almihdhar and Nawaf Alhazmi, lived with an FBI informant in San Diego.[10] Furthermore, the CIA had seen both men attend an Al Qaeda meeting in Malaysia in January 2000, just prior to arriving in California.[11]

There were a dozen mock drills that morning. Fighter pilots were forced to ask whether it was a drill or the real thing. Who arranged all of these mock drills? The DoD, of course!

The debris at the World Trade Center was cleared out in a week even though the site was a crime scene and at any other crime scene, the evidence would be held indefinitely for forensic analysis by law enforcement agencies. The debris, which may have contained evidence of controlled demolition, was rapidly transported to Asia where the steel would be recycled into new products.

In addition, during the week before 9/11 there was a tremendous spike in the stock market on put options and call options for companies directly affected by the attacks

Put options are instruments that pay off when a stock drops in value. On Thursday, September 6, 2001, there was huge surge in put options for the following companies: American Airlines (operator of Flight 11 and Flight 77), United Airlines (operator of Flight 175 and Flight 93), Morgan Stanley (which occupied 22 floors of 1 WTC), Merrill Lynch (headquartered near the WTC), Bank of America, and reinsurance companies Munich Re of Germany, Swiss Re of Switzerland, and AXA Group of France (that had to pay out billions to cover losses from 9/11).[12] Between September 6th-September 10 the sale of put options on United Airlines was 90 times higher than normal and 285 times higher than normal on September 6th; on September 10 the sale of put options on American Airlines was 60 times higher than normal; between September 7th-September 10 the sale of put options on Morgan Stanley increased 27 times; during the four trading days before 9/11 put options for Merrill-Lynch increased 12 times the normal level.[13]

Conversely, call options are instruments that pay off when a stock increases in value. There was a spike in call options on Raytheon (the defense contractor, maker of Patriot and tomahawk missiles, and parent company of E-Systems, whose clients include the CIA and NSA).[14]

Moreover, Deutsche Bank Alex Brown, the American investment arm of the German giant, Deutsche Bank, purchased put options on United Airlines. Deutsche Bank Alex Brown was formerly headed by A.B. "Buzzy" Krongard, who left that company to join the CIA. In 1998 he was counsel to George Tenet; in March 2001 he became the Executive Director of the CIA. Deutsche Bank also was directly involved in insider trading relating to Munich Re.[15]

I was dumbfounded. I gazed at the floor in utter dejection. However, eventually the Internet would apprise me of even more sordid news: the CIA overthrew the government of Greece twice and that of Cyprus once. The US was responsible for the death of my beloved Uncle Dionysus who had sent me money to attend Columbia. It 1974 it staged a coup over two waves, on July 20 and August 14, and then gave the green light to the Turks to parachute into the island and take over the homes of the 160,000 Greek Cypriots who lived there; 50,000 Turks moved into the homes of Greek Cypriots who were forced to leave their homes; the Turks took over the house that I inherited from my father and they forced my Uncle Dionysus to sleep outside during the cold winter months. He fell ill and died in the cold. This is what Turkey did at the behest of the Secretary of State Henry Kissinger. Three documents pertaining to US and NATO involvement in the Cyprus tragedy of 1974 are on the Internet: one is from the Secretary General of NATO to the U.S. Secretary of Defense; two are from the U.S. Secretary of State Henry Kissinger authorizing the assassination of Archbishop Makarios.[16] These documents have been declassified and published. I returned to the Internet each day and discovered one ugly fact after the next.

It was during this time, in our new lodging, when I started receiving burn marks to my arms and legs. I distinctly remember sitting in my new cubicle and rolling up my pant leg to locate the site of the latest assault. I discovered a burn mark in my skin: it was a tiny saucer-shaped crater. When

I examined it closely, I found that something had burned a hole into my skin. I gazed up at the ceiling tiles and wondered if it had come from there. Then I looked around the room. Where could this have come from? I was starting to happen more and more frequently. After a while the small crater filled with blood; then it turned dark brown and I was left with a permanent brown mark. With time my arms and legs were covered with brown marks. I distinctly remember that the pinpricks and burn marks started in October 2001 at my new work site.

Was this a government psyop that was part of a behavior modification experiment? Did it have anything to do with the fact that I was using the Internet to uncover all of the atrocities that America had committed? Was the government trying to break me down psychologically so that it could build me back up into a different person? Or was it trying to see whether it could cause cancer long distance via EMs? Was the government imaging into the office tower from an unmanned drone or orbiting satellite by sending down electromagnetic waves? Or had the government put something in my food or drink that was causing me to attract EMs? By November 2009 I would ascertain that not only does the government burn holes through people's skin via laser pulse technology directed through brick and concrete, it would also take a nick out of the crown of my head and rifle my aluminum tarpaulins with hundreds of holes as I lay beneath them!

The big day came when we reopened for business. At last, things were back to normal. Or were they? I had never been assaulted by an invisible force that burned a hole in my skin the diameter of a pin before.

(Endnotes)

1   Sun Tzu, *The Art of War, Strategic Assessments*, translated by Thomas Cleary (Boston: Shambhala Publications, Inc., 1988), 49.

2   Ramon Gilsanz, Edward M. DePaola, Christopher Marrion, and

Harold "Bud" Nelson, *World Trade Center Building Performance Study: Data Collections, Preliminary Observations, and Recommendations* (Washington, DC: Federal Emergency Management Agency, 2002), Chapter 5, page 5–2.

3   James Risen, "A NATION CHALLENGED: THE INTELLIGENCE AGENCY; Secret C.I.A. Site in New York Was Destroyed on Sept. 11," *New York Times*, November 4, 2001, 1B.1.

4   "CIA Office near World Trade Center Destroyed in Attacks," November 4, 2001, http://archives.cnn.com/2001/US/11/04/inv.newyork.cia.office/ (February 18, 2009).

5   "CIA Office Lost in Terror Attack," November 4, 2001, http://www.bbc.co.uk/2/hi/americas/1637454.stm (February 18, 2009).

6   This incident in Dallas is one example: "...Rhonda Lucich, a director of elementary education for the Garland Independent School District...said the boy approached his teacher on the afternoon of Sept. 10 and casually told her: 'Tomorrow, World War III will begin. It will begin in the United States, and the United States will lose.' Lucich said the child's statements were passed along to the FBI. She said she did not know whether the agency had acted on the tip. An FBI spokesman could not be reached for comment." R.G. Ratcliffe, "Boy in Dallas Suburb Predicts Start of WW III Day Before Attacks," *Houston Chronicle*, September 20, 2001, 33. This occurrence in Brooklyn is another example:

At Brooklyn's New Utrecht High School, the FBI was notified that a Pakistani student in a bilingual class "made a comment to a teacher the week prior about the twin towers," said Karen Finney, spokeswoman for the Board of Education.

Finney would not reveal the nature of the comment, but the Journal-News of Westchester reported yesterday that the student pointed at the tower during a heated political argument and declared, "Look at those two buildings. They won't be here next week."

School officials would not release the name of the student, but said he was still attending classes at New Utrecht. They said they notified New York police and that the matter was turned over to the FBI." Greg B. Smith, "Some Got Warning: Don't Go Downtown on Sept. 11: Feds Probe Whether Mid-Easterners Knew of Danger," *Daily News*, October 12, 2001, http://www.nydailynews.com/archives/news/2001/10/12/2001-10-12_some_got_warning_don_t_go_d.html (February 27, 2009).

7   "Transcript of President's Address to Joint Session of Congress,"

New York Times, September 12, 1990, A20.

8   Larry D. Hatfield, "Growing Web of Evidence Points to Bin Laden," *San Francisco Chronicle*, September 13, 2001, A1; "Details on Hijacking Suspects," *Chicago Tribune*, September 15, 2001, 13; Lenny Savino, "Assault on America/How They Did It/No Extraordinary Means Needed for Terrorist Mission," *Houston Chronicle*, September 16, 2001, 41; Joel J. Smith and Charlie Ramirez, "Two Suspected Hijackers Took Lessons; Novice Can Steer a Large Jet Plane, Instructor Says," *Detroit News*, September 13, 2001, 3.

9   "Two of 19 suspects named by the FBI, Saeed Alghamdi and Ahmed Alghamdi, have the same names as men listed at a housing facility for foreign military trainees at Pensacola. Two others, Hamza Alghamdi and Ahmed Alnami, have names similar to individuals listed in public records as using the same address inside the base. In addition, a man named Saeed Alghamdi graduated from the Defense Language Institute at Lackland Air Force Base in San Antonio, while men with the same names as two other hijackers, Mohammed Atta and Abdulaziz Alomari, appear as graduates of the U.S. International Officers School at Maxwell Air Force Base, Ala., and the Aerospace Medical School at Brooks Air Force Base in San Antonio, respectively." Guy Gugliotta and David S. Fallis, "2nd Witness Arrested; 25 Held for Questioning," *Washington Post*, September 16, 2001, A29. In addition, the *Los Angeles Times* reported, "A defense official said two of the hijackers were former Saudi fighter pilots who had studied in exchange programs at the Defense Language School at Lackland Air Force Base in Texas and the Air War College at Maxwell Air Force Base in Alabama." H.G. Reza, Evan Halper, and Lisa Getter, "Suspected Hijackers: 19 Quiet Lives That Shattered the Word; Inquiry: 'Nice,' 'Normal' Guys Had Few Belongings But Access To Lots of Cash. Tantalizing Clues Show Path to Destruction," *Los Angeles Times*, September 15, 2001, A1. Also see Dan Eggen and Amy Goldstein, "FBI Names 19 Men as Suspected Hijackers: Some Lived in U.S. for Several Years," *Washington Post*, September 16, 2001, A12.

10   Robert J. Lopez, H.G. Reza, and Rich Connell, "Hijackers in San Diego Weren't Hiding," *Los Angeles Times*, July 25, 2003, A25.

11   Ibid.

12   "Insider Trading: Pre-9/11 Put Options on Companies Hurt by Attack Indicates Foreknowledge," http://911research.wtc7.net/sept11/stockputs.html (February 26, 2009).

13   Ibid. The website refers the reader to Michael C. Ruppert, *Cross-*

ing the Rubicon: The Decline of the American Empire at the End of the Age of Oil, foreword by Catherine Austin Fitts (Gabriola, BC: New Society Publishers, 2004).

14   Ibid.

15   Michael C. Ruppert, "Suppressed Details of Criminal Insider Trading Lead Directly into the CIA's Highest Ranks: CIA Executive Director 'Buzzy' Krongard Managed Firm that Handled 'PUT' Options on United Airline Stock," http://www.hereinreality.com/insidertrading.html (February 26, 2009). On the other hand, in 2004 the 9/11 Commission totally whitewashed the issue: "Highly publicized allegations of insider trading in advance of 9/11 generally rest on reports of unusual pre-9/11 trading activity in companies whose stock plummeted after the attacks. Some unusual trading did in fact occur, but each such trade proved to have an innocuous explanation. For example, the volume of put options—instruments that pay off only when a stock drops in price—surged in the parent companies of United Airlines on September 6 and American Airlines on September 10—highly suspicious trading on its face. Yet, further investigation has revealed that the trading had no connection with 9/11. A single U.S.-based institutional investor with no conceivable ties to al Qaeda purchased 95 percent of the UAL puts on September 6 as part of a trading strategy that also included buying 115,000 shares of American on September 10. Similarly, much of the seemingly suspicious trading in American on September 10 was traced to a specific U.S.-based options trading newsletter, faxed to its subscribers on Sunday, September 9, which recommended these trades. The SEC and FBI, aided by other agencies and the securities industry, devoted enormous resources to investigating this issue, including securing the cooperation of many foreign governments. These investigators have found that the apparently suspicious consistently proved innocuous." *The 9/11 Commission Report: Final Report of the National Commission on Terrorist Attacks Upon the United States* (New York: W.W. Norton & Company, 2004), 499n130.

16   American Duplicity IV: The CIA Files," http://www.greece.org/cyprus/Takism8.htm (February 21, 2009).

Chapter Seven

The Reign of Terror of King George II: The Second Year and Third Years (2002–2003)

No Government can be long secure without a formidable Opposition.[1]

—Benjamin Disraeli, *Coningsby* (1844)

We had two instances of temporary lodging. When we first arrived, our managers rented some used furniture from a private contractor. We used the rented lodgings for several months as a group of employees formed a team and selected and purchased permanent new furniture. When the new furniture finally arrived, our managers moved us temporarily to another floor so that workmen could install it.

My first temporary office was characterized by frequent burn marks to my skin. I rolled up my sleeves and pant legs and studied the tiny wounds with puzzlement. I asked my coworkers whether they had experienced these phenomena and they responded in the negative. It appeared that for some reason, I was attracting electronic signals, and I was the only one in Customs who was. Had the government put something in my food? Was it experimenting with me? It would have been the easiest thing in the world to do because I found so much to eat outdoors. I started to pay attention to people who happened to be standing nearby whenever I discovered untouched food. For example, on one occasion I was walking on 5th Avenue and I found a brown paper bag with an uneaten pastrami sandwich sitting squarely atop a telephone booth. I looked around. Sure enough, as usual, there would be someone close by with a cellphone; the moment I made eye contact with the person, he would turn off his cellphone and hurry away. It always happened. Was it a coincidence? Or was the government feeding me something?

There was something else significant about our first temporary office space: as I sat in my cubicle early in the morning, I would hear a thunderous CRACK! lash down on the metal cabinetry in a cubicle down the hall. Or I would hear a SNAP! whip across the paperwork left on someone's desk. A few times when I arose from my desk and walked to the point of origin to investigate, I discovered that the office was unoccupied. I surmised that perhaps it was static electricity emanating from the monitors.

Months later. The lighting was dim upstairs in the second temporary setup. Furthermore, when I arrived in the morning at 6 AM, I started noticing more strange squeaks punctuated by violent metal taps off the cabinets in unoccupied cubicles. As I sat in my office in semi-obscurity and I would hear a fierce, vehement CRACK! lash against a metal cabinet several cubicles away from mine. It sounded like a loose wire on a telephone pole had delivered 40,000 volts to a tree. When I would get up to investigate, I always found that the cubicle was empty. This happened every morning.

The electronic physical assaults continued and proliferated: they became increasingly more violent and hurtful, and eventually they took place in my apartment and on the street, as well as at work. As I sat at my desk, writing, a violent electrical burst of energy would explode against my hand, arm, face or the back of my head. The man-made fiber covering on the modular walls, highly hydrophobic, continually exuded a violent snapping sound. BZZZT! BZZZT! BZZZT! This continued throughout the day. I thought that surely it must be static electricity due to the fact that man-made fibers are hydrophobic, that is, they do not absorb moisture; I surmised that electrical currents were rippling across the surface of the textile wall coverings.

I buttonholed strangers in the elevators that worked for private industry on other floors and asked them whether they had experienced these phenomena on their floors. The answer was invariably always the same: "What? Are you kidding? No, never!" Soon I ascertained that all of these occurrences transpired only on the floors that Customs occupied. I became increasingly suspicious of The Man with the Beady Eyes on the stepladder who had his hands perpetually in the ceiling.

I received one pinprick to my skin after the next as I was working at my desk. Every time I examined the site of the wound, I found that something very thin, with the diameter of a pin, burned a hole into the surface of my skin. Then it started happening as I lay in bed at home. Then it occurred in every room in the apartment. Then it started happening on the sidewalk, on subway platforms, on subway steps, in train cars, in buses, in department stores, at the local library, at the post office. I could find refuge nowhere.

It was during this time at our second temporary lodging when my coworkers started finding objects in places where they had not left them the night before. One woman had left her monthly report face up on her desk and when she arrived at work early the next morning, she found it upside down and pushed into her pencil holder. For some reason, this incident bothered her tremendously: she talked about it all morning and was outraged that someone had invaded her own personal office space. I was surprised that she cared at all about the placement of her monthly report and I wondered why it bothered her so much. I wanted to be helpful, so I advised her that I, personally, did not have any expectations of privacy in Customs and that I never left anything that I had paid for at work because I did not expect to find it in the morning. Looking back on this, could it be that she was part of the control group and that normal people do care about the items in their workspace, while the experimental group, bathed in microwaves, are lulled into indifference and docility?

The day that we moved out of there and returned downstairs, I packed a report cover in a box containing an electric lamp. After we moved downstairs, I discovered that the report cover was missing. Looking back on it, I now believe that I was part of the experimental group; if so, the observers ascertained that the theft was of no consequence to me. Actually, I didn't care about the report cover because I had not paid for it, it was government property. However, if I had paid just one penny for it, I would have been very upset by the loss.

Then I was very surprised when the woman sitting just a few cubicles from me informed me that someone had stolen five dollars from her desk drawer. I had no idea that this was going on. This made me very sorry that I had the habit of going into her cubicle and taking chocolate kisses from her candy dish. If she had reported this, and if there were a pinhole camera somewhere, I could be suspected of wrongdoing when all I was doing was pacifying my sweet tooth.

There were also bizarre occurrences in which sound was thrown long distance into bathrooms that had a single occupant. One day I asked a coworker whether he had ever noticed any strange taps and thumps emanating from unoccupied rooms.

"It's funny that you should ask," he said. "I came in very early one morning to use the gym before starting work, and I was alone in the shower. Suddenly I heard a woman's high heel shoes walking loudly across the tiles just outside of my shower stall. I was very embarrassed because I was in the shower and I didn't know what to do. I wrapped myself in a towel and stepped outside the shower to see who was there. I discovered that no one was. This bothered me enormously because I had distinctly heard high heel shoes going tap,

tap, tap, against the floor just inches from me. I was certain that someone was nearby. I looked up at the ceiling and saw that there are air vents up there. I figured out that the sound must have emanated from the air vents above. There are offices on the other side of that wall and the sounds must have come from there through the vents."

"It's funny that you experienced this in the shower," I replied. "One morning at 6 AM I was alone in a bathroom stall on this floor and I heard keys drop loudly on the other side of the door. I came out and discovered that there was no one there. I checked every stall, but I was the only one in the bathroom."

"The sound must have traveled through the air vents," he repeated. I did not want to get into an argument with him. There are no offices on the other side of the bathroom that I used. In fact, there are none anywhere in the vicinity, either on that side of the hall or behind it.

The few months spent on that floor were creepy indeed, but nothing compared to what was on the horizon, either at the office or at home. There were several more robberies on that floor of both personal and government property. This perplexed everyone because we all made a nice living and could afford to buy anything we wanted. Furthermore, we could not imagine that anyone among us was a thief. The fierce snapping continued to pummel the cabinets in unoccupied offices at 6 AM, as did the electrical shocks to my arms and head and the burn marks in my skin.

Every time I was in the elevator with people who worked in private industry on other floors, or met office employees standing outside, smoking a cigarette, I inquired as to whether they, too, were experiencing electronic phenomena on their floors. I wanted to know whether the real world was putting up with this. I even met people who had worked on several other floors because they had gotten transfers within their companies. I was repeatedly told by every stranger I interviewed that no one on his floor was getting burn marks in his skin, that there were no loud thuds emanating from empty offices, violent metallic taps clicking off the metal bookcases and cabinets, or loud sounds in bathrooms occupied by one individual.

Looking back on this, I find this to be the smoking gun. We were being bombarded by more than static electricity emanating from monitors. Private corporations on other floors were packed with highly sophisticated computer systems, more advanced and modern than what the government was giving us. If the employees of the private companies in the building did not hear violent taps snapping off their cabinetry or get shocks or burn marks, it was because no one was experimenting with them.

It was during our second temporary lodging that I also noticed a severe personality change in one of my colleagues. One day I was stunned to catch him talking to himself uncontrollably. As he came out of the men's room, he repeatedly uttered very, very low pitch sounds like the monks do in Tibet when they meditate. He sounded like water gurgling down the bathtub drain. Because my cubicle was situated opposite the men's room, I heard all of these utterances. As I did so, I sat perfectly still in my cubicle, frozen, eyes closed, and listened with great shock and astonishment. I had to know who this was. I leaped up and quietly tiptoed around the divider to see who was making these sounds. When I identified him, I wondered what had happened to him.

Before we left that floor, I discovered that there was something else that had changed about this guy: he lost his ability to control his anger. One day when I entered his office, he walked in behind me and slammed the door so hard that the doorknob almost went through the sheetrock. That was the first occasion that I saw that he had lost his impulse control. However, there was another time, also. On another day he spontaneously and uncontrollably pushed a wheeled chair across the room with such vehemence, he could have seriously hurt the man who was sitting opposite him. He had never hurled a chair across the room before. Nor had he ever smashed a door against the wall. I wondered what had happened to him. When did he lose his impulse control and self-restraint? He was not like this when I had first met him in 1978. Clearly, something had changed in his brain and I needed to know what it was. Soon I started going out of my way to observe the behavior of all of my coworkers. I discovered that the people that surrounded me were losing their impulse control, left and right, to beat the band.

Had I been the first to lose self-restraint? I always had a proclivity for saving money, but I had never done a tap dance on dumpsters before. One might say that I had developed a compulsion for saving money. Had I, too, lost my impulse control, but regarding different issues? Were my coworker and I both part of the experimental group? Did our names appear on experimenters' charts somewhere that were broken down by gender, race, ethnic group, and education?

PERMANENT OFFICE FURNITURE AND THE PICTURES ON THE WALL

The big day came and we moved downstairs to our permanent furniture. After we did, there was no overhead electricity on many mornings in my section. Other parts of the floor were fully illumined, but my cubicle and the surrounding areas were not. The employees in my section had to work in semi-obscurity during many mornings. Back then it did not occur to me that there was any significance to this. Back then, I did not suspect that The Man with the Beady Eyes, in overalls, was doing anything special to my cubicle. OK, so the rest of the floor was fully lit and my section was not. It was no big deal. Or was it? I would not become suspicious of this until a year later, when I would be moved to another part of the floor and when the electricity in that section would also be cut off in the early morning, when the rest of the floor was fully lit. Something would be done to my section overnight.

One morning as I sat in my new office working with a set of imported items comprised of many component parts, I realized that I needed to walk down to the end of the hall to confer with a colleague. As I traversed the long corridor, workmen in blue denim overalls were busy drilling holes in walls. Then they bolted framed pictures to the spots where they had drilled the holes. Little by little, day by day, elegant pictures of beautiful natural landscapes, encased in glass and wooden frames, sprouted up all over the hallway along its entire length. I decided to make a tour of the hallway.

The pictures were gorgeous. New England forests. Stormy waves on the high seas. Ethereal mountaintops partially obscured by clouds. The wooden frames were thick and looked costly. The paintings were indeed very classy. It looked like the Louvre. I was surprised that the government had spent the money. I was told that they were gifts from FEMA.

I noticed a painting of a stormy sea bolted to the wall by an exit. It faced the door. Then I spied another scene that had been bolted directly opposite another exit door. More pictures were arranged all around the receptionists by the glass doors at the main entrance. The profusion of artwork struck me as unusual and suddenly I felt that we were being watched. I decided to take another walk down the hall. The hall was shaped like a "U" or a horseshoe. There were two very long corridors connected by a smaller one at one end.

As I walked around the "U," I noticed that the pictures were evenly spaced apart and that there was not one part of the wall, anywhere in the vast expanse of hallway, that did not have a picture. Pictures had been placed at the dead ends at either end of the "U." Wherever there was a corner, there were two pictures at a 90^0 angle. Every spot I visited had a painting.

As I sat in my cubicle, I wondered whether we were being spied upon. I got up and walked over to the exit. Facing the exit squarely there was a raging storm on the high seas with waves swelling to monstrous heights. I scrutinized the texture of the painting. Even though it was covered by glass, I could discern that it was not evenly textured. I wondered whether there might be a camera hidden somewhere either in the texture or in the wooden frame. After several minutes of intense scrutiny I discerned a little glass spot, a tiny glass orb, barely visible amongst the bumpy textures of an ocean wave. It looked like glass. It was shiny and smooth. The area around it was blue ink. A glass dot embedded in blue ink, I thought. Was that the eye of a pinhole camera?

I returned to my cubicle and hurriedly finished my assignment. Then I deposited it on my GS-14's desk. Hopefully that would do for the time being. I hoped that I could have the next fifteen minutes to myself.

I returned to my office and signed on to the Internet. An obnoxious banner appeared advising that this computer was the property of the U.S. government and that employees had no expectation of privacy. The obnoxious message was getting longer and longer and there were more and more facets to the warning. It became something along the lines of "all transmissions can and will be intercepted by the government and the user forfeits all rights to privacy; if you agree to this, continue."

This warning banner did not intimidate me in the least because I identify as a scholar and I am exceedingly proud of that identification. One of the greatest things that a human being can be is a searcher of truth, a propagator of knowledge. I have spent my life asking questions and knocking myself out acquiring facts.

I signed on to the Internet. In the search engine I typed in the keywords "surveillance equipment" in quotation marks. I quickly got an eyeful: a cornucopia of spy machines.

I saw wall clocks that contain tiny pinhole cameras that receive video and transmit it to a remote location. The ads read "Bosses: would you like to keep an eye on your employees?" Home pages grabbed the reader's attention with icons featuring fire exit signs that contain pinhole cameras, pens, smoke alarms, the traditional silver globes, wall paintings...

Wall paintings? My heart beat accelerated as adrenalin coursed throughout my bloodstream. I clicked on that icon. And there they were. All of the paintings on our hallway. They cost $299.00 on the Internet. New England forests. Waterfalls. Stormy seas. In luxurious wooden frames. Each picture contained a minute pinhole camera that captured video and then transmitted it to a remote location.

A word about pinhole cameras: they are so infinitesimally minute, they can fit in the center of the "X" on the head of a Phillips screw. I arose from my seat and returned to the painting of the stormy seas bolted at a 90^0 angle to the exit door. The little glass dot was still there in the midst of the thick blue ink of the ocean's texture. Returning to my desk, I bent over the mouse and clicked "Print."

I went straight to my GS-14 and gave him ten color prints of the ads—paintings of landscapes, smoke alarms, exit signs, wall clocks. I announced that I thought that another government agency, a covert intelligence agency, was conducting experiments, using us as subjects, and was bugging our worksite to observe our responses. Without speaking to me, he grabbed the pictures, jumped out of his chair, and ran out of his office and straight into the GS-15's office. He closed the door behind him. The two men conversed for a full half hour. Finally, my GS-14 emerged and returned to his assignments.

"Well? What did he say?" I asked.

"He denied it," he tersely replied. I contemplated his words in silence for a few moments and returned to my desk.

For the next several days I spent all of my spare time walking through the hallways. I assumed that everything that transpired in front of the pictures was being simultaneously transmitted to a remote location via audio and video.

Several people asked me whether I loved artwork, and then in order not to appear intrusive, quickly added that a lot of people did. I replied, "Not particularly. I think that these are surveillance cameras and that we are all being watched."

"But why?" asked my coworkers.

"Why? Because we make the ideal laboratory mice. We work in the same place for 30 years. No one gets fired. No one quits. Where else can the government keep the same group of people together and watch them uninterruptedly for 30 years? The opportunity is too good to pass up. Do you remember those four people who died around the same time on the 7th floor of the Customhouse? As I recall, two mysteriously dropped dead over the weekend. I think that the government is experimenting with us and is watching us." I articulated my concerns to several people whom I knew would spread the word for me. Then I wondered what would happen when what I had said had eventually been processed in the office of whoever it was that was watching us. As it turned out, I would very soon find out. Electrical shocks to the brain and heart and burn marks all over my skin were on the horizon, unbeknownst to me.

Today I believe that that day marked a turning point in my life. It was a watershed moment, the proverbial beginning of the end. I had noticed something and had made a spectacular discovery. Now I had become a threat to the experimental program of the government agency that was watching us. Previously, all I had encountered was semen on the rug and swastikas around my desk. Now things were about to take a sharp turn towards physical assault.

I asked a supervisor, a GS-14, if she thought that it was possible that another agency was bugging our office. She vigorously shook her head.

"Impossible. Out of the question. Everything that is done has to go through me."

"But what if it is a covert intelligence agency that is compiling data?"

"Impossible. It can't happen. That is not allowed. Everyone has to go through me." I thanked her cordially and ended the conversation. What an imbecile, I thought. She thinks that a covert military intelligence agency conducting experiments is going to go directly to her first and ask for her permission. What a retard. She is an iconic representation of why Customs employees make ideal lab mice.

I thought then and there that if I were to ever write a book about my experience as an experimental subject, perhaps I should call it *Lab Mouse with a Badge*. I visualized what the cover might look like: a white mouse clad in a trench coat, collar turned up, fedora hat, dark glasses, and the palm of his little mouse hand extended towards the reader bearing a U.S. Customs badge. I have since decided that I would not use this title: it would make light of something that is, quite conversely, terrifying to the utmost degree: the military's use of non-consenting, unsuspecting federal employees for Nazi experimentation. A humorous cartoon would undercut the stunning and horrifying reality that we have lost our democracy and our freedom forever in this country and that with the advent of globalization, fascism, controlled by electronics, will become a global phenomenon. You can run, but you can't hide.

THE GUSTY SQUALL

At 2:30 AM a thud dropped on my comforter directly over my right ankle and woke me up. Having been assaulted thus by electromagnetic radiation, it was impossible to return to sleep. I snapped on my walkman, donned my headphones, and listened to the BBC. I was progressively permitted to get less and less sleep.

As I exited the subway that morning, I discovered a large brown paper bag containing a roll filled with ham and eggs and a cup of black coffee. They appeared to be untouched. The coffee was all in the cup and it was piping hot. Little plastic vials containing cream and milk lined the bottom of the bag, along with packets of sugar, stirrers, and napkins. What, I thought, they did not want this? Only in America! A woman stood at the edge of the platform as if she were waiting for the subway. The moment that I picked up the brown paper bag, she turned on her heels, and disappeared up the steps. Are they watching me? I wondered. Nah! Couldn't be. Down the hatch went the ham and egg sandwich. Down the hatch went the black coffee. I sipped the milk and cream separately from their little vials. Then I tore open the sugar packets and poured the sugar in my mouth. I made everything disappear that was ingestible.

That night something highly unusual and significant happened. I was asleep in the middle of the night and as I slept, I felt a great wind blow across my head from left to right. Whoooosh! My hair blew in the gust from left to right; my clothing flapped wildly in the strong wind like a flag on a blustery day. This continued for five minutes, I think. Whoooosh! Whooosh! Eventually I woke up. I stared across the dark room. That had felt so real, I thought. I had felt a powerful, gusty, blustery, windy squall. Back then I wondered whether it was electronic. It blew from left to right. One of the two bedroom windows is situated directly to the left of my bed. I wondered whether the government do it from a parked car, van or an adjacent apartment.

However, now I have the answer. On November 9, 2009 at 1:45 AM I experienced the exact same gusty wind as an aircraft hovered directly over my building and thoroughly perforated the aluminum foil on my bed and walls. The aluminum blanket on my bed is 11 layers thick and yet it is completely saturated with pinholes that permeate all 11 layers. It is done by terahertz technology, the same technology that permits imaging through suitcases at airports. It is delivered from aircraft flying at a distance. Do you see how out of control the Pentagon is? They fund their black ops experiments by trafficking narcotics into the country. They hire operatives to train highly impressionable and uneducated

Muslims to commit ugly acts. They use a combination of drugs, mind control techniques, the transmission of sound at a low frequency that can be heard in the head without the benefit of the human ear, and they destroy the human brain with EMs to get people to carry out atrocities so that the government can say to us, "You need government to keep you safe." I heard on NPR that young blond haired, blue eyed German males, 20 years old, are going to Pakistan to train with the Taliban: yeah, sure, they are neoNazis who are training the Taliban to scare us into being reliant on government, not vice versa.

The powerful wind that I experienced in 2003 and again in 2009 is actuated via extremely high frequency radio waves that we already know are deleterious to human health. Project Pandora proved that microwaves directed at people on an ongoing basis cause cancer, leukemia, blindness. Three American ambassadors to Moscow died of cancer after having been exposed and the American government deliberately left its employees in Moscow for 30 years to profit from the Russian experiment. The nightly radiological assaults perpetrated on the residents of Queens are conducted by terahertz waves, a frequency that is even higher than the gigahertz associated with cancer. Nice government we have.

THE EARTHQUAKE IN BAM, IRAN

On December 26, 2003 an earthquake measuring 6.3 on the Richter scale devastated the city of Bam, Iran. There were 26,271 deaths and 30,000 injuries. The more I learned about the tragedy, the more I was convinced that the U.S. government had done this with electromagnetic waves.

Previously, George Bush had called Iran part of the "axis of evil" and had unsuccessfully tried to introduce CIA operatives into the country. However, after the earthquake, the U.S. succeeded in offering humanitarian aid to the country in exchange for compliance with the International

Atomic Energy Agency monitoring of its nuclear program. I thought that the following were telltale signs that the U.S. had created the earthquake: 1) it happened at the precise time when the U.S. wanted to introduce CIA operatives into the country disguised as humanitarian workers, 2) it had selected Bam because of its name—everyone knows that spooks have a sense of humor, 3) it occurred the day after Christmas as a message to Iran: often warring countries have a temporary one day truce until Christmas has passed and then they resume their hostilities, 4) it is scientifically feasible to use resonance to shatter solid objects above or below the ground by focusing an electromagnetic wave on it that resonates at the same frequency as the object: Nikola Tesla had done it in 1887 or 1888 in the building that housed his laboratory at 48 East Houston Street, NY, NY; resonance caused the collapse of the Tacoma Narrows Bridge on November 7, 1940; the paperwork for Bernard J. Eastlund's patent, number 4,686,605, indicates that electropulse directed at the ionosphere can replace thermonuclear weapons; because a very delicate balance exists between the electromagnetic field surrounding the earth and that beneath the surface, a concentrated electromagnetic pulse directed at the ionosphere and then deflected down can shake tectonic plates beneath the ocean and bring about earthquakes; Raytheon, the defense contractor, currently holds the patents to Eastlund's weapons of mass destruction; on April 28, 1997 Secretary of Defense William Cohen warned us that terrorists have the ability to create earthquakes remotely via the transmission of electromagnetic waves.

Furthermore, on March 16, 2007 a sandstorm hit Bam killing 5 people, 3 of them children, and injuring 14 others. The sandstorm packed winds of 78 mph and it came suddenly and without warning. This tells me that the Pentagon has fined tuned its ability to effect weather manipulation with its HAARP heaters in Gakona, AL.

Throughout the years I discussed my suspicions that the earthquake in Bam was generated by human beings. Most of my colleagues did not believe that modern science can create an earthquake and they laughed when they heard my hypothesis. However, I made it no secret that I thought that the Pentagon uses weather control in its military theater: it can achieve its desired ends and the people under attack do not even suspect that they are being targeted.

(Endnotes)

1 Benjamin Disraeli, *Coningsby or the New Generation* (New York: The Century Company, 1905), 62.

Chapter Eight

The Reign of Terror of King George II: The Fourth Year (2004)

Power tends to corrupt, and absolute power corrupts absolutely.[1]

Lord Action, *Letter to Bishop Mandell Creighton* (April 3, 1887)

CATASTROPHIC FIRE AT SERBIAN ORTHODOX MONASTERY ON MOUNT ATHOS

On the night of March 3, 2004, a fire erupted at the 12th-century Chilandar Monastery on Mount Athos in northeastern Greece. The fire spread by rooftop and destroyed a portion of the monastery extending from the abbott's cell through the hospitality rooms, to the Tower of Saint Sava. This was the northwestern part of the monastery, erected in 1821 and recently renovated: the administrative section, hospitality room, and guest rooms, were housed there. The northeastern portion, White Residence, erected in 1598, was also destroyed. Parts of the monks' living quarters, dating back to 1188, were decimated; frescoes from the 16th and 18th centuries were damaged. The Church of King Milutin, the treasury, archives and monastery library remained out of the fire's range. Whatever had caused the fire, it had focused the damage in the northwestern and northeastern portions of the monastery.

It appears that a laser pulse was used to destroy the monastery in order to shock and disorient the Serbian Orthodox world and to send it a message regarding the introduction of private corporations and international banks in Kosovo: the devastation had assaulted Serbian Orthodoxy's most holy and sacred site on the Greek promontory Chalcidice, thus extending the shock of the Serbian nation from its own territory into the Adriatic. The signature of the occult actors whose sole objective was the extension of empire was evident: the fire occurred after dark, on the night of 3/3, two prime numbers.

The advance of fascism across the planet is a slow, gradual, deliberate progression comprised of individual chess moves. The strategy is to assault from all directions. However, unlike chess, the economy of moves is unnecessary. The globalists have all the money in the world and they control land, sea, air, and near space. Their moves do not have to be few or inexpensive.

In 1997 Prince Charles took an interest in Mount Athos and began visiting frequently. In March 1999 Clinton and his NATO thugs began a war against Belgrade: NATO used 1,000 aircraft in 38,000 combat missions. The assault continued into June 1999. NATO leveled hundreds of Serbian Orthodox churches and destroyed holy, miracle-working relics dating back to the earliest years of Christianity. The purpose was to destroy the Serbs' economy, extend empire and introduce private corporations and banks. To accomplish this it had to demolish its ethnicity and religion. Then the globalists would proceed to the next country. In 2007 the victim was Greece and the method of delivery was again laser pulse: between 6 PM Friday, August 31, 2007 and 6 AM Saturday, September 1, 2007, several hundred fires broke out simultaneously in Greece; 63 people died and thousands were left homeless.

The West has an agenda and Serbia is just one pawn to be taken on the chessboard. Strobe Talbott, Deputy Secretary of State under President Clinton and the lead U.S. negotiator during the Kosovo War, disclosed the real reason for NATO's assault on Serbia and it was not to liberate the Albanian Muslims: "As nations throughout the region sought to reform their economies, mitigate ethnic tensions, and broaden civil society, Belgrade seemed to delight in continually moving in the opposite direction. It is small wonder NATO and Yugoslavia ended up on a collision course. It was Yugoslavia's resistance to the broader trends of political and economic reform—not the plight of the Kosovar Albanians—that best explains NATO's war."[2] Hence, the West's obsession with shocking and subjugating Serbia was to extend the empire of the international banking community and private corporations.

It is significant that just six months prior to the disastrous fire, on September 12, 2003, Prince Charles had made a private visit to the Chilandar Monastery; he was accompanied by another man, purportedly his bodyguard. Did they go to take pictures of the layout and secure the floor plan? Suddenly Charles claimed to have taken an interest in Orthodox Christianity; he and his father, Prince Philip, were members of The Friends of Mt. Athos. Charles also took a keen interest in other religions, i.e., Hinduism and Buddhism. This was used as an excuse to gain a foothold in those worlds. After the disastrous fire, on March 9, Charles sent his condolences and a message of support to the Serbia-Montenegro Embassy in Great Britain.

We know that a laser pulse directed through brick wall from an aircraft flying at a distance can cause a flash fire to simultaneously erupt because it was done at the Koresh compound in Waco, TX. The objective of the destruction of the Chilandar Monastery on Mount Athos was to warn the Serbs to leave the Kosovars alone, let them have sovereignty and elections, and not interfere with the establishment of the New World Order in Eastern Europe.

Mount Athos has existed in relative peace in 2,000 years since it was discovered by Mary, the Mother of Christ, on a voyage to Cyprus in the first century AD.[3] With a few rare exceptions in history, it was not until the Prince of Wales suddenly took an interest in it that calamity occurred on the promontory. The fire destroyed the northeastern and north-western rooms that housed the monks' living quarters with surgical precision, but left the Church, archives, treasury and library untouched. NATO, the Brits, and the Pentagon image and strike with absolute accuracy. We know that this is a fact because NORTHCOM imaged and thoroughly per-forated the aluminum shielding in my apartment on Sep-tember 29, October 16, October 29, October 30, October 21, and November 9, 2009; I have the aluminum shielding riddled with pinholes to prove it.

The globalist agenda is to methodically erode and eradi-cate every last vestige of national identity and religion on the planet. When that has been accomplished, men will no longer unite to defend their tribe against those at the cor-porate top because there will no longer be any identity to defend.

3/11

On March 11, 2004 ten bombs exploded in trains and stations along a commuter line in Madrid; 191 people were killed and 1,800 were wounded. I found it significant that the explosions occurred just three days before Spain's national election, slated for March 14. Obviously, it was an attempt to scare the Spanish population into voting for Conservative incumbent Prime Minister José Maria Aznar, of the Popular Party. His conservative platform boasted strength on antiterrorism efforts and law enforcement, fa-vored sending troops to Iraq, and supported the use of ex-tensive counter-terrorism laws to crack down on the Basque separatist group ETA. If it was the CIA's intention to terror-ize the Spanish into voting for the Conservative candidate, then the false flag operation failed miserably: Spain voted for the Socialist and as soon as he took office, the new So-cialist Party government of Prime Minister José Luis Rodriguez Zapatero withdrew Spain's 1,300 troops from Iraq; it also set out to improve relations with neighboring Morocco.

One morning as I entered through the electronic doors with two coworkers, I was quite vocal about the fact that I thought that the purpose of 3/11 was to Nazify Europe: the Nazis in the CIA wanted to flip Europe from left to right and they would do it with fear. They had succeeded in the U.S. Now it was time to shut up all the people on the left on the Continent who urgently wanted the United States to get out of Iraq, get involved in ending global warming, do away with gasoline-powered cars, and destroy its 15,000 nuclear warheads.

"You think that the CIA did this?" one woman asked.

"Oh, for sure!"

"Why?"

"They want to Nazify Europe just like they succeeded in doing here. First they scare the uneducated, uninformed masses with a terrorist attack, then they saturate the air waves with conservative talk radio. They want to flip Europe from left to right." One woman winced, proffering a thoroughly disgusted look. However, the other, who was a conservative and cautious thinker, did not buy my theory so quickly.

"I just hope that al Qaeda doesn't do it here," she said ominously. Al Qaeda? I was taken aback by how gullible she was.

"Relax. There won't be any more terrorist attacks here," I prognosticated.

"How can you be so certain?" she asked.

"Because if there were, then the Nazis in the Bush crime family couldn't brag that they have succeeded in keeping us safe. They commit their atrocities abroad in order to scare Americans into voting for them; they continually regurgitate that there has not been any terrorist attacks since 9/11. You just wait and see what the mantra will be in the next election."

"It's not far away," was the reply. "2004 is an election year. Let's see, in eight months."

"That's right," I continued. "Then the false flag on 3/11 kills two birds with one stone: it uses fear to flip the Europeans from left to right and it scares Americans into voting Republican because after all, George Bush has kept us safe and there have not been any terrorist attacks here since 9/11."

I entered my cubicle and sat down. A thunderous CRACK! resonated against my metal clothing closet inches from where I sat. Then there was a SNAP! bouncing off the plastic countertop in front of me. Then I got a sharp pinprick to the center of my chest just beneath my neck. It stung like a needle-thin dagger that had penetrated deep beneath the surface of the skin. I lowered my head to see where it was, but it was useless: the site of the attack was a blind spot and therefore, I needed a mirror. I stepped into my neighbor's cubicle and positioned myself a half inch from her mirror. There was a tiny hole in my skin, just like all the ones on my arms and legs. Was this an essay in behavior modification, conducted in real time, via a network, from a remote location?

As my neighbors started to arrive at work, I asked them, one by one, whether they had every received any pinpricks while they were sitting in their offices. The answer was always "No."

"Maybe there is something in your system that attracts electronic signals. Maybe you have a lot of metal in your body. Why don't you get a blood test and find out if you are full of mercury from tuna fish," one coworker suggested. That was an idea, I thought. However, what was even more significant was the fact that I was the only one at work who admitted to getting pinpricks. Everyone heard the violent snaps and clicks that resonated off the furniture. Several people called them "pings." Everyone heard them, they all acknowledged that they were surrounded by them, and yet no one admitted that he was stung by them. Back then I wondered whether I had ingested a state of the art, dust-sized RFID tag. Today, judging from the aluminum foil in my apartment that is riddled with holes as aircraft hover overhead, I understand that the pinpricks to my skin had everything to do with the fact that the pictures on the wall were bugged and were relaying audio and visual data to a remote location where the decision to strike was made in real time.

THE MOVE DOWN THE HALL

I was not getting along with my supervisor and so, I requested a transfer down the hall to fill the first vacancy that arose. I did not have to wait very long: one employee retired and another died. Although I was assigned to do the work of the retiree, I was not permitted to sit in his cubicle. I was assigned to sit in the cubicle of Bart, a 54-year old married Jewish man who had just died of liver cancer. After I moved in to my new office, two more employees died: Andrea, a single Christian woman, and Freeman, a married Jewish man. Hence, the Customs supervisors had to attend three funerals.

Bart had undergone surgery for pancreatic cancer and subsequently he returned to work; unfortunately, the cancer metastasized to his liver and it killed him. He was not the only person to contract pancreatic cancer. Vivian also developed pancreatic cancer and had to have her pancreas removed. Soon after my arrival in my new office, Freeman, seated not far from me in my section, died of kidney disease. He had had a kidney transplant and seemed to be doing well for a while, but died months after returning to work. He was 52 when he died. I believe that his ability to accept the foreign organ had been severely impeded by the assaults of large amounts of microwave radiation that we were all getting. Concurrently, Sean, a handicapped, single Christian man, developed intestinal cancer and had to have a portion of his intestine removed.

We had already had a case of colon cancer in the World Trade Center when Raymond required a colostomy.

It was around that time when Andrea died of obesity. It is highly significant that so many single women living alone had died and/or developed OCDs or autoimmune diseases; and that so many people developed cancer.

The morning after I moved into my new cubicle down the hall, the one that had previously been occupied by Bart, who had just died of liver cancer, all the lights were turned off in my ceiling. This was a fine welcome, I thought. The lights worked all right the week before. However, the morning after I arrived, suddenly there was an unexplained emergency. The lights were off every morning for a full two weeks until around 9 or 10 AM, when they would be restored. Now that I look back on this, clearly, something was being done electrically overnight, every night, in the ceiling directly over my cubicle. After two weeks, the lights came on at 6 AM. Were our experimenters adjusting the electronics in the ceiling?

As time elapsed, a new form of harassment began and it was nasty indeed: every morning at 6:30 AM thick, strong cigarette smoke would be blown into my cubicle from the air vent directly above my chair. It was highly significant that cigarette smoke was not being filtered into anyone else's cubicle but my own. The smoke was so strong, it seemed that someone was sitting alongside me puffing cigarette smoke into my face. Immediately I started coughing. My lungs could not take it.

It became a challenge to see how much work I could accomplish in the morning before the cigarette smoke overwhelmed me at 6:30 AM. When my cubicle filled up with stench, I was forced to run out into the hallway and fill a cup with water to take away the scratching in my throat.

I walked around adjoining offices, but no one else was getting cigarette smoke. Looking back on this, I find it very significant. While it could certainly be deemed to be harassment, it could also be thought to be an experiment to ascertain whether I would continue focusing on my work and ignore it.

I sent my supervisor an email message, but my effort proved to be futile. I had to live with the stench emanating from the vent over my head until the day I retired. Today there is no doubt in my mind that this was part of a military intelligence experiment. Moreover, I asked strangers that I met in the elevator, who worked in private industry on other floors, if they ever had cigarette smoke coming out of their air vents. Again, they all exhibited surprise and invariably gave the same response: "Are you kidding? Why, no, never!" Of course not, I thought, private industry would never tolerate that. Yes, I was a lab mouse with a badge.

REUNITED WITH NELSON

I was uneasy about the fact that my new cubicle was situated directly in front of the employee who had forced me to move out of my office in the Customhouse in the 1990s. I wondered how he was behaving these days. I did not have to wonder very long.

The first few weeks Nelson was introverted and I did not hear a peep from him. Over the course of several weeks, however, the ice gradually broke and we started saying good morning cordially to one another. He started to hang out in the hallway by our offices and converse with others. Occasionally he brought a box of cookies to work and set it next to a pile of paper napkins on the tabletop on the other side of my cubicle. This generated conversation among everyone who happened to walk by.

"Good morning!" he greeted me loudly and boisterously as he abruptly poked his head into my cubicle. I was startled and jumped back in my chair.

"Good morning," I replied politely. Because I no longer had a door with a lock on it, I wondered how this was going to work out. I did not have to wonder very long.

"Surpra-eeeeeeeeeeese!" he shouted and thrust a box of baked cookies beneath my nose.

"Oh, how nice! What a thoughtful thing to do!" I took a piece.

"Go, on, take another piece!"

"All right," I said and did so. Then he disappeared and made his rounds like a doctor going from office to office.

Soon this became a morning ritual and there was no stopping him. Every morning for the next three and a half years he brought food to work and either carried it around from office to office or else he left it on the tabletop for employees to see. I do not know what happened after those three and a half years because I retired. He was one of the reasons that I did. He gradually spent more and more money; there were more and more dishes; they were more and more expensive. I think that it would be valid to say that he had an OCD.

I did some research on the Internet and I discovered that a team of Russian scientists bragged that they were able to get a man to feed everyone in his company merely by flashing the instruction momentarily on his computer every 25th frame. The brain registered the command even though the subject was not consciously aware of it. Soon the human lab mouse was bringing food to work and would not rest until everyone in his company had taken a portion. Very soon I suspected that perhaps my coworker was the subject of a CIA experiment on subliminal suggestion. Indeed, he did seem to exactly mimic the experiment that I had read about on the Internet. Then the strangest thing happened.

Three years later everyone in my division was required to attend a movie sponsored by the Equal Employment Opportunity Office. The topic of the movie was harassment at the federal worksite: we were instructed as to how to identify harassment, what the laws are, and what course of action we should take when we felt that we were victims of it. The conference room was darkened and the movie began.

And then what I saw on screen caused my jaw to drop open in astonishment.

On screen there was featured a male in a business suit walking around his office balancing a silver platter of baked cookies in one hand and a tray of chocolate fudge brownies in the other; he was walking from table to table asking people whether they wanted to eat something. "Go ahead," he coaxed, "It's delicious!" The guy in the movie looked just like Nelson. Everyone in the audience commented on the similarity.

During the ride home on the "E" train I wondered whether the government had shown us this on purpose as a joke. Was this hubris carried to an exponential power? I wondered who had made this film. Was it made by the same people who were experimenting with us? The next morning Nelson brought two shopping bags of food to work and laid it out on the table. He was a movie star.

THE TELEPHONE CONVERSATION

June 2004. A Customs inspector called from Texas. He was holding up release of a shipment; he asked about the distinguishing characteristics of illegal weapons and how he could discern a legal item from an illegal one. Soon the subject turned to terrorism.

As the inspector was eager to converse, I found myself stating that it appeared to me that the greatest terrorist country in the world was the United States. It has a long history of intruding in the affairs of sovereign nations. I mentioned that during 1946–2001 the DoD trained more than 61,000 Latin American soldiers and police at the School of the Americas at Fort Benning in Georgia. I added that what outraged me personally was what America had done to the Greeks.

"Oh, really? What has it done to the Greeks?" he asked.

"It overthrew the government of Greece twice and that of Cyprus once. The Nazis in the CIA staged a coup in Cyprus in 1974 over two waves and killed everyone on my father's side of the family."

"Oh, no, Ms. Gregory...I am very, very sorry to hear that."

"Yeah, and I lost the house that I inherited from my father. The Turks, at the behest of Secretary of State Henry Kissinger, invaded the island; they occupied my house and threw out my uncle, who was an elderly man and a retired college professor. He died of pneumonia sleeping outdoors in the winter time."

"Oh, no...this is devastating to hear...I'm so sorry."

"I'll never forgive the Nazis in the CIA for staging a false flag operation and killing my family. The Turks, with the support of the United States, ethnically cleansed Cyprus of 160,000 Greek Cypriots and invited 50,000 Turks to take over their homes. The USS Little Rock was stationed in the Mediterranean to assure Turkish victory. Can you imagine that? The occupation continues until this day, it is illegal, and it is in violation of the United Nations Charter and numerous Security Council resolutions demanding the end of military action and the removal of Turkey's army from the island. When I think about all the evil things that the U.S. has done in the world, it makes me want to go home and take a shower. I am ashamed to be an American."

The poor guy didn't know what to say after that. Eventually the conversation wound down and I returned to my work. What I did not know was that immediately after the 2000 presidential election, the DoD began running every domestic telephone conversation through the DARPA computer looking for key words. If a flagged key word was articulated in a conversation, the entire conversation would be later recalled for scrutiny. It would be safe to assume that "Nazi" and "CIA" would be good words to flag.

The more that I thought about my dead uncle, the more that I wanted to know about what the Greek Cypriots were saying about what had happened.

I signed on to the Customs computer. I moved past the obnoxious banner informing me that by proceeding I was surrendering all rights to privacy. I inserted the key word "Cyprus" in my search engine and what I discovered was very tragic, indeed. All right, I thought, they can access my electronic queries. What did I care?

I learned that in 1974 the Turks destroyed artifacts of Greek civilization going back to antiquity. The elderly were being held in concentration camps on the eastern fork of the island. There was a media blackout on this tragic injustice in America.

Three government documents are posted on the Inter net that have since been declassified and published. They reveal the U.S. and NATO's complicity in staging the coup in Cyprus, their plot to assassinate Archbishop Makarios between May and June 1974, and their facilitation of the illegal Turkish invasion. The first document, from Joseph Luns, the Secretary General of NATO, to the U.S. Secretary of Defense, states, "The Assistant Undersecretary of State...showed the decision of the American government to finish the Cyprus problem. We agreed...for supporting the Turkish army during the landing, as well as, in the violent expulsion of Makarios."[4] The second document, from U.S. Secretary of State Henry Kissinger to the American Embassy in Nicosia, says, "You will proceed to the final cure of the Archbishop Makarios. The final cure is a decision of the National Security Council/PRM-42. Follow the special directions."[5] The third document, from U.S. Secretary of State Henry Kissinger to AMCOS/MIDEAST, says, "Clean the table of our ambassador in Cyprus, the cleaning is a decision of the National Security Council/PM-36. Follow the program directly."[6]

I surmised that the oil companies intend to build refineries on Cyprus one day. In 1975 the Union Oil Company of California, dba Unocal, made plans to construct an oil pipeline across the Middle East through Afghanistan, Iraq, Iran,

Syria, underneath the Mediterranean, and through Turkey. Unocal was acquired by Chevron in 2005. Hence, one must necessarily extrapolate that the U.S. has divided Cyprus so that one day it can stage another false flag operation and legitimize occupation and subsequent use of the island for offshore oil refining.

I was furious at the Nazis in the Pentagon and took advantage of every opportunity that came my way to articulate my feelings. Back then I did not yet know for sure that the pictures on the wall were bugged and that decisions could be made in real time as to how employees would be harassed.

One morning two of my colleagues and I chatted as we entered through the electronic doors, traversed the lengthy corridors, signed in, and picked up our mail. As we were walking past the pictures hung in the hallways, I said in a loud voice that Rummy and the other Nazis who infest the upper echelons of the U.S. military gave mustard gas and the nerve agent Talbun to Saddam in 1983; because Nazis are control freaks, no matter how much they control, it is not enough; it must be an evolutionary thing stemming back to the fact that Attila the Hun deposited his DNA with so many women in northern Europe.

"Did Rumsfeld give mustard gas to Saddam?" one woman asked.

"Yes, and the nerve agent Talbun, too. I read it on the Internet. On December 19–20, 1983, Rumsfeld went to Baghdad and gave Saddam mustard gas and nerve agent."

"You have a very good memory," she said. "How do you do it?"

"Well, actually, I printed a newspaper article about it yesterday and was reading it in the subway this morning. It's still fresh in my mind." I removed the news article from my Columbia shoulder bag. "The salient point is that Saddam got mustard gas and nerve agent from Rumsfeld." I glanced at the news story. "President Ronald Reagan dispatched his Middle East envoy who was Donald Rumsfeld. Rummy met with Saddam on December 19–20, 1983 and gave him bis-(2-chlorethyl)-sulfide, also known as mustard gas and ethyl N, N-dimethylphosphoroamidocyanidate, a nerve agent known as Talbun. And then in March 1984 Saddam used these two chemicals on Iranian soldiers. Then in 1988 he dropped poison gas on Kurdish civilians, his own people, from American-built helicopters. Isn't that interesting? He got it from Rumsfeld." I made sure that I enunciated clearly into the painting on the wall. Back in 2004, I had strongly suspected that the pictures were bugged, but had not yet proven it.

Could the electrical shocks that I would one day get be an essay in behavior modification? Does the method used consist of first tearing down the subject with shocks and then building him up into something different?

THE DISCOVERY OF CHIRP AND MISTY

June 2004. I had a rough weekend rescuing animals. Saturday morning I happened to look out of my bedroom window and I spied a sparrow trapped in string that was dangling from the fire escape across the alleyway. The bird swung back and forth in a desperate, but fruitless attempt to extricate itself from the string. I grabbed my keys and bolted out of the door.

Soon I was entering my neighbor's apartment and given permission to go out on her fire escape to rescue the bird. Lying on my stomach and reaching down the side of the fire escape with a pair of scissors, I managed to cut the string. The bird survived and flew away. I ripped the seat of my pants and had to do a little needlework.

Then on Sunday morning I was walking to the supermarket saw a large white shopping bag on a strip of grass on a lonely side street. I wondered what was in the bag and so I peeked inside. I was hoping for a few six-packs of soda, but this was not the city. Two little green eyes looked up at me and then I heard a tiny meow. It was a beautiful black Persian cat. I carried my new little friend around the Drive asking if anyone wanted to adopt it. There were several senior citizens sitting on the window ledge in front of the bank and one woman agreed to adopt the cat. I made two life-long friends that day, one human, and one from the animal kingdom.

Soon the woman and I were conversing on the telephone. I gave her my number at work, she called me there, and we discussed our favorite subject, politics. She and I shared an antipathy for U.S. intervention in the affairs of sovereign nations. Very soon I was telling her that the Nazis in the Bush crime family should be put on trial for treason and crimes against humanity. Over the course of the summer, on the U.S. Customs telephone, I enumerated every atrocity that ever happened on 9/11; everything that I knew about Skull and Bones; that I was convinced that the terrorist act that occurred in the Russian gymnasium during the week of the Republican National Convention was a CIA false flag operation designed to bolster the ratings of candidate Bush during the convention because they would significantly drop two weeks afterwards;[7] that NPR had reported that the guns and ammunition had been hidden beneath the floorboards of the gym months before, when the gym was under construction, and that that was the smoking gun. Why would Muslims hide them there and suddenly whip them out during the week of the RNC? One must ask who profited from the event. It was a CIA operation designed to bolster Bush's ratings. What I did not know was that our conversations were being sifted through DARPA's computer as the government was searching for the articulation of certain preselected key words.

BURSTS OF ENERGY OVER MY BED

One Saturday morning in July 2004. I was laying in bed, ready to snap on my walkman to listen to 1010 WINS, when the sound of BZZZT! resonated across the room. The sound materialized in midair in the middle of the bedroom, equidistant between the ceiling and floor. I dismissed it as the sound of a paint chip falling to the floor somewhere in the room.

After I listened to the news for 15 minutes, I removed my headphones and wondered what I would do that day. Suddenly another crackle materialized in midair right over my bed equidistant between the ceiling and the floor. It was several feet above me and did not touch my body. I wondered what was going on with the electrical wiring in the building.

The next day it happened again, but this time the electrical burst touched my right arm as I lay in bed. It felt like a tiny burst of energy, an explosion of air on the surface of my skin. I looked at my arm and wondered what to do. Should I tell the landlord?

A half hour later I arose from my bed to get a snack. An electronic burst struck my ankle before I reached the doorframe. I looked down at my leg. Then I walked over to the window and gazed up at the antennae peeking over the side of the roof. Was it coming from there?

MY NEIGHBOR'S MISSING DOORKNOB AND ELECTRONIC PHENOMENA

My neighbor who lives across the street and I met on the sidewalk. We were on our way to the supermarket and we parked our shopping carts on the sidewalk for a while as we visited.

"So, what are you going to call the kitty?"

"Misty."

"That's adorable. May I ask you something? Are you getting little electrical bursts, little BZZZTs! that explode in midair in your apartment?"

"A lot of strange things have been happening to me lately. I don't know where to begin."

"Really?"

"Yeah. First I came home from the doctor and someone had removed the door knob from my door. They left it on the floor, right in front of the door."

"You're kidding!"

"No. Then I had put a metal bar in the window to keep the window open, but something whacked it out of its place and it went flying across the room."

"No!"

"Yeah, and I find all of my things on the floor in the morning. They roll off the tables and dresser by themselves. No matter what I put on the table, socks, a pile of neatly folded sheets, whatever, it rolls off and ends up on the floor."

"Do you think that Misty is doing this?"

"Oh, no! It's much too high for her. Things roll off of high shelves! From the top of the refrigerator! She is not doing this. But now that you mention her, there is something that she does that is very strange."

"Yeah, what?"

"She jumps up into the air and tries to grasp something that is not there. She senses something. I can't see it but apparently she sees it or senses it and she leaps up and tries to hit it with her paw."

"I think that it is electromagnetic phenomena. I think that the government is experimenting from the planes or orbiting satellites passing overhead."

"That very well may be. Whatever this force is, it knocked the metal bar out of my window where I had it wedged tightly and it throws all of my stuff on the floor."

"Keep me posted. I would like to know what my neighbors are experiencing."

THE ASSASSINATION OF THE PATRIARCH OF ALEXANDRIA

Saturday, September 11, 2004. 11 AM. I was lying in bed listening to the Greek program, "Cosmos FM" on WNYE 91.5 FM. The show's regular programming was interrupted for a special announcement. It was then, on the morning of September 11, that I heard that a helicopter had just crashed into the Aegean moments before. I was stunned to learn that inside that helicopter, there was the entire hierarchy of the Greek Orthodox Church on the African continent: Petros VII, Patriarch of Alexandria and All Africa; the Metropolitan of Carthage; the Metropolitan of Pilousion (Port Said); the Bishop of Madagascar; two archimandrites; a deacon; the Patriarch's legal, technical, and press advisors; the Patriarch's brother and personal guard; five crew members. The entire hierarchy of the Greek Orthodox Church on the African continent had been eviscerated that morning.

The helicopter was a twin engine U.S. Army Chinook helicopter that was only 1 ½ year old. Visibility was good that morning. It carried 12 passengers and 5 crew members; everyone aboard died in the crash. The helicopter went down en route to Mount Athos, a monastic community in northern Greece, located about 60 miles southwest of Thessaloniki. Petros was due to arrive shortly after 11:00 AM, making his first official visit to the 2,000 year old monastic enclave. However, his helicopter disappeared from radar at 11 AM. Hours later, bodies and wreckage were found about 5.5 miles from the Mount Athos coast.

The Patriarch of Alexandria was well known throughout the world both for his missionary work and for preaching peace between Christians and Muslims. He was a key figure in Christian-Muslim dialogue in the Middle East.

The Patriarchate at Alexandra, Egypt, was established by Saint Mark in 42 AD. Hence, Petros VII was an Orthodox leader directly in the line of Saint Mark.

I listened attentively to my walkman all afternoon for updates on the tragedy. The more I thought about it, the more I was convinced that it was highly significant that the crash had occurred on September 11. 9/11 is the telltale sign of U.S. intelligence agencies carrying out covert activities and false flag operations; 9/11 is the hallmark of occultists who believe that the prime number, 11, and 9, the square of the prime number 3, possess magical powers; they carry out their significant operations on 9/11 because they hold fast to numerology.

My list of 9/11 events was getting longer now. We can add the following to the material listed in Chapter Six:

• On September 11, 2001 the U.S. government staged a false flag operation that ultimately obliterated the balance of power, the checks and balances, that had been in place since the Constitution was ratified on June 21, 1788. The Bush administration used the event to leverage despotic power that was hitherto unseen: it ran all domestic telephone calls of U.S. citizens through the DARPA computer and listen for keywords; it opened citizens' mail; it entered and searched citizens' homes when they were away at work; and very soon we could add that it uses powerful microwave weapons to image inside homes and deliver powerful shocks to the people inside—here on domestic soil. A few of the telltale signs of the false flag operation are enumerated below.

• The 9/11 Commission was a whitewash. The sale of put options on American and United Airlines spiked during the week preceding 9/11 and the government never reported on those sales.

• On September 11, 2004 the U.S. government skewed the electronics in an American Chinook helicopter and assassinated the Patriarch of Alexandria, the Metropolitan of Carthage, the Metropolitan of Pilousion, and the Bishop of Madagascar. The Patriarch was an international figure known for his dialogue of peace between Christians and Muslims in the Middle East.

The Bush administration wanted the Patriarch of Alexandria dead because he was a vociferous opponent of the U.S. invasion of Iraq. As a successor to Saint Mark, he pointed out to George W. Bush that the Orthodox Christian world and the Muslim world were enjoying a relatively peaceful, albeit fragile, peace. On January 2, 2003 Petros wrote Bush a letter and pleaded with him not to invade Iraq because Christians and Muslims were getting along in the Middle East and a war would disrupt the peace. Here is his letter:

Alexandria, 2nd January 2003
Ref. No. P.V./3
His Excellency President George W. Bush
President of the United States of America
The White House
Washington D.C., USA
Your Excellency

"Glory to God in the highest, and on earth peace and goodwill toward men." (Luke 2:14)

From the historic city founded by Alexander the Great and where Christianity was preached by St. Mark the Apostle and Evangelist; from the land of the Nile river and a country which is a model and example of harmony between Christians and Muslims, I wish to make an earnest call to Your Excellency to avoid any attacks on Iraq. If Iraq is attacked, the negative consequences of such an attack would not only be felt by the peaceful land of Egypt but the whole world as well.

As the Primate of the Greek Orthodox Church of Alexandria and All Africa, a Church that has existed for the last two thousand years, I call on Your Excellency to try and find a peaceful solution rather than that of war. The Middle East is a sensitive area that already is suffering greatly. Such a war would be seen as an attack against Islam. Such an impression, though false, would have unjust far-reaching and long lasting consequences upon religions, their faithful and their reputations. Religions, in essence, have nothing to do with politics, terrorism, and war.

From this holy place, I invite Your Excellency to offer up intense prayer to the Almighty God, who created us all, that peace may reign in the whole world. I also ask our Lord to enlighten all the leaders of all nations to work to build a world without violence, a world that loves life and grows I justice and solidarity.

May the New Year be a joyful, peaceful, graceful and blessed one for Your Excellency, the members of your beloved family, the people of the United States of America and the whole world.

With the love of our Incarnate Lord Jesus Christ
+ Petros VII, Pope and Patriarch of Alexandria and All Africa
In the Great City of Alexandria
January 2, 2003

And there it is, the reason that the Bush administration wanted the Patriarch of Alexandria dead: he was an embarrassment to the Nazis in the White House that were currently promulgating a false religious war, one based on phony premises; here was the successor to Saint Mark who warned Bush that the U.S. should not spoil a fragile peace. The portion of the letter that must have particularly gotten the Nazis' goats was the statement, "Religions, in essence, have nothing to do with politics, terrorism, and war." It is precisely the antithesis of this statement that Bush was using as an excuse to extend empire.

The timing of the assassination is the smoking gun. First, the occultists act on 9/11. Secondly, 2004 was an election year and the presidential elections would be held in two months. They wanted the Christian who got along with Muslims out of the way before Election Day 2004. Note that Petros wrote the letter on January 2, 2003 and made his position clear then. The Bush administration waited as long as 1 year, 8 months before it killed him; it did not choose 9/11/03 because 2003 was not an election year.

(Endnotes)

1   Lord Action, *Letter to Bishop Mandell Creighton*, April 3, 1887, in Louise Creighton, *Life and Letters of Mandell Creighton: D.D. Oxon. and Cam., Sometime Bishop of London...by His Wife*, 2 vols. (London: Longmans, Green, and Company, 1905), 1:372.

2   John Norris, *Collision Course: NATO, Russia, and Kosovo.* Foreword by Strobe Talbott. Westport, CT: Praeger Publishers, 2005, xxii–xxiii. John Norris is Strobe Talbott's former communications director. This highly revealing citation was unearthed and cited by Naomi Klein, *The Shock Doctrine: The Rise of Disaster Capitalism* (New York: Picador, 2007), 415n. Klein brilliantly shows how shock is the first step in defeating and then subjugating a country.

3   According to tradition, Mary, the Mother of Christ and Saint John the Evangelist had left Joppa and were sailing to Cyprus to see Lazarus, the first bishop of a city that is now Larnaca. She was struck by the great beauty of the promontory and asked Her Son to give it to her as a gift. See Mary Efrosini Gregory, *Miracles of the Orthodox Church* (Minneapolis: Light & Life Publishing Company, 2009), 118–27. Available at www.light-n-life.com.

4   American Duplicity IV: The CIA Files," http://www.greece.org/cyprus/Takism8.htm (February 21, 2009).

5   Ibid.

6   Ibid.

7   The Republican National Convention took place August 30-September 2, 2004. The atrocity in the Russian gymnasium occurred September 1–3, 2004. Bush got a huge bounce in his ratings because Americans were scared; after the Convention, the ratings dropped as expected.

My right arm, as the rest of my body, has multiple burn marks effected long distance
via through-the-wall imaging and striking. One EMP punctured my lower left eyelid,
leaving a perfectly circular pinhole.

03.07.2010 11:

Chapter Nine

The Reign of Terror of King George II: The Fifth Year (2005)

The struggle of man against power is the struggle of memory against forgetting.[1]
—Milan Kundera, *The Book of Laughter and Forgetting* (1980)

NAZI MONETARY CERTIFICATES UNDERWRITTEN BY BANKSTER – February 2005

I was having coffee with several colleagues when they delivered the stunning news: Customs had once looked inside the diplomatic mailbags at JFK Mail Branch and had found monetary certificates with swastikas across the top, underwritten by a major financial institution. The corporation will remain nameless because I do not want to endure the aggravation of a lawsuit and the need to round up witnesses to substantiate the facts. Now, no one is ever permitted by law to open the leather mail pouches that the diplomats use, not even Customs. However, one day, the word came down from the top of the pyramid that the time had come to open them. And that was what Customs employees found.

I asked the key question: I wanted to know whether a name—George Herbert Walker or Prescott Bush—appeared on the Nazi monetary certificates. The answer was negative. I explained to my colleagues that George Herbert Walker had brought millions of dollars worth of Nazi war bonds into the U.S. and that American corporations had purchased them. The government took him to court and the case is in the law books. The Trading with the Enemies Act of 1917 was amended because of him. My friends assured me that there were no names—just a flying eagle across the top of each and at the bottom, they were underwritten by a big company.

I returned to my cubicle to do my work. However, the more that I thought about it, the angrier I became. So, I thought, it is, indeed, all true! There really are Nazis in the Bush family tree, after all! That clinched it: the assassination of the Patriarch of Alexandria and 11 others in the helicopter was a chess move in the quest for empire. I was ashamed to be an American; I felt even worse about what the government was doing with the million dollars that I was lending it through my purchase of Treasury bills.

THE TOWN CRIER AT 5 AM

I asked my supervisor whether the law permitted me to have a blog on the Internet. My supervisor shook his head vigorously and his face turned apoplectic crimson.

"No, no, not allowed."

"I'm not allowed to write on the blogs on the Internet?"

"No."

"May I call a radio talk show and air my opinions?"

"No."

"Don't I have the First Amendment right to freedom of speech?"

"No." That was the end of that. Everyone in America has constitutional rights except federal employees. I remember hearing on Air America that a nurse at a VA hospital in the southwest lost her job because she had written a letter to the editor of a local newspaper about ending the war in Iraq.

As time elapsed, and American massacres continued to increase in frequency and magnitude, I grew more and more livid. America was the greatest terrorist nation on earth. I needed to vent, but I was not allowed to. I considered screaming messages in the streets. Should I do it? Would I get arrested? At Grand Central, Times Square, Penn Station and Union Square, probably, but elsewhere?

I departed my apartment building at 4:30 AM. I knew the location of a pizza joint that piled its unsold pies in a tall stack for the garbage truck. As I headed out of my building and proceeded through the alleyway, a car raced past me. When I got to the sidewalk, I saw that his was the only car on the street; there were no others as far as the eye could see. How did they manage that? How did they always get a car to pass the alleyway just as I stepped into it? Suddenly, the lava that had been percolating beneath the surface, rose to the top and exploded into a public service announcement.

"George Bush is a Nazi!" I screamed at the top of my lungs. "The Nazis in the Bush crime family transport Nazi monetary certificates in the diplomatic mailbags at JFK Mail Branch!" I cried as I walked up the street, headed for the subway. A black car turned the corner and stopped abruptly in the middle of a street. The driver rolled down his windows and looked at me. I was delighted to have an audience.

"George Bush is a Nazi!" I repeated. "I work for the U.S. Customs Service and we found monetary certificates in the diplomatic mailbags at JFK Airport. They have swastikas at the top and are underwritten by...!" The driver listened attentively and then stepped on the gas and disappeared down the street.

I headed for 63rd Drive. At 4:30 AM people were returning home from their night jobs. I stood on the corner and delivered my message in a powerful voice.

"Ladies and gentlemen, your attention please. I work for the United States Customs Service. My coworkers have found Nazi monetary certificates in the diplomatic mailbags at JFK Airport. They have swastikas across the top..." It felt good to vent. Someone came out of an all night store. I delivered the message. Then the two of us engaged in conversation. After that I descended the subway steps. I stood at the edge of the platform and blurted my message out across the platform. As the minutes elapsed, more and more people descended to catch the 4:45. I remained on the platform and screamed some more. I could always catch the 5:07. Another crowd gathered. I educated them until they boarded the 4:55. When the 5:07 came, I boarded it and did my thing in the train.

This became a habit. Every morning when I left my building, just as I was walking through the alleyway, a car raced past me. When I stepped onto the sidewalk and looked up and down the street, I discovered that there was no other traffic, as far as the eye could see. Livid, I metamorphosed into the town crier and galloped along, waiving my lantern, like Paula Revere. I met a number of people on the street who felt the same way that I did: the men delivering the morning papers; cleaning people and food service employees rushing to their jobs in the city; exhausted people returning home from their night jobs; undercover cops. I introduced myself and we exchanged ideas. Almost everyone I met was as thoroughly disgusted with the American government as I was. I had a lot of support. And it was very healthy for me to be able to exchange ideas.

The freedom that I enjoyed as I screamed my head off every morning in Rego Park contrasted sharply to the Nazi environments of Grand Central, Times Square, Penn Station and Union Square. The minute I stepped into large subway terminals, I found men wielding tommy guns, cops with dogs that appeared to dine on humans, and other assorted characters clad in face masks and hazmat gear. I resented them tremendously. Why don't they tie a yellow police tape around the ranch at Crawford, I thought. They are at the wrong address. The hypocrisy made me seethe even more. And the next morning I shouted my message even louder in Queens. I dared not do it in Manhattan, because if I got arrested, I would not only be fired, I would forfeit my pension. My career screaming through the streets of Queens and in subways lasted for three years. It ended when I retired.

My Password

I changed my password in the Customs computer to "1nazi." I had George Bush in mind when I devised it: George Bush is one Nazi. It occurred to me that anyone who had a copy of a master list of passwords might think that I was trying to express the idea that I was one Nazi. After I chose this as a password, I had the impression that someone, somewhere, knew what my password was.

Back in 1987, before my promotion, my supervisor had a list of employee passwords on the top of her desk. One day she called me into her office to discuss my rating and invited me to sit in her visitor's chair adjacent to her desk. When the topic of conversation turned to passwords, she showed me that she had a master list of everyone's password. Although this occurred in 1987, it proves that password information is somewhere in the automated system and that it is just a question of who has the ability to access it. Perhaps "1nazi" did inspire more electronic assaults, or perhaps not. I decided that if I had already been chosen to be the subject of a psyop, my password was irrelevant.

Followed By A Helicopter

5:30 A.M. I was just walking away from a mailbox in Manhattan after I had dropped my rent check down the chute. A postal employee happened to be standing on the sidewalk staring fixedly into the gutter and I struck up a conversation with him.

"You see all of these white box trucks on every corner? They are surveillance trucks. 60,000 of them came north after 9/11." He snapped out of his lethargy.

"Oh, yeah?"

"I really resent being watched."

"Me, too, baby. Me, too."

"You know, I work for the U.S. Customs Service and my coworkers found Nazi monetary certificates in the diplomatic mailbags at JFK airport. They had swastikas across the top and they were underwritten by a major financial institution."

"Really?"

"Yeah. That means that everything you read about on the Internet about the Bush crime family trading with Hitler is true. They bought war bonds from Hitler and kept them for 50 years and then transported them out of the country."

"I'm not surprised one bit."

"Federal employees are not allowed to express their views publicly, so I am telling everyone by word of mouth." The man grinned broadly from ear to ear. A gold cap twinkled beneath the street lamp.

"You go, girl!"

Suddenly a helicopter peeked over a roof and hovered directly overhead from me. I looked up at it and flew into a rage. I screamed at the top of my lungs, "What are you looking at, you Nazis? You're in the wrong state. Why don't you tie a yellow police tape around the ranch in Crawford?" The man to whom I was speaking became frightened, excused himself, and hurried away. I looked up at the helicopter above and screamed, "I know all about the Nazi monetary certificates in the diplomatic mailbags and as soon as I retire from my federal job, I'm going on 60 Minutes and you can catch my act with Morley Safer! Then I am going to write a book!"

I stopped for a moment and wondered whether there indeed existed a causality between my conversation with the man and the fact that there was now a helicopter overhead. I could think of only one way to find out.

I crossed the street when the light turned green. The helicopter followed me across the street. Then I crossed back to where I was before. The helicopter followed me back. I metamorphosed into a seething cauldron of indignation and screamed up at it, "Ya Nazis! What are you looking at me for? Why don't you put Bush, Cheney, and Rummy on trial for treason, convict them, and then tie them up to Old Sparky?"

I decided to walk the length of two long blocks between city avenues to see what would happen. The helicopter followed me the length of the first block. I looked up at it and screamed, "I know that Henry Kissinger ordered the assassination of Archbishop Makarios in 1974! His telex from the State Department bearing his name is on the Internet!" I looked around. Hip-hop people, clad in jeans sagging half way to their knees and sporting as much gold as an Egyptian pharaoh, were watching me while they were talking on their cellphones. Of course, I thought, I should not jump to the conclusion that they are undercover cops. The fact that they are everywhere is no proof of causality.

I crossed the street and walked the second long block to the next avenue. The helicopter followed me there. "O.K. ya Nazis, I get it. You're spending your Middle Eastern gas on me," I screamed up at the sky. I was getting tired of this.

This concretized my suspicion that the white box trucks parked on the corners around the subway station had equipment that permitted them to listen to conversations on the street. The whole reason that this was taking place was because they had heard me. Well, I thought, I'll give them something to listen to. I walked the long blocks back to work and as I did, I clearly enunciated into my nonexistent cellphone, affixed to my imaginary earpiece, that the TV station had expressed great interest in doing a documentary on our discovery that George Bush is a Nazi and that his family transports Nazi monetary certificates in the diplomatic mailbags at JFK Airport; I recommended that we procure legal counsel to advise whether the financial corporation could sue if we disclosed that it had underwritten the Nazi monetary certificates with swastikas at the top.

When I got to work I had the urge to change my password to "4osama." However, I did not dare. I really did want to retire and I did want to sleep in my own bed that night.

The NSA Bugs The Phones In Greece And Hangs The Man Who Made The Discovery From The Ceiling

March 2005. My coworkers were sipping their morning coffee: some were chatting, while others read the news on the Internet. I decided to do the latter. I sat down at the computer and moved past the obnoxious banner that warned me that I have no expectations of privacy in the government automated system. I accessed the BBC. Seconds later I became apprised of a news story that had just broken and was blazing across the world like a flash fire: it was the most extraordinary wiretapping scandal of the post-Cold War era; the victim was a democratic sovereign nation, a nation that was proud of having invented democracy thousands of years ago by casting seashells inscribed with the names of candidates. As I continued to read, I became increasingly livid with every passing second. Then I accessed multiple news sources to get as many details as I could.

On March 9, 2005 a Greek man was found hanging from the ceiling in his Athens apartment. Apparently, he had just made the discovery that someone had been bugging the mobile phones in Greece. The means employed were highly sophisticated electronic wiretapping techniques, most certainly the fingerprint of the National Security Agency (NSA): the NSA is America's signal intelligence agency and no other group exhibits the level of acumen in electronic eavesdropping that had been employed. Wow! I thought, the U.S. was bugging the phones in Greece and then hung the man who discovered it from the ceiling! Suddenly my inner world exploded into a seething miasma of rage and indignation. I raced through various news sources, acquiring more and more facts.

Each morning I returned to the story to pore over new developments just as they became public: the lawsuit filed by the family, the lawyer's call for an exhumation and postmortem examination of the body; the opinion of an American who had once been employed at the American embassy in Athens, but then resigned after the U.S. invaded Iraq in 2003: he said that it was the hallmark of the NSA; computer experts who provided in-depth analyses of the techniques that were employed the moment that the press reported on them. Finally I had learned all that I wanted to know.

Costas Tsalikidis was an electrical engineer who was employed by Vodafone Greece, the national cellular company, as a network engineering manager. Shortly before he was found hanging in his apartment, he had made the discovery that someone with inside access to Vodafone switches had bugged more than 100 high-ranking Greek government officials including Prime Minister Costas Karamanlis and his wife, cabinet ministers, security officials, and the mayor of Athens; besides the mobile phones of the country's political and security elite, it was also discovered that those of journalists and Arabs residing in Greece, military personnel, and that of a U.S. embassy employee were illegally monitored. The conversations were diverted to 14 shadow pay-as-you-go phones were they could be recorded. This went on for about nine months between June 2004-March 2005, beginning before the 2004 summer Olympics that were to be held in Athens. The European press strongly suspected that it was the U.S. National Security Administration (NSA) because of the remarkable degree of sophistication that was used. The surveillance was accomplished by exploiting software created by Ericsson, the Swedish manufacturer of the cellular switches that Vodaphone used.

More than two years later, in July 2007, the *IEEE Spectrum*, a journal of the Institute of Electrical and Electronics Engineers, described in detail how the wiretapping was performed. In an article entitled, "The Athens Affair," Vassilis Prevelakis and Diomidis Spinellis explain:

> ...the scheme did not depend on the wireless nature of the network. Basically, the hackers broke into a tele-

phone network and subverted its built-in wiretapping features for their own purposes.

We now know that the illegally implanted software, which was eventually found in a total of four of Vodafone's Greek switches, created parallel streams of digitized voice for the tapped phone calls. One stream was the ordinary one, between the two calling parties. The other stream, an exact copy, was directed to other cellphones, allowing the tappers to listen on the conversations on the cellphones, and probably also to record them. The software also routed location and other information about those phone calls to those shadow handsets via automated text messages.

Nowadays, all wiretaps are carried out at the central office. In AXE exchanges, a remote control equipment subsystem, or RES, carries out the phone tap by monitoring the speech and data streams of switched calls. It is a software subsystem typically used for setting up wiretaps, which only law officers are supposed to have access to. When the wiretapped phone makes a call, the RES copies the conversation into a second data stream and diverts that copy to a phone line used by law enforcement officials.[2]

In July 2007 the *New York Times* reviewed Prevelakis and Spinellis' article and summarized it thus:

The two researchers explored the methods used by the surveillance operation as well as analyzed the weakness in the security of the cellular telephone switching systems that may be inherent as a result of software extensions added to permit so-called "lawful intercept" by law enforcement agencies.

The surveillance was done with a remarkable degree of sophistication, exploiting software developed by Ericsson, the Swedish manufacturer of the GSM cellular switches, which were used by Vodafone. Shortly before the bugging of the cellular system began, the telephone equipment maker had provided a software update to the computerized switches that route cell-phone calls.

The article raises fascinating unanswered questions by noting that the Swedish phone equipment firm supplied only a portion of the lawful intercept system—which had not been purchased by Vodafone Greece. The control interface software module was not included in the upgrade. However, because the modules necessary to essentially target and "clone" phone calls came with the upgrade, the attacker was able to control the modules inside the system, while effectively hiding from Vodafone Greece technicians.

That code permitted someone—who almost certainly had physical access to the computerized switches—to install at least 14 "shadow" cellular phone accounts. Whenever a call was made or received by one of the targets of the surveillance, one of the secretly created cellphone accounts could listen in.[3]

Back in 2005, just as the story broke, the evidence suggested that Tsalikidis had not committed suicide. He was 38, engaged to be married, and he had his whole life ahead of him. He was found dead two days after the tapping was uncovered and one day before Vodafone informed the government. A former American diplomat advised that he was certain that the U.S. had done this.

I was upset. I visited my GS-14 and advised of her of all of the sordid details of the story. I added that making the area safe for the Olympics could not have possibly been the reason for the wiretapping: how did monitoring the Prime Minister, his wife, cabinet members, security officials, and the mayor of Athens, make Greece safe from terrorists? Why don't they reopen the 9/11 Commission instead and find out why the hijackers received diplomas from U.S. military programs?; why they lived at housing facilities for foreign military trainees at Pensacola?; graduated and received diplomas from Lackland Air Force Base and the U.S. International Officers School? (see Chapter 6, note 21). The globalists in the Bilderberg group want to destroy the nation state that is Greece because geographically, Greece is the gateway to the Middle East and the globalists want to facilitate massive immigration in order to bring about one world government; they seek to destroy Greece's ethnic identity and the Orthodox Church. However, Christ proclaimed, "… upon this rock I will build my church; and the gates of hell shall not prevail against it" (Mat 16:18). Senators and House representatives should vote to defund all intelligence agencies, but they have Swiss bank accounts thanks to the lobbyists in the military-industrial-oil complex. My GS-14 felt very badly that I was aggravated. I, in turn, regretted that I had shared my unhappiness with her.

"I'm sorry," I apologized, "I'm such a bundle of joy today. I didn't mean to depress you."

"It's O.K.," she replied and changed the subject to work. She gave me an assignment to do. After I left her office I looked around for someone else to tell.

I decided to visit another coworker. She listened intently and shook her head back and forth in dismay.

"The Nazis in the Bush crime family are way of control," I concluded.

"Oh, yeah, WAY out of control. WAY, WAY out of control. And you know something?" she asked. "There is nothing that we can do about it." I was stunned by the truth of her statement. I nodded assent. Then there was a very long pregnant pause as we both contemplated what she had said, eyes fixed on the rug, heads shaking from side to side. Her philosophical point was brilliant indeed.

"How do you deal with it?" I asked.

"I just live my life, one day at a time. What else can you do? I'm not going to ruin my health over it," she replied. I thanked her for her opinion and returned to my cubicle to do my work.

At 6 AM the following morning I entered through the electronic doors with a coworker Very soon the subject turned to politics. I apprised her that the NSA had bugged the phones in Greece and then hung the man who made the discovery.

"That is so disgusting," she said, shaking her head in dismay.

"Yeah, it is, and you know what I heard on NPR last night?"

"What?"

"That the Italians threw the CIA out of Italy," I squealed gleefully. "Isn't that great?" She pumped an arm in the air twice as if our team had just made a basket.

I headed for my cubicle to find out the news from Alex Jones. I loved Alex Jones. I could not get enough of his websites. I wondered whether he was getting electrical shocks from the government in his house, too.

THE WALL COLLAPSE

I heard on the radio that there was a wall collapse on the Henry Hudson Parkway. On May 12, 2005 a 300 by 100-foot section of a retaining wall in Washington heights collapsed; no one was injured. Thousands of tons of dirt were spilled onto the northbound lanes of the Henry Hudson Parkway and the ramp connecting Riverside Drive and West 181st Street to the parkway.

The first thing that I thought was that the government was having target practice either from an airplane or from space. Apparently a plane or an orbiting satellite could be sending down an electromagnetic wave that resonated at the same frequency as the retaining wall; the principle in physics that applies here is the same one that permits opera singers to break a glass when they hold a note for an extended period of time; this is how the U.S. caused the earthquake in Bam, Iran, at the time when it wanted to gain entry into the country. I articulated my thoughts to my coworkers in their offices and standing in front of the lovely pictures in the hallway.

THE MYSTERIOUS CASE OF THE PERPETUALLY BROKEN ELECTRONIC DOORS

Meanwhile, at work, there was another significant occurrence that indicated that covert operatives were free to enter and do their dirty work at night. We had some very expensive and highly sophisticated electronic glass doors at the main entrance. It was such a high tech setup that employees were given swipe cards to enter. However, strangely enough, the mechanism in these high-tech doors was perpetually broken and the swipe cards did not work.

The managers requested that the man in the blue denim overalls come over with his step ladder and toolbox and fix the fancy electronic glass doors at the main entrance. And he did so, many, many, many times. Every other day we would see him laboring in the ceiling and fooling around with wires sticking out of the walls. However, as soon as he had fixed the doors, they broke again.

It became a Kabuki dance. He set up the ladder and fixed the doors, the employees got in, they did not get in, the clerk made the telephone call, he came back, set up his step ladder, and on and on, ad nauseam.

Now, dear reader, do you get the impression that someone, somewhere, wanted to keep the mechanism that controlled the electronic glass doors perpetually broken? That perhaps a covert operative in an intelligence agency was using high-powered microwave technology to skew the electronics in the doors remotely with a zap? I believe that a military intelligence agency skewed the electronics in the glass doors so that it could enter at night and set things up so that the experimental group would get the exact dose of EM waves that it was supposed to get and the control group would not.

It is significant that the Kabuki dance abruptly ended the moment I mentioned my suspicions to my supervisor. I told him that I believed that another agency was experimenting with us and that its operatives were able to enter at night because the electronic doors were broken. I said that a 6 AM. At 7 AM the man in the blue denim overalls stood on his stepladder at the main entrance and worked in the ceiling. The next morning the doors worked perfectly. And the morning after that. This efficiency lasted for a full week. Then the doors did not work again. I am convinced that it was a microwave zap that did it.

During the months preceding my retirement, the expensive doors managed to remain fixed permanently. The electronics in the wall and the swipe cards worked perfectly. Had our experimenters in the Pentagon evolved to the next step in evolution, namely, administering the EMs long distance via orbiting satellites or unmanned aerial drones? Perhaps they did not need to get in as often.

7/7

On July 7, 2005 four bombs detonated on three London Underground trains and a double-decker bus during a 57 minute period; 3 bombs exploded at 8:50 AM; the fourth, on the bus, at 9:47 AM; 56 people died and 700 were injured. My coworkers were terrified that it might happen in the New York subway system and they talked about it endlessly. Even as they sat at their desks and worked, they shouted comments about it over the modular dividers into their neighbors' cubicles.

I sat down at my computer and scoured numerous media outlets. In a few minutes, I had all the information that I needed to know. That morning, Visor Consultants, a crisis management consulting firm, had been staging mock simulations of a terrorist attack at precisely the same time and at the exact same train stations that had suffered the explosions. Visor Consultants trains FBI personnel at Quantico, VA, and the company has a website. On its homepage, an advertisement states that Visor Consultants "has helped many organizations to better anticipate and prepare for whatever crises, risks and threats they might face. All of our consultants have many years of real-time experience dealing with actual crises..."[4] On another webpage, we find "We are a team of experts located in the heart of London, but with international coverage, dedicated to helping you maximize your corporate resilience in an uncertain world. This includes: Running complex exercises, or simple table top rehearsals for your Business Continuity (BC) and Crisis Management Teams."[5]

Peter Power, managing director of the firm, was giving an interview on the BBC that morning and was surprised that there had been a real terrorist attack at the same time and at the same Underground stations where he was conducting his mock drill. His interview on the BBC became the subject of radio programs and newspaper articles. The video has since been posted on You Tube.[6] O.K., I thought, I get it: the U.S. and England, acting in concert with one another, staged the event at the precise time of exercises, just as there were a dozen different mock drills going on concurrently in the northeast on 9/11. Apparently, mocks drills are the best time to do this.

I jumped up from my desk and dashed into various cubicles announcing what I had discovered. People were surprised as they had not heard about Visor Consultants' drill or Peter power's interview on the BBC. Then they narrowed their eyes and nodded assent. They got it.

Subsequently I learned that the baby-faced Muslim who entered the London Underground with a backpack filled with explosives was a schoolteacher of young children. As the days progressed it became evident that he had agreed to participate in what he thought was a mock drill for the purpose of educating others. Wow, I thought. He believed that he was participating in a training exercise and they had substituted the rags in his backpack for real dynamite. I dashed into the cubicle of a coworker. I explained everything that I had learned and gave her the hard copy of an Internet article.

"But why now? Why London?" she asked in a low voice. "It was timed to coincide with the G8 summit that convened Wednesday, July 6 in Gleneagles, Scotland. George Bush is at the summit and he is on the verge of embarrassing himself in front of the whole world. Everyone else wants to discuss the U.S. invasion and occupation of Iraq under false pretenses, the Kyoto agreement, global warming, disarmament, the supervised destruction of nuclear missiles, and AIDS. There are protests and demonstrations bringing these issues to the attention of the media. However, the U.S., whose war machine is well oiled and running, needs to draw attention away from Iraq; it is not willing to burden corporations with finding alternate fuel sources and modifying their manufacturing processes; it is against every issue that the rest of the world advocates. Now that the London bombings have occurred, George Bush can radically change the topic of conversation to terrorism: this is his forte; the topics of Iraq, Kyoto, global warming, nuclear disarmament, and AIDS, have vanished into the ethers and Bush is dictating what the new topic of conversation will be." My coworker thought about it.

"They did change the topic of conversation," she admitted.

"Yeah, they did, and there is something else about the timing. First, it stopped George Bush from having nothing to offer at the G8 Summit. But also, bear in mind that the day before, London was awarded the 2012 Olympics. Now their minds have switched from protests to worrying about terrorism."

"Oh, that's right, they did just get the Olympics."

"Yeah, they did, and I have an Alex Jones article here that says that the CIA and England, working in concert, planned and carried out bombings in Iran in 1953 and bragged about it 40 years later on the radio; and furthermore, it is also a historical fact that in 1980 the CIA was behind the bombing in Bologna in which 80 people were killed.[7] Here, I made a copy of the article from the prison planet website." She took the article and slid it into her briefcase.

"I'll read this on the train home."

"Here is some more material. I printed pages from Visor Consultants' website. They stage mock drills related to terrorism; this is what they do for a living. Look here, it says, "running complex exercises, or simple table top rehearsals." And here is a page from boingboing.net.[8] They have some dialogue from Peter Power's interview on the BBC." I gave her the pages and she slipped them into her briefcase with the Alex Jones material.

When I returned to my cubicle it occurred to me that perhaps I should spread the word around. I made a few more copies and gave them to people whom I thought would pass the world along for me.

The moment that I returned to my cubicle, loud cacophonic snapping commenced. CRACK! An electrical dagger struck and resonated off the metal cabinet over my desk just inches from my forehead. SNAP! a thunderous clatter emanated from my metal clothing cabinet a few feet from my back. One minute later I got a sharp pinprick to the crown of my head. It felt like a needle had dug into my cranium. Instinctively I raised my hand and covered the site of the assault with the palm of my hand. It started again, I thought. The site burned for several minutes.

Looking back on this now, I have come to correlate the shocks that I receive in my apartment in Queens with each day's activities on the Internet. Now that I am retired and am engaged in researching this book, I spend each day at the Rego Park Library, Elmhurst Library or Forest Hills Library triangulating terms such as "CIA," "7 WTC," and "moved at 6 AM." A cogent argument could be made that I am the subject of an experiment in behavior modification and that triangulating search terms such as these triggers negative reinforcement afterwards.

There is no more privacy in public libraries than there is in the government computer system: a personal identification number (PIN) is required to use public libraries and name and proof of address must be supplied to get a PIN number. The government knows who is accessing what, all the time.

DRIVERLESS CARS IN REGO PARK

On July 30, 2002 DARPA announced the Grand Challenge for American auto teams: the goal was to get a vehicle to navigate a course in the southwestern U.S with out the benefit of a driver. In March 2004 the DoD offered a $1 million prize to the first team that could get a driverless car to traverse a 142-mile desert course from Barstow, CA, to Primm, NV; no one was able to complete the course; the vehicle that managed to go the farthest traveled only 7.4 miles. However, another competition was held in October 2005 and the first prize increased to $2 million. Five teams completed the course. In a third competition held on November 3, 2007, six teams completed the course.

In October 2005 five robotic cars without drivers completed a rugged 132-mile course. DARPA awarded the $2 million prize to the fastest one that completed the course in less than 10 hours. The taxpayer-funded Grand Challenge was part of the Pentagon's effort to reduce the number of causalities on the battlefield by fulfilling a congressional mandate to have a third of all military ground vehicles unmanned by 2015.

Currently there are three clusters of activity relating to free-ranging, off-road, driverless cars. These programs include the FROG passenger vehicles from Holland, the ARGO research project from Italy, and DARPA's Grand Challenge in the US. All of these projects are military-oriented. The driverless car is equipped with sensors, lasers, cameras, and radar that provide data to onboard computers. These electronics make decisions that include distinguishing between large objects and small and deciding whether a chasm to too deep to cross.

In June 2007 the team of Stanford engineers that had won the $2 million prize in 2005 unveiled a driverless, computer-packed Volkswagen Passat station wagon that can maneuver in city traffic. It passed tests on an artificial course that require it to navigate on a city block at no more than 15 miles per hour, negotiate a four-way intersection, stop at the intersection and waiting for other vehicles before proceeding, and pass a stationary car immediately after an intersection. In the Fall 2007 53 teams participated in DARPA's Urban Challenge, a 60-mile timed race in which driverless cars were required to follow a course and perform simulated military missions in urban traffic.

In August 2005 I saw an article on the Internet that advertized the upcoming October Grand Challenge. After I was apprised of the event, I decided to be more observant of local traffic in an effort find out whether there were any driverless cars in Rego Park. Once I started going out of my way to peer directly into the driver's seat of cars stopping at intersections, I was astonished at what I discovered.

A few days after I read the article, when I was returning home from work, I saw four driverless cars in a row. I was standing at the intersection of Saunders Street and 63rd Avenue. A parade of driverless cars stopped at the intersection at which I stood, permitted traffic to pass at the intersection, then accelerated and proceeded past me, went south on 63rd Avenue, and then made a left turn Austin Street and proceeded east. The windows were clear and there was no mistake about what I saw. It was then that I surmised that Rego Park must be the test site of a secret Pentagon project—both on the ground and in the air.

The Rego Park-Forest Hills police precinct ranks among the safest precincts in New York City. Because the residents are well to do and above average intelligence, our area was selected to be the test site of the recycling pilot program. The city wanted the recycling program to succeed, so it conducted its trial project in an area where the citizens were most likely to comply with the rules. From this one may extrapolate that because our town is safe, the DoD does not have to worry about people stealing its driverless cars. The Internet advises that these cars carry $200,000 worth of electronic equipment.

I saw many driverless cars on Saunders Street after that because I was looking for them. Whenever I stood at a corner, waiting for the light to change, I always glanced at the driver's seat of the car in front of me. I saw a minimum of two driverless cars per week.

However, soon the DoD started installing darkened windows on its expensive test vehicles. Although it is more difficult to see through a darkened window, it is not impossible. Whenever I saw a car with black or dark blue windows, I approached it and strained to see whether there was anyone in the driver's seat. Many times I succeeded in identifying vehicles that were driverless.

I became friends with a local postal clerk and I asked her whether she had ever seen a driverless car in Rego Park. I was very surprised at the information that she divulged:

"I have seen a lot of driverless cars in Rego Park. Have you seen any? You drive."

"What? No, well, I've never seen one, but now that you mention it, I'll tell you something strange that happened here. There was an accident on Queens Boulevard and someone was struck and killed. And when the cops opened the door, there was no one inside."

"I'm not surprised. Now when I cross the street, I will no longer assume that the driver will slow down and stop. There may not be a driver in the car and apparently they are crashing them."

"You say that you've seen a lot of them?"

"Yes, I have seen about two dozen, so far."

"Two dozen! Well, now I am going to start looking for them, myself."

"The cars themselves do not cost more than regular cars. However, the sensors, radar and lasers that they carry on board cost $200,000."

"This must be a test site for the government."

"Yeah, well, it's a safe neighborhood. They don't have to worry about people stealing their expensive toys."

THE BLOND GUY ON THE STEPLADDER

I was returning home from the Rego Park library when I saw my neighbor standing on the sidewalk.

"Listen, I want to tell you something. Yesterday morning there was a blond guy on a stepladder doing something to your window."

"Which window?" I asked. She pointed to my bedroom window.

"That one over there. Is that your bedroom window?"

"Yeah."

"Well, he was doing something up there. He stood on a stepladder and he was doing something. He was up there a long time."

"How long?"

"A long time. I would say a half hour."

"Do you think that it had something to do with cable TV? They are putting cables up all over the place."

"Do you have cable TV?" she asked.

"I don't even have a TV. I listen to my walkman."

"So then how could he be the cable guy?"

"Well, now that you mention it, I guess that he can't. I wonder if he implanted something in the windowsill from the outside that is causing me to get electrical shocks to my brain."

"Maybe. I just thought that I'd let you know."

THE CRASH OF HELIOS FLIGHT HCY 522 IN GREECE

On August 14, 2005 a Boeing 737 Helios airliner took off from Larnaca, Cyprus, and headed towards its destination, Athens International Airport. The plane crashed near

Grammatiko, Greece, 25 miles north of Athens, killing all 121 people aboard, 115 passengers and 6 crew; the airline reported that among the victims there were 48 children, most of them Greek-Cypriots; the passenger list indicated that 20 were children.

Two highly significant facts about the tragedy made me livid. First, it occurred on the 31st anniversary of the CIA sponsored coup in Cyprus. 31 years to the day! Surely, that was no coincidence!

Secondly, the Associated Press reported that the pilot, Hans-Jürgen Merten, 58, was a former East German who was an employee of Direct Personnel International, a Dublin-based agency that supplies pilots to airlines.[9] Furthermore, the AP reported, "The German pilots union Vereinigung Cockpit said it had no information on Merten or his background. He had a valid airline pilot's license, said spokeswoman Cornelia Eichorn from Germany's Luftfahrt-Bundesamt aviation authority, who could provide no further information."[10]

Then more details surfaced: two Greek F-16 military aircraft flew alongside the plane and saw the copilot, Pambos Charalambous, slumped over in his seat, but there was no sign of the pilot! The oxygen masks could be seen hanging from the cabin. There had been a loss of cabin pressure. They also saw a young cabin steward trying to regain control of plane. Each day I poured over the news looking to see if the pilot's body had been found. Each day I read that search efforts had failed. I was convinced that this German worked for the CIA, had sabotaged the plane, and then had parachuted out. Finally, 13 days later, on August 27, 2005, the *New York Times* reported that the pilot's body had finally been "identified through DNA testing and dental records" and "All but one of the 118 bodies recovered so far have now been identified."[11] Oh, really? They finally found and identified the body of the pilot, which was among the very last to be recovered? Was it really that of Hans-Jürgen Merten or had the CIA dug up a corpse from a graveyard and planted it at the site of the crash? Why did it take two weeks to find and identify the body of the pilot? To this day I am convinced that the CIA sabotaged the plane on the 31st anniversary of the coup in order to send Greek Cypriots the message not to stand in the way of Turkish accession to the EU: either it was done by hiring a German pilot to sabotage the plane and then parachute out or by having an operative disguised as a maintenance man incorrectly set the pressurization control on manual rather than automatic. It was either/or. No one can convince me differently. The CIA has a long history of viciously running in circles around the Greeks, like bums on motorcycles, and because they always employ high technology, no sovereign nation on earth can do anything about it.

Apparently, I was not the only one who was haunted by the specter of air masks dangling from the ceiling, the co-pilot slumped over in his chair, and no sign of the pilot. The *Guardian* reported that the pilot's remains were identified around the same time that the copilot's diary was discovered; the diary was found at the scene of the crash: "The discovery came as forensic experts identified the remains of the airline's German-born pilot, Hans-Jeurgen Merten. This ruled out one of the more bizarre theories that have abounded since the crash: that Merten had parachuted out of the plane."[12] Bizarre? No, not at all: quite understandable and logical given the fact that two F-16 fighter jets accompanied the doomed jet until it crashed and the men inside the F-16s saw as many as four people in the cockpit, but no pilot:

> Greek F-16 fighter pilots, who were ordered to shadow the airliner during its final minutes in the air, say they saw an unidentified man grappling with the controls moments before the plane plunged to earth, as the co-pilot lay slumped in his seat.
>
> It has since been reported that four people, including Charalambous, were in the cockpit at the time of the crash.[13]

It seems that the whole world was in there except the pilot. If Merten did die in the crash, although I do not believe that he did, then the sabotage was effected by moving the pressurization switch from automatic to manual, as indicated in the paragraph below.

More than a year later the *New York Times* reported that a Greek inquiry had determined that human error was responsible for the Helios Airways crash: "...the two pilots... failed to competently operate controls regulating cabin pressure and misinterpreted a subsequent warning, which eventually led to the crew's passing out and the crash...the crew had failed to recognize that the pressurization switch was on manual rather than automatic, which would have allowed the cabin to pressurize by itself. Maintenance officials in Cyprus left pressure controls on the incorrect setting..."[14] This is the official story and the final findings. Perhaps the pressurization switch had been deliberately moved when the plane was being maintained between flights.

I discussed this with my colleagues. When I pointed out that the tragedy had occurred on the 31st anniversary of the CIA sponsored Turkish incursion of Cyprus, they agreed that the timing sounded suspicious. However, I noticed that one coworker had difficulty remembering the facts that I was telling her and she was unable to focus; it was becoming more and more of a struggle for her to retain information lately, even for a few minutes. Many of my colleagues, who had shown interest in world events in the past, did not seem to care about anything lately except eating, watching movies, and going shopping. Their horizons have diminished into concentrically smaller and smaller circles. Looking back, I realize that their docility, loss of interest in world affairs, and inability to focus, were all results of high concentrations of EMs focused at them.

Today there is a proliferation of material on the Internet that indicates that EMs have been proven in the lab to cause docility and that the Pentagon would love to exploit this military advantage to control large populations. How much of it is true? How can we discern fact from fiction when the government is actively engaged in disseminating misinformation in order to maintain supremacy? The government knows that the Internet is a powerful tool of mass education and hence, that it poses a threat to its dominance; it has succeeded in disseminating so much rubbish, people do not know what to believe anymore.

THE VETOES TO TURKISH ACCESSION TO THE EU

I was awakened from my sleep in the dark solitude of the early morning hours by a wave moving up my blanket. I froze and pretended to be asleep. I wondered whether those doing this had the ability to image inside my bedroom. Was there a bug slipped down from the ceiling above? I did not yet know that it was possible to image inside a building from an aircraft passing at a distance and deliver a stunning blow with a laser pulse. I did not yet know that the Pentagon was aggressively and obsessively pursuing microwave weaponry.

I remained motionless. The sensation of the moving pencil continued as the microwave pulse rapidly glided up the blanket alongside my torso and up to my shoulders. There was a short momentary pause and then suddenly, a strong puff of air was blasted against my upper lip. This startled me and I instinctively shook my head. It was an evolutionary response.

When the body is assaulted by high-powered microwave (HPM) radiation, its natural Circadian rhythm is disrupted and the subject becomes energized. Then it becomes impossible to return to sleep. Over the course of time, the person who does not get a sufficient amount of sleep visibly and significantly ages. This is a scientific fact. And this is what has happened to me. I am not permitted to get more than 4 hours of sleep each night. When I look in the mirror, I see an old woman. I have just celebrated my 59th birthday. This is what they must have done to the young man with whom I worked during my agents' detail. He looked like he was 80 when he could not have been more than 40.

Because I was abruptly awakened night after night, I became accustomed to putting my headphones and listening to the BBC over NPR radio. This is how I was apprised of current events in Europe; it turned out that some of these events would be highly significant and would leave me wondering.

On one particular night in 2005 I was brusquely awakened by a sudden puff of air blown against my cheek. Dear reader, imagine what it must be like to be fast asleep and then to be awakened by a sudden blast of air in your face. You know that it could not have come from an open window because your windows are closed. It could only be electronic in origin.

I lay in bed and struggled in vain to return to sleep. After an hour of repeated attempts to return to sleep and persistent failure, I decided to turn on my walkman and listen to the BBC. An English broadcaster announced that a few countries were opposing Turkey's proposed accession to the EU. France, Germany, and Austria were three nations that had spoken out: they made the case that Turkey did not belong in the EU for many reasons.

The subject of the broadcast on that particular night was Chancellor Wolfgang Schüssel of Austria. In September and October 2005 Schüssel had adamantly insisted that the EU could open membership negotiations with Turkey only if a status other than full membership were offered. Austria refused to be pressured by the US and other nations in the EU and firmly held its ground that Turkey had no business joining the EU. I was delighted to hear this and I silently cheered in the darkness of my bedroom when I heard it.

The BBC stated that Turkey's European adversaries point out that Turkey is not located in Europe and that therefore it cannot be part of the EU. Historically, the Ottoman Empire has remained outside of Europe and there is a significant dividing line between Christian and Muslim culture. Secondly, Europe, plagued with unemployment and huge immigration, cannot absorb 70 million more Muslims who would be able to travel freely and work in the EU. Thirdly, Turkey's economy is dismal and its admission would certainly be no asset to Europe; it is a lower middle-income country and it would greatly increase the disparity between regions in the EU. Moreover, Turkey should get out of Cyprus because its invasion and occupation of a third of the island is in violation of multiple UN resolutions. Lastly, Turkey is engaged into a battle against the Kurds, a nation without a state, and it flagrantly disregards minority rights.

Because of the arguments enumerated above, France, Germany, and Austria have recommended a "privileged partnership" or an agreement that offers less than full membership in the EU. In 2005 only 31% of the French, 29% of Austrians, and 21% of Germans favored Turkish accession to the EU. I found this information fascinating and I filed it away in my mental hard drive. I snapped off my walkman, removed my headphones, and returned to sleep.

Little did I suspect that night that in the months ahead I would learn very disturbing news: suspicious roof collapses in Austria and Germany in the future would indicate that Rumsfeld's Pentagon took revenge on these two countries for blocking Turkey's accession to the EU. Furthermore, France had already suffered a suspicious roof collapse in Paris!

I was only able to get another hour of sleep that morning: I was again abruptly awakened by a vigorous tap on my ankle from an invisible wave of energy. I was energized and alert and ready to get up and go to work, except that it was too early. Again, I snapped on my walkman and listened to the BBC some more until it was time to get up and go to work. I was averaging five hours of sleep per night; in the years ahead, the number would be reduced to four, and then three.

As of this writing, it is now known that laser pulse can bring about a roof collapse such as those in France, Germany, and Austria. This raises the highly disturbing specter that the American government is using laser pulse to punish countries that resist the gradual advance towards complete globalization. The residents of Queens know full well that laser pulse can shake a roof to the ground: my neighbor, who lives on the top floor of the building across the street from me, has a metal roof, and a NORTHCOM aircraft that passed directly overhead delivered two powerful thumps to the metal roof, causing the entire top floor to shake and opening fissures in the walls and ceiling. They rifled holes in my aluminum foil eight times; my aluminum blanket went flying off the bed at 5:15 AM and upon examination, it was thoroughly perforated. A week later, a 1:45 AM a NORTH-COM aircraft hovered directly over my building and thoroughly perforated a metal blanket of aluminum foil and a 9 x 12 wall covering. The clatter of the laser pulse against the metal was so loud, my next door neighbor heard it! It sounded like continual gunfire that lasted for ten minutes! The most disturbing aspect of this violation of our bodies, homes and right to privacy, is that microwave radiation causes cancer.

(Endnotes)

1   Milan Kundera, *The Book of Laughter and Forgetting*, translated by Aaron Asher (New York: HarperPerennial, 1996), 4.

2   Vassilis Prevelakis and Diomidis Spinellis, "The Athens Affair," *IEEE Spectrum Online*, July 2007, http://www.spectrum.ieee.org/jul07/5280 (February 26, 2009).

3   John Markoff, "Engineers as Counterspies: How the Greek Cellphone System Was Bugged," *New York Times*, July 10, 2007, http://bits.blogs.nytimes.com/2007/07/10/engineers-as-counterspys-how-the-greek-cellphone-system-was-bugged/ (February 19, 2009).

4   "Visor Consultants: Home," http://www.visorconsultants.com (March 1, 2009).

5   Visor Consultants: About Visor Consultants," http://www.visor-consultants.com/businesscontinuity.htm (March 1, 2009).

6   There are two videos. First, "Peter Power 7/7 Terror Rehearsal," http://www.youtube.com/watch?v=JKvkhe3rqtc (March 1, 2009). The second is "BBC Radio-Drills Ran on Day of London Bombings 7-7-05," *BBC*, http://www.youtube.com/watch?v=sEbUQiYOGjU&feature=related (March 1, 2009).

7   Paul Joseph Watson and Alex Jones, "London Underground Bombing 'Exercises' Took Place at Same Time as Real Attack," http://www.prisonplanet.com/articles/july2005/090705bombingexercises.htm (March 1, 2009). The article contains portions from a BBC transcript of Peter Power's interview.

8   Mark Frauenfelder, "London Bombings Coincide with Security Exercise," http://www.boingboing.net/2005/07/10london-bombings-coin.html (March 1, 2009). This article also contains portions from a BBC transcript of Peter Power's interview.

9   "Pilot in Crash Had Been E. German Pilot," August 16, 2005, http://www.redorbit.com/news/technology/210071/pilot_in_crash_had_been_e_german_pilot/index.html (February 19, 2009).

10   Ibid.

11   "World Briefing Europe: Greece: Crash Pilot's Remains Identified," *New York Times*, August 27, 2005, A4.

12   Helena Smith, "Diary Find Could Solve Greek Air Crash Mystery," *Guardian*, August 28, 2005, http://www.guardian.co.uk/business/2005/aug/28/theairlineindustry.internationalnews (February 27, 2009).

13   Ibid.

14   "World Briefing Europe: Greece: Human Error Caused 2005 Helios Crash," *New York Times*, October 11, 2006, A6.

Chapter Ten

The Reign of Terror of King George II: The Sixth Year (2006)

BIG BROTHER IS WATCHING YOU...[1]
—George Orwell, *1984* (1949)

THE ROOF COLLAPSES IN EUROPE

1:45 AM. I was abruptly awakened from my sleep by a blast of air across my face. No matter how many times this happens, it is always an eerie experience. The evolutionary response is to shield yourself with your blanket.

I snapped on my walkman and listened to the BBC. It was then that I learned that on January 2, 2006 there had been a roof collapse in Germany. The roof of an ice rink caved in the town of Bad Reichenhall, Bavaria, near the Austrian border. Fifteen people were killed, including twelve children; thirty-two people were injured. The Europeans thought that the incident was highly suspicious: the Germans are the best engineers in the world and they certainly know how to build roofs that do not cave in when there is snow accumulation. Moreover, officials had tested the weight of the snow on the roof and had pronounced the structure to be safe.

As the weeks progressed and interrupted sleep continued, I began to notice that there were an inordinate number of roof collapses in Europe. On January 27, 2006 the roof of a town hall in the southern Austrian village of Mariazell collapsed under snow; there were no injuries. On January 28, 2006 the snow-covered roof of a trade hall in Katowice (in southern Poland) collapsed during a racing pigeon exhibition. Sixty people were killed and 140 injured. Meanwhile, Georgians endured a seventh day without heat after there was an explosion that severed gas supplies from Russia. On February 23, 2006 a market roof collapsed in Moscow killing 66 people. I counted four roof collapses during the period January 2-February 23, 2006 and one explosion of a gas pipeline. I quickly surmised that there must surely exist a causality between the roof collapses in Austria and Germany and these governments' vociferous opposition to Turkish accession to the EU. It was also obvious that the gas pipeline in Georgia had been blown up so that Russia could not transport its gas to market.

Every morning as I heard about one more roof collapse, I resolved that as soon as I arrived at work, I would sign on to the Internet and get the specifics related to the tragedies. The following question arises: was there a causality between my Internet searches at work and the interruption of sleep and electrical shocks at home? The government had access to all of my computer queries—searches that paired "Austria" and "roof collapse," followed by the triangulation of "Austria," "veto," and "Turkey."

That morning I signed on to the Customs computer as my coworkers were reading the morning news on cnn.com. I rapidly moved past the obnoxious banner informing me that I had no expectations of privacy and inserted "roof collapse" in my search engine. What I discovered concretized my thesis that there existed a causality between the disasters and the vetoes.

Back on May 23, 2004 Paris had a roof collapse, too! The roof collapsed in terminal 2E, a newly-constructed part of Charles de Gaulle Airport; five people were killed and three injured. The roof was brand new. I thought that it was significant that the previous year, on February 10, 2003 France, Germany, and Belgium had vetoed Rummy's plan to arm Turkey to the hilt "in case it was attacked by Iraq." French President Jacques Chirac bore the brunt of the criticism because he blocked Rummy's decision to authorize NATO to send AWAC surveillance aircraft and Patriot missiles to Turkey.

I wondered how the Americans did it. How can one effect a roof collapse on demand? Two years later, when I researched what electromagnetic waves can do when steadily resonated at a specific frequency, I discovered that a building can be shaken to the ground long distance via EMs. In 1887 or 1888 Nikola Tesla invented a device that caused the building housing his laboratory, located at 48 East Houston Street, New York, NY, to shake.[2] The principle in physics that applies is the same as that which permits an opera singer to shatter a wine glass with his voice. And that was back in the 19th century. In the 1980s the use of ultrasound to break up kidney stones from a distance was a byproduct of Pentagon science. That paved the way for imaging and striking humans situated on the other side of barriers.

It is significant that the U.S. Army Corps of Engineers (USACE) has a "shake table" in Champaign, IL, that it operates via electromagnetic waves. It uses the device to shake objects such as military equipment and structures in order to test their ability to withstand shock and vibration. This apparatus is called the Triaxial Earthquake and Shock Simulator (TESS). TESS creates longitudinal and transverse waves to initiate a shaking motion; it increases the frequency until it matches the particular resonant frequency of the object; when that frequency is reached, the shaking begins. The USACE provides a detailed explanation of how the system works and a picture of TESS on its website.[3]

The Internet is also filled with pictures of small shake tables that students make as school science projects. If you insert "shake table" in your search engine, you will see pictures of science fairs featuring elementary school children and their teachers working with these homemade devices.

I skipped lunch and returned to the search engine. I wanted to know the exact dates that France, Austria and Germany had cast their vetoes in Brussels. As I clicked on various websites, electronic crackles began to resonate from the metal cabinets just over my desk. SNAP! BZZZT! Soon the electromagnetic activity in my cubicle became too powerful to ignore. A violent metallic tap struck off the metal cabinet inches from my head. I jumped back in my chair and stared at the cabinet. I wondered whether this was an essay in behavior modification. I decided to find a small notepad and begin keeping a log of the date, time, and description of the phenomena. I wrote, "12:11 PM metallic snap resonates off the cabinet." Two minutes later an electrical shock hit me on the crown of my head. It was painful and felt as if a dagger had penetrated my cranium. Immediately I looked at my watch and entered in my log, "12:13 PM: a sharp electrical shock strikes me on the head from directly overhead." Unfortunately, since I started working in Customs I have become obsessive-compulsive about cleaning (I never was before) and after several weeks of maintaining the log, I came to work one morning, robotically headed straight for the shredder, and destroyed it. Why did I do that? I found myself continually beginning a new log and then shredding it when the notepad was completely filled. Was this an attempt to make the unpleasant reality go away? Was it because if I shredded my log, I would not have to deal with the fact that a lot of people would not believe me? Were my experimenters forcing me to do this somehow? Since I retired, I kept a log of electromagnetic phenomena in my apartment (see *Microwave War*). My compulsion with log shredding ended when I stopped working in that environment.

Since I started communicating with my publisher about writing this book, I have begun to receive electrical shocks to the heart and brain sequentially every few seconds. This constitutes an innovative and more aggressive assault: before I got a shock once a night, now I am getting them in a series, one after the next, spaced apart by only a second or two. It has also become obvious, today as I am inserting this text in the manuscript, that the assaults are originating from commercial carriers equipped with electronics that permit imaging and strikes in real time from a remote location. If I recorded the strikes that I get every time a commercial carrier approaches, I would have little time to do anything else. Moreover, my neighbor, who has a metal roof, gets a very violent THUD! against the roof when a commercial carrier flies overhead. Now the Pentagon is obsessed with cracking metal roofs.

A deep sharp needle penetrated my right leg just beneath the knee. I stopped what I was doing and rolled up my pant leg. There was a tiny dish-shaped crater on the surface of my skin. It looked as if someone had burned a hole into it and left a minute, circular-shaped incision. Hours later when I checked it again, it was red, having filled up with blood. In the days following it turned dark brown and remained there permanently as a dark brown mark.

I returned to the computer. This is what I gleaned: France, Germany and Austria told Rummy to go fly a kite regarding his love affair with Turkey. Subsequently, these countries suffered roof collapses resulting in many deaths and injuries—France, on May 23, 2004; Germany, on January 2, 2006; Austria on January 27, 2006.

Raindrops In The Living Room

March 2006. I came home from work one afternoon and discovered that my living room floor was inundated with water: drops of water were steadily descending from an area in the ceiling directly above the radiator. Fortunately I had a large bucket in the house and I set it down on the floor beneath the rupture. At the rate that the drops were falling, I ascertained they would fill a quarter of the bucket in a 24 hour period.

Back then I did not consider the possibility that a connection might exist between the emergency that had suddenly arisen in my living room ceiling and the electrical shocks to my brain and burn marks in my body. It did not yet occur to me that the crack in the radiator in the apartment above may have been effected by a burst from a laser pulse weapon. Today I believe that it was a test to see how I would respond in a crisis situation: most certainly, my experience at home would become the topic of conversation at work the next day. Our watchers could see my reaction to stress and how fast I would resolve the problem. In the months ahead I would discover that all of the conversations at work were indeed being recorded by electronic bugs hidden in the wall paintings.

At 6:15 AM the next morning I called the landlord from the office and left a cordial message on his answering machine. I advised him that water was steadily pervading from the living room ceiling and asked for the super to stop by any time after 2 PM. The landlord never returned my call; neither the super, nor a handyman ever stopped by to investigate the problem.

The following morning I called again and left another message. This time I told the landlord that I had a bucket on the floor and that I thought that I could handle the problem at my level until he could locate and repair the leak. Again, he never returned my call, nor did the super or handyman stop by. That day when I returned from work I went straight downstairs to the basement and spoke to the building's handyman. He came over to the apartment, witnessed the leak, and assured me that he would inform the super. The super never appeared.

After three months of emptying the bucket once in the early morning hours and once after work, I realized that it was just a matter of time before the ceiling would decay and collapse. I had no choice but to take immediate action. There was only one way to force the landlord to make the repair: remove the bucket and let the water fall on the floor. Then he would have to contend with the people living beneath me, who might not be as docile and self-effacing as I was. This was a trick that I had learned from working for

216

the federal government: over the years my coworkers had frequently used the expression "squeaky axles get greased."

This approach proved to yield immediate and permanent results. Not only did the people beneath me complain about the water that was emanating from my apartment, they found a place to live on the other side of town and moved out of the building in less than 24 hours. My landlord had lost his tenants.

When I came home the next day, the super rapped vigorously on my door. He entered and saw that the water that had soaked the apartment downstairs was coming from the ceiling in my living room. He produced his cellphone and called the landlord. The conversation was all in Arabic and his speech was lively and animated, punctuated with occasional hand gestures with his free hand. Finally, he said in English, "Yeah, it's for real. Believe me, it's really happening."

Before he left, he advised me that he might need to gain access to my apartment the next day. Would I be home? I said that I was going to work, but would leave the door unlocked: all he had to do was push it open. Very good.

Then he told me that he had another problem: the woman upstairs did not live there and the landlord did not have a key to her apartment. Did I have her telephone number? I said that I did not, but I would try to find it on the Internet when I got to work the next day and I would call the landlord.

The next day at work I signed on to the Internet and discovered that my upstairs neighbor was a famous antique dealer; she had written a coffee table book on antiques; she lived outside of New York State; she had a business associate in London and they scoured Europe in search of the best and most valuable antiques; she had attended many antique fairs. I called the landlord and gave him the telephone number at which I thought that she could be reached.

Moments after I arrived home from work my doorbell rang. When I opened the door, I discovered my upstairs neighbor standing at the door frame, looking very sheepish and apologetic. She said with great regret, "Oh, Mary, I am so sorry. Really, I am. Can you ever forgive me?" She advised me that, for some mysterious reason, the radiator in her living room had suddenly burst. Neither one of us had ever heard of a metal radiator suddenly bursting. Indeed, the radiators in our building were very old and they appeared to be as impenetrable as army tank material.

Question: what is the statistical probability that her radiator would suddenly burst, when she did not even live there to turn the valve? Was this caused by the same people who caused the taps on my blanket, the wave moving up the bed, the bursts of sound next to my ear, the puff of air against my face? Was it the same source as that which caused the plaster and paint to crack and fall from the ceiling all over the apartment, dropping with loud snaps against the wooden floor, concurrently as I was being assaulted by electromagnetic waves? Something was causing the paint and plaster to come down. It was always in the corners of a room, by an exterior wall, that is, inches from a wall that also served as the façade to the building. This indicates that there had been an aerial attack at an angle, directed at the brick façade and that it penetrated the wall. I always discovered the fragments on the floor the morning after an assault. Was it the same group of people that had caused fissures to suddenly appear on every wall in my apartment? Each day when I returned from work I found a new deep gash, running diagonally down a wall—in the kitchen, living room, and bedroom. Each day the gashes became longer and deeper. Then large rectangular pieces of plaster became disengaged from the living room wall and fell on the floor.

The following year I was researching a book on the fulfillment of Biblical prophecy entitled, *Christianity and 21st Century Science.* It was while I was investigating state of the art weaponry that I discovered that the U.S. has the technology to effect a violent blow from an airplane flying at a distance via high-powered microwave (HPM) and laser pulse technology (see *The Science behind Microwave War,*

Chapter One, section entitled, "Strike a Person from a Distance"). In 1987 the *Washington Post* reported that the Russians were able to kill a goat at a distance of 1 kilometer with radio frequency (RF) weaponry; the Pentagon had already been researching this since the 1960s.[4]

If an intelligence agency were bombarding my body with EMs over time, night after night, and this incident was planned to see how I would react to stress, what was learned? The results showed that I emptied the bucket of water and remained docile for three months before I got fed up and decided to address the situation. In other words, I was submissive for three months before I rebelled. This coincides with the length of time that it took me to do something about the fire escape marauders.

As I am writing this, it is becoming evident that over time, I have been steadily shocked into remaining docile for longer and longer periods of time; the same person who once treasured Kenneth Blanchard and Spencer Johnson's *One Minute Manager* has become a three month manager. Moreover, I have been inhaling poisonous fumes from a cracked steam pipe since 1987 and have not initiated a lawsuit to get it repaired.

A Rude Awakening

2 AM. I am dreaming: the feathery wind is brushing against my face like rose petals. I am delighted to be sitting on top of a locomotive as it is speeding through the countryside. The sun is shining and there is a carpet of green all around me as trees line the valleys on either side of the train tracks below me. I like sitting on top of the train.

Suddenly, a violent electrical jolt jars my consciousness, my upper torso jumps off the bed, and my head involuntary jerks from left to right. I awaken from my sleep fully aware that my shoulders have just been physically lifted off the mattress and that my head has uncontrollably moved from one direction to another.

I sit up and swing my legs over to the side of my bed. I stare vacantly down at the wooden floor in the darkness. I have just been electrocuted in the brain: now what am I going to do? I arise and walk around the apartment in the darkness of the night. Is it safe to go back to sleep in that room? Should I move the bed into another room? Should I move it now or tomorrow? The electrical shock has energized me. My body's entire metabolism has been disrupted. I cannot return to sleep now. I decide to put on my headphones and listen to the walkman until it is time to go to work.

At 9:30 AM Nelson arrived at work carrying two shopping bags filled to the brim with food. The whirlwind stormed down the hallway as his coattails flapped behind, and he loudly hummed, "Hmmhmm, hmmhmm." He swept into the cubicle behind mine and rummaged loudly through his multitude of shopping bags. Everyone on the floor, impeded from concentrating on work, sat immobilized, listening to him continually rustle his plastic bags for a full half hour. The crackling and crunching of the polyethylene supermarket shopping bags was doggedly persistent and sadistically unrelenting. Just as we were all falling into a meditative, anesthetic stupor, he exploded out of his office and dashed down the hall to the kitchen.

I was typing on my computer when Nelson thrust a tray covered with chocolate cookies between my face and the keyboard. I looked up to see that he had an abnormal, pathologically intense expression on his face. He looked as if his entire happiness in the whole world was contingent upon my accepting a sample. I took a cookie and politely thanked him. "Go on, take two! Go ahead, don't be shy!" he goaded me. I took another one and he disappeared around the corner to the next cubicle. He walked around the floor, invading every office, as he persuasively enticed people to take a piece. Then he refilled the tray and left it on the counter on the other side of my cubicle.

I resented the fact that he chose the countertop on the other side of my cubicle wall to display his food: it always attracted a commotion and the continual conversation made it impossible to think. Why couldn't he exercise his obsession in the kitchen, I thought. One day one of my coworkers supplied the answer: the other employees did not want him in the kitchen because he ate smelly fish covered with an even more odiferous topping that made them nauseous. They had thrown him out of the kitchen.

Nelson returned to his office and rummaged through plastic bags again. I found the sound of the rustling plastic to be intolerable. There was no end to it and it invaded by consciousness just as I was desperately trying to concentrate on a complex legal issue. Without warning he materialized next to me and thrust a tin of assorted nuts beneath my nose.

"Would you like some assorted nuts? Take some! Go ahead and take some!" I glanced into the tin. They did look tasty and they were free, so I softly conceded, "O.K." Thereupon, he suddenly produced a paper napkin from nowhere like Houdini and poured some nuts into the paper napkin and deposited it on my desk. I thanked him cordially and returned to my work. He occupied himself after that by continuing on his rounds asking everyone to take some nuts.

The sound of rustling plastic bags erupted once more and this time, it was accompanied by "La, la, la, dee, dee, dee, la, la, la!" I looked up from my monitor towards the modular wall that separated my cubicle from his. The rustling stopped, but the humming continued a cappella. Then the sound of boxes popping open and plastic spoons and forks dropping on the melamine table top was heard on the other side of my wall. Then I heard employees exclaim, "Oooooh!" and "Aaaaah!" These apostrophes were punctuated someone's cry, "Would ya look at that!" The curiosity got the better of me and I arose to see what was going on.

There was a smorgasbord on the tabletop: baked cookies, jam, jelly, biscuits, assorted nuts, chocolate kisses, and marshmallows. Crowds gathered and the employees egged him on. They articulated their personal preferences and asked if he would please try to bring their culinary favorites to work tomorrow. I thought that it was unforgiveable that people were encouraging him. It was obvious to all that he had an obsessive-compulsive disorder, but my coworkers, as selfish as they were, were delighted to profit from it.

I could not think in the midst of the hubbub; my work required introspection and analysis. Therefore, everyone morning after Nelson arrived, I was forced to gather up all of my work off my desktop, retrieve my portable chair from my closet, and escape down the hall to the library where I could be by myself. I used my swipe card to beep myself into a tiny closet containing a few Customs law books. That was our library. It was my sanctuary, the only place where I could find any peace.

It is highly significant that I never received any electrical shocks or burn marks in the Customs library. Evidently, it had not been wired up to deliver electronic assaults. That area was not part of the experiment. I spent most of my time sitting in my portable chair in the tiny closet until the day I retired.

DHS Wants To Know Whether I Have A Cell-phone

On one particular morning I received an unusual email message from someone that I did not know. The person identified himself as an agent from DHS and informed me that his records indicated that I had borrowed a cellphone from Customs and had not returned it. I had to return it right away or I would be subject to legal action. What kind of nonsense is this, I thought. I made the decision not to dignify his nasty letter with a response. I left it in my in box for several days and then deleted it.

A week later I received a duplicate message. Now I was annoyed again. I decided once more not to answer it. What would they do to me?

However, after a full week of seeing its presence every time I signed on to e-mail, I resolved to answer his stupid inquiry and then delete it. But what should I say? I decided to ask my supervisor. I printed a copy of the e-mail message and showed it to him.

"I don't have a government cellphone," I protested. "I don't have any cellphone. I don't own a cellphone."

"It must be a case of mistaken identity, that is all," he suggested. "Just tell him that you did not borrow a government cellphone and that you would appreciate it if he would correct his records. Make sure that you tell him to correct his records." I thanked him and followed his recommendation.

I composed an e-mail message and returned it to the agent. Then I noticed that he had left a cellphone number in his e-mail message with an area code. I decided to look up the area code to find out where he was from. It was a suburb of Maryland. I thought that it was significant that my first name appeared within the name of the state. Could this be a psyop? Or was the government worried that I was in constant communication with another and would one day sue, go on TV or write a book?

I went on to research his exchange (the first three digits of the telephone number after the area code). His exchange was indeed a Maryland exchange. Then I inserted his telephone number in www.refdesk.com to see if I could get his address from a reverse search. I was unable to get an address or business name. The results of my inquiry indicated that it was a non-existent telephone number in Mary-land.

ELECTROCUTION IN THE LIVING ROOM

The moment that I came home from work, I dismantled the bed and moved it into a far corner of the living room, as far from the window as possible. I was afraid to spend another night in the bedroom. I discovered that sleeping in the living room was a bizarre experience: I started to notice fresh gashes that were surfacing in the living room walls. All of my efforts proved to be fruitless: I discovered that I was not safe in the living room either. I was safe nowhere.

I went to sleep. I dreamt that I was in a neighborhood that I had visited before. I knew that it was a labyrinth. Nonetheless I proceeded walking forward and got lost in the maze. There were some country homes with apple trees in the front yard and white picket fences. Every block was like every other block. I wandered around and stumbled onto a college campus. It looked like Queens College. I walked through the student lounge in an effort to get to Kissena Boulevard. I could get the bus there and go home, although I vaguely remembered where home might be. I approached the rear entrance to Academic II, walked through the complex adjoining it to Academic I, and exited the front door. The bus was waiting for me on the corner by the gas station.

I boarded the bus and as the bus made a sharp curve around a field, I swung to the side, clutching the hand rail. Tall apartment buildings brushed the sky through the bus windows. I bent down to see the view through the driver's windshield. Suddenly my consciousness was shattered into a miasma of bright white and yellow light and pain permeated throughout; concurrently I felt my torso rise in the air and then descend on the bed. The light preceded a sharp piercing dagger to the right side of my brain. My head involuntarily moved from left to right. I awoke from my sleep.

It happened again. I distinctly remember my head involuntarily move on the pillow from one side to the other. I was not safe in the living room either. Where could I move the bed?

The Midget With A Cellphone

It was 5:00 AM at the 63rd Drive subway station. I was waiting for the "E" train to depart 71st and Continental in Forest Hills at 5:03. It would be in Rego Park at 5:07.

I was standing near the edge of the platform facing east. Suddenly I felt a needle go through my back equidistant between the shoulders. It was a piercing, penetrating burn that dug into my skin and beneath the flesh. I whirled around to see where it could have come from.

At that moment a very short man holding a cellphone was walking directly behind me; he held a cellphone in his hand parallel and it was pointed at my back. He casually stepped around me and fastened the cellphone back on his belt. I wondered whether he had just turned it on. Then I wondered whether it even was a cellphone. I had no idea was kind of a device it was. I wanted to ask him. The train was coming. It was the 5:07. I discarded the thought as I boarded the train.

I boarded an "F" train at Roosevelt Avenue because it arrived before the "E" and set my little portable chair at one end of the car by a door. A woman boarded the train, looked around, and sat down right next to me. I thought that this was a very odd thing to do because the car was otherwise empty and usually people like to space themselves apart from one another. I opened up my copy of *Metro News*, one of the free newspapers that are distributed at subway stations and street corners in the morning, and scanned the headlines.

Suddenly a dagger pierced my left ankle. I looked up from my newspaper and saw that the woman was holding her cellphone so that it pointed directly at me. She was staring at me squarely in the eyes. I thought that that was a very bold thing to do. Not only had she had the audacity to sit right next to me when the rest of the car was vacant, but she was staring at me, too!

"Excuse me," I asked, "did you just turn on your cellphone?" She continued to stare at me with cold indifference.

"Yes, I did," she replied without expression.

"The reason I ask is because for some reason, I seem to attract electronic signals. When people point their cellphones at me, I get a burn mark in my skin." I rolled up my pant leg and located the site of this most result assault. Sure enough, there was a newly formed bloody dot on my ankle. I pointed to it.

"See?" I asked. She looked at it without registering any expression on her face.

"Do you have a cellphone?" she asked matter-of-factly. She stared at me intensely.

"No," I answered.

"No? You don't have a cellphone?" she asked, raising her voice.

"No," I said.

"Are you sure?" She looked at me suspiciously as if she did not believe me. What did she mean, am I sure? Who was she, anyway? And why did she ask me whether I was sure? She was getting on my nerves in a big way and as soon as we pulled into the next station, I dashed out onto the platform and rushed into the next car.

As I set down my portable chair in the next car, I thought about the fact that more than one person wanted to know whether I had a cellphone. First I got an e-mail message from an agent in Mary-land and apparently that did not convince whoever it was who wanted to know. I was sure that the Mary-land area code to the nonexistent cellphone number had a subtext of humor. Now I was convinced that the woman in the next car was either a fed or a cop who was sent to find out whether I had a cellphone. Apparently, my experimenters needed to known how well connected I was and whether I was planning to go public with a lawsuit. Dear reader, do you see the danger that exists when the federal government recruits local police to carry out its affairs under the guise of homeland security? The cops are given only a little information on a need to know basis. Hence, they fully participate in the Pentagon's Nazi experiments, get much needed information for the feds, and yet they remain oblivious to their complicity.

The White Box Truck

Summer 2006. 5:30 AM I was sitting in my portable folding chair in front of a department store. I was just about to open the morning's *Metro News*. I glanced at my watch. In another half hour they would turn on the lights upstairs and I could go to work.

Then, just as I lowered my head and began to pour over the newspaper, I felt a sharp needle penetrate my right leg, just beneath the knee. Instantaneously I looked up to see where it was coming from. There was no one around holding a cellphone. However, an unmarked white box truck, with two men seated in the cab, had rapidly just swung around the corner and was now speeding past me. I looked at the truck suspiciously. I had heard on the radio that after 9/11, 60,000 white box trucks came north. This was a white box truck. Was it a security truck? Were there men inside taking pictures through tiny pinhole cameras in the chassis? In the years ahead a large white box truck would stand in the middle of the street in front of my apartment building. No one would get out; no one would enter. After a long period of time, the driver would step on the gas. One day I would learn about the government's ability to image through brick walls.

When I went upstairs, sat down in my office chair, and rolled up my pant leg. Sure enough, just as expected, there was a tiny crater at the site where I had felt the pinprick. It looked like a burn mark. It was filling up with blood. Something had burned the surface of my skin and had left a tiny, bowl-shaped crater that was now bleeding. In the days ahead the crater would dry and turn dark brown. It would leave a permanent brown mark on my skin. Since 2001 when the electronic assaults began, I have become covered with brown dots. I would like to sue the government for disfigurement and pain.

CONFLUENCE

I began to notice that there were an inordinate number of white box trucks in Queens that passed me everywhere I went. Surmising that they were among the 60,000 that had come north, I strongly resented being watched as if I were a criminal. I tried my best to avoid them by staying off the beaten path and using quiet, sleepy little side streets. Then the strangest thing happened.

I noticed that every time I approached a corner on a back street, a vehicle would suddenly appear and make a left turn or a right turn directly in front of me. It was always a white box truck. As this happened more often, I became more and more indignant. Why were they following me around? Resolving to remain on sparsely trafficked side streets in order to avoid them, each day I took the long way home, the long way to work, the long way to the store. What would normally be a ten minute walk turned into an affair that often lasted several hours. Once I was angry, I set up my portable chair on the street and refused to get up. Instead of taking ten minutes to walk home from the subway, I ended up sitting on a corner several blocks out of my way, watching cars drive around me. This was good, I thought: let them worry that I might be a drug dealer. I resolved to drive them insane any way I could. The same white box trucks, with the same people in the cab, drove around and around the block, turning the corner and glaring at me as I obstinately sat in my folding chair on the corner.

Then I noticed something else: just as I was walking to a corner and I looked down the street, I noticed that a white box truck would be approaching the corner on the next parallel street a short block away. Invariably, the white box truck always made a turn, came up one block to where I was standing on the corner, and then made a turn directly in front of me. It looked like the driver was circling the block. This enraged me. I knew that there was a police camera hidden at one particular intersection because someone knew about it and had pointed it out to me. It suddenly became apparent that the white box trucks were taking their cues from hidden cameras at intersections. I resolved that if they were going to watch me, I was going to watch them. Now that I look back on this, I understand that the Pentagon was using Rego Park as a test site for urban warfare. That is where the entire robotic car program was headed: towards navigating the urban environment while carrying military weapons aboard; that is what DARPA's Urban Challenge was all about; that is what the British Ministry of Defense's Grand Challenge sought to accomplish.

Watching the watchers was the simplest thing to do: I always conveniently carried a tiny portable chair for the subway, so all I had to do was open it up and set it firmly on the ground on a street corner. I was conducting an experiment and I wanted to see what would happen.

Invariably, a parade of vehicles materialized. One after the next, all in a conga line, they turned the corner a block away, came up one short block to where I was perched on my seat, drove around me, and back in the other direction. I noticed that the same parade, comprised of the same cars, was circling the block over and over again.

I started to notice license plates; unusual looking drivers, and decorations dangling from rear view mirrors. Soon I became adept at calculating how many times each car had passed me.

Then I noticed something even more unusual: whenever one or more pedestrians approached the spot on the street where I was sitting, a car would materialize and stop squarely in front of us. The driver would turn and stare at us as if to ascertain whether anything was changing hands or record words that were said.

Moreover, I noticed the following phenomenon as I stood watching the street from a stairway window in my apartment building: whenever a tenant left my building and approached the sidewalk, a car raced by. This discovery made me feel better: a car sped by whenever anyone came out, not just me. Moreover, from the same stairway window I noticed that whenever one or more pedestrians approached the intersection, one or more cars would suddenly appear on a previously empty street.

In August 2006 the strangest thing of all happened: I had set my little portable chair on a corner on a remote side street and I sat down. There were no cars or pedestrians. Suddenly, a male pedestrian appeared and he was going to cross the street. Just as he approached me, four large SUVs appeared from four different directions and they skidded to an abrupt halt at the intersection in front of us. The drivers sat frozen and did nothing for ten minutes. During that interim, the pedestrian and I remained side by side on the corner, conversing; he was standing and I was sitting.

"Look at that," I said to him.

"Looks like they almost cracked up. It would have been a four car collision, if they had."

"Yeah," I said watching the cars. None of the drivers moved, nor made an effort to back up, the entire time that the pedestrian and I shared the corner together.

"I like your chair," the pedestrian said. "Where did you get it, may I ask?"

"Paragon Sports at Union Square."

"Oh, I know where that is."

"Broadway and 17th Street. Second floor, camping department. It comes in a little case and folds up like a little umbrella."

"Nice! I have to get one! Well, have a nice day," he said and continued along his way.

"You, too." I waved good-by. It was at that precise moment, when the pedestrian started to walk away, that the four drivers saluted each other through their windshields. Each extended a right arm, index finger next to middle finger, briefly touching the right temple and then extending the arm out, as in a military salute. They instantly backed up and sped off as quickly as they had materialized.

It looked like a Pentagon experiment to me. Why were they targeting me? I was livid. I started screaming at the top of my lungs, "George Bush is a Nazi! George Bush is a Nazi!" as I sat in my little portable chair, victimized by the watchers. Then I got tired of it all and returned home. This was more or less the existence that I led outdoors in my neighborhood until the day I retired. Once I retired, I was much too busy writing, researching, and formatting texts according to publishers' specifications, to waste my time sitting on street corners watching the watchers.

The Russian At 96th Street

I took the subway up to Columbia to use Butler Library. I was writing a book about how Diderot had a notion of evolutionism a hundred years before Darwin. I hoped to get it published and then present it to the French Department at Columbia as a doctoral dissertation. I needed them to wave the ten year rule: Ph.D candidates are given 10 years to get a book published. In my case it was 31 years. Would they wave the 10 year rule for me? It was worth the old college try.

In order to save time, I took the express to 96th Street and then got off at 96th to transfer to the Number 1. As I stood on the platform a sharp needle penetrated my chin just beneath the left side of my mouth. Instantly I looked up. A tall man was pointing his cellphone at me. I wondered whether he was an undercover federal agent or perhaps, an undercover city cop, who had been assigned to procure a recent photo of me. There was only one way to find out, not that I expected him to own up to it, if he was. I just wanted to talk about it. And show them all, if I were being watched, that I was on to them. I initiated a conversation. It turned out that he had a thick Russian accent.

"Excuse me, may I ask you a question?" Startled he looked up.

"Yes."

"Are you an undercover cop?"

"No, I am not. Why do you ask?" he asked with a wide grin.

"I just felt a pinprick to my face when you held up your cellphone. Did you just take my picture?"

"No, Miss, I did not take your picture. I was just checking for a text message."

"Did you just switch this device on a moment ago?"

"Yes, I did." That was the answer that I was looking for: an outgoing electromagnetic signal hit me in the face near my chin and it happened the precise moment that he had turned on his device. The Number 1 train roared into the station and the doors opened. Suddenly I felt overwhelmed by embarrassment and the only thing that I wanted to do was to duck into another car so that I could avoid this guy. Question: was I attracting electronic signals or did I just happen to be standing in the path of one?

THROWING SOUND LONG DISTANCE

2 AM. Dreaming. I am bicycling past white picket fences. A repetitive ping...ping...ping creeps forward from the dark recesses of my mind. I hop off the bike and chain it to the front entrance of Queens College. I slowly walk uphill on the tar-covered road to Academic Tower, briefly stopping to gaze up at the glass and silver complex. It glistens brightly in the noonday sun, blinding me. As I enter inside the building I hear ping...ping...ping. I vigorously shake my head. I wake up. Stone silence. The sound has stopped. The pinging was just like the sonar on the old television program "Voyage to the Bottom of the Sea." That was the sound that the TV audience heard as the submarine stealthily swept across the ocean floor. That was the sound in the background when the show's actors leaned over their controls and scrutinized their screens.

It was a mechanical sound that is heard only when the subject is asleep. I have since learned that sounds can be transmitted at the precise frequency that the brain uses during the sleeping state.

The brain communicates with the organs of the body via extremely low frequency (ELF) waves. For example, it tells the heart precisely when to beat via ELFs and concurrently directs other organs in the same manner. The brain is a multitasking machine. Researchers have discovered that the frequency on which the brain operates varies depending on whether the person is awake, asleep, alert and active, in a quiet state, or remembering a past event. The myriad frequencies that the brain uses in various states have been all been identified and categorized.

When I arrived at work that morning, I told my coworkers that I had heard a repetitive pinging sound in my sleep. They adamantly held that I had dreamt it. I did not argue with them, but I silently rejected their hypothesis: it was a distinct repetitive mechanical sound; I was certain that it must have been electronic in origin.

Over the next few months I heard other cyclic, rhythmic sounds in my sleep that disappeared the moment that I awoke. One such sound was a recurrent tapping against the window glass directly to the left of my bed, heard on many nights. I thought that the smoking gun was that it was always gone the instant I stirred. Deeming that the government was experimenting transmitting sounds that could only be heard when the subject is asleep, I resolved to ask all the neighbors on the block whether they heard distinctly electronic sounds that vanished the moment they awoke. It turned out that several women living alone did and that over time, they found it extremely annoying. They quickly added that the furniture and appliances often shook. Then things started to get progressively more creepy at night.

THE TAP ON THE COMFORTER

I was fast asleep when I was awakened by the sensation of someone pulling down hard on a corner of my comforter at the foot of the bed. When that happens, the instinctive response is to move one's leg. This must be an evolutionary response to get whatever pest or animal has landed on one's body off immediately.

This phenomenon recurred night after night and it has been going on to the present day since it first began in 2005 (see the logs in *Microwave War*). On subsequent nights I was awakened by a tap on my comforter either next to my ankle, or directly over it. It was then that I realized that the pulling sensation was not caused by the comforter actually by pulled down, but rather, by a tap at the very edge of the bed.

It is significant that the tap on the comforter on my bed was repeated like clockwork and that it always happened just moments before the alarm clock was set to go off at 4 AM. Apparently someone wanted to make sure that I arose promptly at 4 AM.

Invariably I always found a box with an untouched pizza in the morning. There was always someone on a cellphone watching just a few feet away from the pizza. Was there something in that pizza that the government wanted me to ingest? A state of the art, microscopic radio frequency identification (RFID) tag, perhaps?

In 2001 Hitachi announced the Mu-chip or μ-chip, measuring just 0.4 mm x 0.4 mm and transmitting at 2.45 GHz with a tiny antenna. It was used during the 2005 International Technology Exposition in Aichi, Japan, to prevent the forgery of admission tickets; it can be imbedded in currency to prevent counterfeiting.

On February 13, 2007 Hitachi announced the advent of an even smaller RFID chip, one that measures 0.05 mm x 0.05 mm, the size of a dust particle—it is called RFID dust. Science articles suggest that one day in the future, RFID dust will be placed in restaurant food and the bill will be calculated by scanning the customer's stomach at the end of the meal. The restaurant patron can eat all he wants and the waiters do not have to bother keeping tabs on what he ordered. Hence, today it is easy to sprinkle RFID dust with seeds or spices in bread products or rice dishes to monitor someone's position from afar.

A cashier in a local drugstore told me that she also gets pinpricks when someone points a cellphone at her. She rolled up her shirt sleeves to uncover the dark brown spots all over her arms. It is also significant that she gets the moving wave across the blanket at night. Did DARPA drop RFID dust from an aircraft to see if it could identify the position of specific individuals in a large urban population? Having read about DARPA's Urban Challenge, in which driverless cars carrying military equipment were tested on city blocks, I now realize the following stunning fact: the Pentagon is actively and obsessively developing surveillance tools that will soon become ubiquitous throughout the United States. The Pentagon admits that on October 1, 2008 it deployed troops domestically within 100 miles of U.S. borders. What is frightening is that the media, because of interlocking directorates, has chosen to ignore this fact. This means that presently and in the future, the government has the technology to clandestinely identify and kill dissidents. Warfare that is conducted remotely, in real time, via a network, was announced in 1996 in *Air Force 2025*.

It is also significant that during the days preceding this domestic deployment, September 16–31, 2008, a car bearing the license plate USMC cruised through the streets of Rego Park. Moreover, there was a parked bright red pickup truck that boldly portrayed, on the back of its cab, a larger than life size picture of a GI garbed in camouflage and helmet, pointing a rifle as he peered through the gun's target finder. People on the street were surprised to suddenly be confronted by a huge picture of someone pointing a gun. At the time it attracted a lot of attention. Since then, I have not since seen this pickup truck.

I also considered the possibility that I may have ingested a metal solution that caused me to pick up electronic signals. I was then and still am a receiver of shocks due to cellphones and passing SUVs. One day I received a sharp pinprick to my leg at the 63rd Drive subway station as I stood at a landing on the stairway at the north side of Queens Boulevard. When I looked up, I discovered a large electrical box riveted to the ceiling directly overhead. I am certain that the shock emanated from there. It could very well be that I ate or drank something that causes me to permanently receive electromagnetic waves. Looking back on it, I allow for the possibility that the tap on the blanket at 4 AM was designed to get me out of the house and introduce me to my daily dose of whatever it was that the government wanted me to ingest.

I was also growing progressively angrier and angrier at the moving wave that rippled across the top of the comforter. It felt as if someone had pressed a pencil point into the comforter from above and run it up the entire length of the bed, from my feet, right up to my shoulders specifically for the purpose of intimidation. This happened when I was wide awake, listening to my walkman or when I was asleep, night after night, and it continues to the present day.

Then they no longer dropped it in the vicinity of my body, but accurately and precisely struck me directly on the legs and torso. Then, appallingly, they targeted the lymph nodes in my armpits and groin with absolute surgical precision. My neighbors are now contracting Hodgkin's lymphoma: the site of the tumor is always either the armpits or groin. What the Nazis are doing now is gathering massive amounts of data that prove that cancer can be caused aerially—the victims in Queens are always Jewish and/or single women living alone.

THE EXPLOSION OF SOUND OUTSIDE MY EAR

Because I received burn marks to my skin when lying in bed, I began sleeping with every square inch of my body covered. I still do. When the experiment begins, it gets intolerably hot, both in the summer and winter. This is because microwave radiation speeds up the motion of water molecules and causes them to heat up; that is how microwave ovens cook food; our bodies are mostly water. Moreover, I have compared experiences with my neighbors and everyone attests to the fact that soon after they begin experiencing an electrical spark against their flesh or movement across the blanket, their intestines are full of gas. Again, this provides evidence that microwave is being used to heat up the water in the body.

When I covered myself with the blanket up to my neck, but allowed my face to be exposed, I got burn marks to my face. Hence, I have no choice but to sleep with the pillow carefully positioned over my head, leaving just enough room to breathe. I should add here that very recently a powerful electropulse dropped onto my pillow, directly above my head. If I had not taken the precaution to sleep with the pillow over my head, I would have been struck in the face. Perhaps I would have been blinded, gotten a stroke, or worse. This is what the government is doing with your money.

However, there are many more reasons that I must sleep with the pillow pulled over my head. One night, as I slept as people normally do, with my face exposed on top of the pillow, I was awakened by a burst of sound that erupted in midair, half an inch from my left ear. It lasted for two seconds. One could say that it was a phoneme, the smallest unit in a language that is capable of conveying a distinction in meaning (as the m in met and the b in bet).

Dear reader, imagine for a moment the following scenario: you are lying in bed fast asleep; it is the middle of the night; you are all alone; it is dark; you live on a quiet little street in a Queens town where they roll up the sidewalk after dark; suddenly, without warning, a deafening loud "WHAAAAA!" erupts in midair, just a few inches from your left ear.

And it happened again a few nights later. This time it was a 2-second phoneme that sounded like a tape recording of a raucous crowd. It could have been a sound byte of a New Year's celebration at Times Square.

Night after night, just before going to sleep, I had to take great care to arrange the pillow over my head and over the bridge of my nose, just so, so that it would completely cover both ears, but leave just enough room for my nose. I hoped that this would provide a barrier to the sound that was thrown from a distance into my bedroom. However, as it turned out, this approach did not end the harassment.

When your nose is exposed between the pillow and the blankets, so is your mouth, chin, and each side of the mouth. I would be abruptly awakened, night after night, by a blast of air directed at my upper lip. Suddenly a thin spray of air would brush across my upper lip to the side of my mouth and across my lower jaw to my ear. Undoubtedly, it was the same technology that caused the invisible wave to move up the comforter. How much more could I cover up, I wondered. I had to breathe.

This reveals the absolute precision with which the Pentagon can image through a brick wall. My experience is corroborated by that of a woman, also single and living alone, who lives across the street from me, and who is also awakened night after night by a scream that erupts just inches from her ear. Our corroborating testimony provides evidence of the following: the flawless accuracy of imaging through barriers; the selection of single women as test subjects; the intention to accelerate the aging process through continual sleep disruption over the course of years; the study of the effects of long term bombardment with EMs on the human body; that this is being done from aircraft flying at a distance; that Nazis infest the Pentagon.

As time elapsed, I grew angrier and angrier. I needed to vent, but was not permitted to contact the media. My only outlet was to continue to scream my message on the streets and in the subways. One morning I arrived early at the 63rd Drive subway station and made my usual public service announcement: "...and the moment that I retire, I am going on 60 Minutes to talk to Dan Rather. The most significant news in the world is not in the free newspapers that they're giving us at subway entrances. The U.S. Customs Service has discovered that the Nazis in the Bush crime family have transported Nazi monetary certificates in the diplomatic mailbags at JFK Airport!"

One morning when I boarded the train, I encountered a young man of 20 who admitted that he had also been experiencing electronic phenomena. He acknowledged that he had been struck in the face with a blast of air in the middle of the night. When I heard this, I wondered how many other Queens residents were experiencing this. Was the phenomenon ubiquitous? Was there anyone else in the train? How many people could I get to own up to this before we reached my destination? Should I purchase a voice recorder and carry it with me everywhere?

"You have experienced a blast of air across your face when you were asleep and it woke you up?" I repeated, incredulous and delighted that I was not the only one.

"Yes, I have."

"Were the windows open or shut?"

"They were closed. I like to sleep with the windows closed."

"Did you wonder why you felt a draft when the windows were closed?"

"No."

"Why not?

"Well, I don't know, these things happen."

"You mean that they happen now and then?"

"Yeah."

"How many times have they happened?"

"A few." His face and expression were sincere.

How many others like him were there? Does Queens make an ideal experimental site because of its demography? Are immigrants less likely to complain to the media, write letters to their senators, or sue the government for harassment? Why large metropoli? Is it done to acquire statistics on resulting diseases from large populations?

THE UNCONTROLLABLE URGE TO MAKE PUBLIC ANNOUNCEMENTS

The sadistic psyop continued in the early morning hours: a car always sped past the alleyway between 4–5 AM, just as I was about to emerge from its shadows. I glanced at my watch. It did not matter what time it was, it always happened and then there would be no other traffic on my sleepy little street as far as the eye could see. Even though I was still in the shadows of the alleyway and I wore a black windbreaker and black pants, the driver would always invariably turn his head and glance directly at me with the accuracy of a champion dart thrower. Back then I thought that either the feds or the cops were checking to see when it was that I departed from my building. I no longer think that. It was a psyop designed to rile me up.

This happened morning after morning, no matter what time I emerged from the alleyway. I decided to vary the times that I exited my apartment building to see what would happen. On some mornings I arose from bed earlier than usual; on others I stayed in bed longer. The result was always the same: the precise moment that I emerged from the alleyway, no matter what time it was—3:07 AM, 3:49 AM, 4:16 AM, 4:29 AM, 5:16 AM—a car would speed past me and the driver would turn and glance straight at me; there was never another car on the street behind it or in front of it, as far as the eye could see. This continued all through the second term of King George II. Now I am retired and it still happens. For example, on Saturday, August 29, 2009, I left the house twice during the morning and twice it happened. There were no other cars on the street.

Since then I have decided to investigate whether this is being done to others. One day I decided to exit my apartment, but not leave the building right away. Instead, I chose to ascend a stairwell and pause by a window that overlooks the street. I noticed that just as people were exiting our building, a car would race past. Whenever several pedestrians approached the intersection, four SUVs with blackened windows approach that intersection from all directions.

I hypothesize that these four SUVs that intercepted the pedestrians from my building may be related to the Pentagon's obsession with perfecting the driverless car. Now that I know about DARPA's Urban Challenge, I know that the car that will intercept pedestrians during urban warfare in the future will be driverless. And thus the Pentagon has realized its goal: it can wage a campaign in an urban setting without suffering any casualties at all.

The following question arises: with technology such as this, will recalcitrant taxpayers will ever be able to stage a Boston Tea Party in the future? Will anyone be able to challenge despotic rule ever again and live to tell the story? It has become evident that the argument that this technology has useful applications for the military theater abroad is not primary reason for its development: with the continual and persistent unification of countries via trade agreements and the eventual arrival of one world government, the enemy is mass populations of people who will rebel against despotic rule. Dear reader, don't you see? The militarization of space, the driverless cars, the surveillance from afar, the attacks from aircraft, performed in real time, from a remote location, via a network, have been developed to control the masses. With interlocking directorates and codependent financial interests, there will be no other side. Don't you get it?

I resolved more strongly than ever that if they were going to watch me, I would give them something to watch. Back then I thought that perhaps they suspected me of wrongdoing and therefore, I resolved to do my best to pique their curiosity to the max. My response to surveillance became automatic, reflexive, uncontrollable.

The next morning, I entered the alleyway and even before I emerged from its shadows, a car sped past me and the driver momentarily glanced in my direction. At that moment, my anger exploded like a seething cauldron. Lunging forward with the spring of a tiger, I screamed at the top of my lungs, "George Bush is a Nazi! George Bush is a Nazi!" I turned 90^0 and ran towards the speeding car in an effort to catch up with it. The driver stepped on his brakes and stopped at the corner. As I approached the corner, out of breath, the driver opened his window and looked me with curiosity. I repeated the mantra. "George Bush is a Nazi! George Bush is a Nazi! I work for the United States Customs Service and my coworkers have discovered that the Nazis in the Bush crime family transport Nazi monetary certificates in the diplomatic mailbags at JFK Airport!" The driver opened his glove compartment and withdrew an electronic device. There was no doubt that he was going to capture this, possibly with both audio and video. I repeated my spiel. As he stepped on the gas and disappeared into the distance, I felt much better.

Morning after morning I chanted the mantra at the top of my lungs on the darkened streets before dawn. I knew that I had lost my impulse control. I was aware that my behavior had become an involuntary response to seeing a car on the street at an early hour when there should be no traffic. I wondered whether it was the same thing that was causing my coworker to uncontrollably feed the other employees.

I gleefully surrendered to the urge to announce to the world the truth about the Nazis in the Bush crime family. Poised on the corner of 63rd Drive and Queens Boulevard, I broadcast my message in a hearty voice. And as I did, I gathered more and more testimony from people indicating that I was not the only person in Queens who was being harassed by microwave technology.

THE MAN WHO HAD A BUG ON HIS BACK

Fall 2006. 5:00 AM. I stood in front of Rite Aid on the corner of Queens Boulevard and 63rd Drive.

"George Bush is a Nazi! The Nazis in the Bush crime family transport Nazi monetary certificates in the diplomatic mailbags at JFK Mail Branch! These financial instruments have swastikas across the top!" Just then a young man about 30 walked past me. A warm and congenial conversation began and soon the subject turned to covert government activities. I asked the stranger whether he had ever received any electronic shocks to his brain in the middle of the night. The response was immediate.

"No, but it's funny that you should ask. Now that you mention it, something very strange happened to me recently. I was standing on the street having a cellphone conversation with a friend of mine. Right here, on Queens Boulevard, in fact. My friend said, 'I'd like to kill George Bush.' Now, mind you, it was not I who said this, it was my friend who said it. And he said it just like that: 'I'd like to kill George Bush.' The moment he said it, all of the sudden, I felt a bug on my back."

"A bug?" I exclaimed. I wanted clarification.

"Yeah, it felt like a big bug had dug its claws into my back and that it was holding on for all it's worth."

"How long did this sensation last?"

"For several minutes. About fifteen."

"They can do it with electronics. It was an electronic phenomenon," I advised.

"Whatever. It happened a few times again after that, whenever I got on the cellphone."

"They're Nazis," I declared. "Now let me tell you about what the U.S. Customs Service found in the diplomatic mailbags at JFK Mail Branch…" I drew a crowd by the subway entrance. I met the men who delivered the newspapers. Very soon I was telling them about the electronic shocks to my brain.

"I work for the federal government and I am considering the possibility that perhaps they have planted a tiny computerized chip somewhere in my apartment—an RFID tag that permits them to locate my apartment from the distance." The newspaper deliveryman's response was immediate and instinctive.

"If you work for the government, it's IN you, baby." He nodded demonstrably in the affirmative to emphasize his point. His coworker vigorously nodded assent.

"Yep, baby, it's in you," his partner agreed.

"It is?" I asked incredulously. I was taken aback by the fact that he spoke with a tone of authority. "Are you certain?"

"Yeah, it's in you. They do it to prisoners all the time. A book was written about Holmesburg Prison." The book to which he referred was Allen M. Hornblum's *Acres of Skin: Human Experiments at Holmesburg Prison.*

"Yep, yep," his coworker agreed. As I gave it some thought, we fell silent.

"You know," I continued, "I think that they direct electromagnetic waves at postal employees and they destroy the frontal part of the brain that governs judgment and impulse control. The government fries their brains and that is why all of the sudden, one day, postal workers snap."

"Oh, for sure. They have been doing that for decades. But I'm telling you, there is something INSIDE of you, baby." The two newspaper men stared at me fixedly and agreed that it was a *fait accompli.*

I descended the steps leading into the 63rd Drive subway station in stunned silence. I boarded the 6 AM. The conversation had been so engrossing, I had missed all of the trains between 5–6.

This was what a log of a typical morning at work looked like:

6:02 AM I arrive at work.

6:03 AM As I am walking down a long hallway, all of the sudden a printer, set on a table in the hall, just inches from me, spontaneously switches on and off by itself. Because I am the only one on the floor, there are no other employees present to press "print" and get the printer started. This happens morning after morning, at the precise moment that I am inches from it.

6:16 AM A violent metallic tap strikes off the metal cabinet directly over my desk. I am sitting at the computer in my cubicle working.

6:17 AM Two loud crackles snap off the textile covering on the modular wall to my right.

6:21 AM Two loud metallic snaps bounce off the metal cabinet in the cubicle opposite mine. I get up and go over to that office. The woman who occupies that office has not yet arrived yet.

6:32 AM Cigarette smoke begins to waft into my cubicle from the air vent directly over my head. In a few minutes, my cubicle is saturated with thick cigarette smoke and I start to cough uncontrollably. I reach for an empty plastic cup and dash out of the office and down the hallway to the water fountain to fill it. I have to sip water every little while as the stench lingers for several hours.

7:02 AM A sharp pinprick pierces the crown of my head. It feels as if a razor-sharp needle has stabbed my cranium. I touch the top of my head to see whether I am bleeding; I am not. Then I carefully scrutinize the ceiling above me. This morning I notice something that I have not discerned before: there is a tiny convex curvature, a bump, jutting out from the metal lighting fixture directly over my head. It is about a quarter inch in diameter. I decide that the thing that caused the bruise in the metal must have struck from above so that what I now see, as I am seated below the ceiling fixture, is the convex side (the surface that bulges outward, as the exterior of a sphere). Greatly intrigued, I get up and walk around the floor to examine the rest of the ceiling. I notice that several other lighting fixtures also have tiny bumps protruding from the surface of the metal. I am wondering if these tiny bulges were caused by a high-powered microwave device shooting a beam down from above. They have the exact same diameter of the pock marks that have surfaced on my walls at home. The only difference is that here at work, I am looking at the convex side and at home, the concave side.

7:17 AM I get a sharp pinprick to the left side of my chin. I look in the mirror and find a tiny saucer-shaped crater in my chin. It is a burn mark. [Today as I am typing this, I have a permanent brown mark on the left side of my chin from that morning].

7:28 AM Two loud crackles bounce off the metal cabinet over my desk.

7:29 Two strident hits resonate noisily off the metal cabinet in Nelson's cubicle directly behind me.

7:30 A violent snap strikes off the metal clothing closet in my office.

7:31 A violent metallic snap emanates from the cubicle next to mine.

7:51 I am struck on the back of my head by a powerful electrical burst of energy. It feels as if I had been whacked by a foam plastic bat. I get up and walk around the floor to investigate. I discover that there is a lot of electrical activity proliferating throughout the area. There are metal snaps, crackles, and bounces emanating from cubicles all over the floor. The people who have arrived at work are oblivious to it.

8:16 AM A coworker pays me a visit to confer on a work-related issue. She sits down in my guest chair and we begin to converse. Suddenly, a powerful metallic SNAP! strikes off of the clothing closet just inches from her head. Startled, she cries out, "What was THAT?" I am glad that I have a witness. I say that this goes on all day long. She recommends that I talk to the supervisor about being moved to another cubicle. Then she picks up her works and quickly leaves.

8:20 AM I walk down the hall to my supervisor's office. I want to tell him that that there is an unusually high amount of static electricity in my cubicle this morning, and that I have been getting pinpricks to my skin and electrical shocks to my head. However, when I reach his office, I discover that it is unoccupied. Someone tells me that he is attending a meeting with people from Washington and that he will be incommunicado all day. In the past, whenever I brought the subject up, the expression on his face indicated that he did not believe me. He has told me on several occasions that the next time it happens, to come and get him so that he can witness the phenomena himself. What is the point? By the time he comes out of his meetings, it is no longer happening.

8:37 AM I get a pinprick to my right arm. It creates a tiny burn mark.

8:38 AM There are two violent metallic snaps that bounce off of the metal cabinet directly over my head. I arise from my desk and return to my supervisor's office. Perhaps he came out of the meeting on a break. No such luck.

9:06 AM Three electronic crackles bounce off the acrylic covering on the modular wall next to me.

9:07 AM Two loud electronic snaps emanate from Nelson's cubicle behind me.

9:08 AM Two metallic snaps resonate violently from an office several cubicles away from mine.

9:10 AM A new stream of cigarette smoke emanates from the air vent overhead. In seconds my cubicle fills up with cigarette smoke and again, I start to cough uncontrollably. My plastic cup is empty. I pick it up and return to the water fountain to fill it. I cannot sit in that cubicle until the stench subsides. This is going to take a full hour. I talk to people in the hallway to pass the time.

9:20 AM I walk around the floor to see whether the other employees are getting cigarette smoke filtered into their cubicles. They are not. I ask a coworker to visit my office and tell me whether she smells cigarette smoke. She comes over but confesses that "she lost her sense of smell when she suddenly became allergic last winter." I ask her whether she has a runny nose that does not stop running. She says that she does. I say that we all got a runny nose that did not stop running during the winter of 2005.

As it turned out, the epidemic of runny noses that occurred at my worksite continued for two full years, even as I retired. My coworkers purchased several different kinds of allergy medications, but to no avail. I never took any medicine because as a rule, I do not take medication and also because I did not believe that it was an allergy. I held that the government had delivered a little present to us through the air vents. The whole city developed congestion that would not go away that winter.

Since then I have learned that in 1998 the U.S. trekked to the Arctic Tundra and dug up the corpses of people who had died of the 1918 Spanish Flu epidemic. Subsequently, scientists sequenced the 8 viral gene segments that comprise the virus and successfully reverse engineered the Spanish flu. By January 2007 it was reported that 7 macaque monkeys had been injected with the reverse-engineered flu. The virus triggered a violent immune response, the monkeys' lungs immediately filled up with fluid, and they had to be euthanized. It is significant that the 1918 Spanish Flu was an H1N1 virus. Moreover, the Mexican swine flu is also an H1N1 virus and it contains portions of swine flu, bird flu, and human flu. Meanwhile, I have a runny nose that has not stopped running since the winter of 2005; all of my coworkers now have congestion and are perpetually taking cold remedies and allergy medication, when they never had allergies before; my neighbors in Queens all have runny noses that do not stop. What is the statistical probability that it is a coincidence that 1) the people of New York City suddenly developed perpetual and incurable congestion after 2) the U.S. dug up corpses of the 1918 Spanish Flu, reverse engineered the virus, and delivered it to monkeys, who 3) developed a violent immune response that filled up their lungs with fluid? That is what happens when the pharmaceutical industry and the government take turns swapping executives. It is called fascism. Dear reader, do what the police do in order to solve a crime: ask who benefits. The answer is the pharmaceutical industry that is selling its decongestants to the public in ridiculous quantities.

10:23 AM Two metallic snaps bounce off the metal cabinet above my desk.

10:24 AM Two snaps bounce off the textile wall covering on the wall behind me.

10:27 AM A tap off the metal clothing cabinet in my cubicle.

10:28 AM A burst of energy bounces off my right cheekbone.

10:30 AM Nelson puts a tray of food out on the hallway counter and attracts a crowd. People congregate and talk about food for a half hour.

ASSAULT, FOLLOWED BY WALL FISSURES, BROKEN PAINT AND PLASTER

That night as I lay in bed listening to my walkman a sharp dagger penetrated my heart. My heart momentarily stopped beating and I gasped for air. Moments later I was able to breathe normally. I removed the headphones and listened carefully. One minute later a large jet approached the house and flew directly overhead.

Early the next morning I stepped on broken plaster and paint chips as I traversed the apartment. They made a crackling sound beneath my sneakers and so, even though I had terminated my account with Con Ed and did not use electricity, I was alerted to the fact that there was debris all over the floor. I took the flashlight and scanned the floor, the ceiling, and the walls. I noticed something that I had never seen before: a huge fissure had appeared in the living room wall. The crack ran diagonally across the wall and traversed the entire the distance from the ceiling to the floor. I surmised that the wall must have ruptured the night before when I was struck by the high-powered microwave radiation that hit my heart. As time elapsed multiple fissures appeared in the walls in the living room, kitchen, and bedroom. They were accompanied by plaster and paint chips all over the floor. I always discovered the new cracks in the walls on mornings after I had been struck in the brain or heart by a powerful microwave that left me gasping for air.

A CONDUCTOR'S ADVICE

I boarded the "E" train at 4:45 AM. Most passengers on subways in the early morning hours choose to sit in the conductor's car for the purpose of safety. I entered the conductor's car just as he peered out of his booth window and closed the subway doors. He exited his booth and stood just outside it at his end of the car. I chose the other end of the car and began my message.

"Good morning, ladies and gentlemen. I am sorry to interrupt you, but I have a message that I want to get out. I am not collecting any money." Newspapers were lowered and eyes were raised. I had everyone's undivided attention.

"I work for the U.S. Customs Service. One day my co-workers opened the diplomatic mailbags at the JFK Mail Facility. Inside they found monetary certificates with swastikas at the top." People looked annoyed and returned to their newspapers. The rest closed their eyes. Their reaction thoroughly stunned me. What I was giving them was real news. Why were they reading the tripe in the free newspapers? The conductor beckoned to me with his index finger to come join him where he was standing because we were approaching Roosevelt Avenue and he had to momentarily enter his booth to open the doors.

"Wait here," he instructed. When the passengers had entered the train and he had shut the doors, he came out of his booth.

"You're wasting your time here. These people are either homeless or else they think you're crazy. Just look at them. If you want to get your message out, write a book. I'll buy it."

THE SECURITY GUARDS CAN'T KEEP TRACK OF THE OPERATIVES

5:45 AM. I decided to visit the bathroom before signing in. As I was walking down the hallway, a large group of eight or ten men, clad in dark blue coveralls, emerged from a rear stairway and walked en masse down the hallway just behind me. I turned around and was startled to see a crowd of men following me at that early morning hour in a darkened hallway. I was also afraid of them as I was the only employee on the floor. As I stood in front of the bathroom door, I reached for my computerized plastic card, turned nonchalantly, smiled cordially, and said, "Good morning," hiding my fear. They returned the greeting: "Hello!" I beeped myself into the bathroom and slammed the door shut behind me. Then I heard laughter on the other side of the door. I waited for a full minute, then opened the door just a little bit, and peered outside. The workers had taken the elevator and departed the floor. The first thought that I had was that they were CIA operatives planting microwave devices in the ceiling. I decided to tell the security personnel in the lobby that I had seen them. I returned to the elevator and descended to the lobby.

The security guard declared that there should be just two workers upstairs, not eight or ten.

"No, I saw eight or ten," I maintained.

"No, you saw only two."

"No, eight or ten," I repeated. "It was a horde like the frogs in Exodus 8:6."

"Really? I am very surprised because I gave permission to just two men at 2 AM to go upstairs." Because the security guard and I had become friends over the years, I felt free to tell him what I thought.

"I believe that the government is experimenting with the federal employees upstairs. We get loud snaps and taps that strike off the cabinets and furniture. We are saturated in a highly dense electromagnetic environment. I am getting burn marks in my skin and electrical shocks to my body all day long. I asked the people that work for private industry on the other floors and they're not getting this. I think that the Nazis in the CIA are experimenting with us." The security guard, struck by my words and intense expression, became concerned.

"I am going to investigate this," he replied, as he produced a walkie-talkie. "I'm calling my boss right now." I returned to the elevator. As I rode upstairs, I remembered the security guard in Seven who said that the CIA arrived at 7:20 or 7:25 when the secretary saw them move out at 6. I surmised that intelligence agencies know how to run circles around security guards.

As I proceeded down the empty hallway past the printers, one printer suddenly turned on and off making an electronic squeal that lasted for about two seconds. This occurred the moment that I was two inches from it. I wondered how they did it and deduced that they must have cameras. Then two coworkers entered through the side door. I asked them whether the printer ever starts and stops just as they pass it in the morning. They said that sometimes it does and that it must be a power surge.

"But the printer is connected to a surge protector. Shouldn't the surge protector prevent that from happening?" They did not know.

6:04 AM I am sitting at my cubicle and I begin the day's work.

6:38 AM A strong stench of cigarette smoke descends from the air vent above my head and fills my cubicle. I begin to cough uncontrollably, jump up from my chair, grab a plastic cup, and rush to the water fountain to fill it.

6:56 AM Two powerful snaps strike off the metal cabinets over my head.

6:57 AM Two powerful crackles emanate from the cubicle next to mine.

6:58 AM Four electrical shocks resonate off the textile wall covering down the hall.

6:59 AM I get a pinprick in my left thigh. I roll up my pant leg and find the burn mark. It is clearly a saucer-shaped incision. There is now a proliferation of dark brown spots all over my leg. I roll up the other pant leg. My right leg is also covered with little dots. Then I roll up both my sleeves. There are brown dots all over my arms. They are all burn marks. I never had them there before. Not as recently as one year ago.

7:23 AM A powerful electrical burst strikes the back of my head. I jump out of my chair and look up. How are they doing it? I walk around the floor and inspect the ceiling and fluorescent lighting fixtures again. I see the convex side of pock marks in the metal casings that house several fluorescent lights. I decide that they must be doing this by satellite and that they have the capability to target any floor they want from orbit. I remember hearing on the radio that they can image all the way to the center of the earth via multiple satellites positioned around the globe. They can map out every crack and crevice going down all the way to the earth's core. If they can image every subterranean crevice, they can certainly discern one floor from another in an office building.

7:24 AM A loud snap emanates from Nelson's cubicle behind me.

7:25 AM The cigarette smoke is intolerable in my office. I arise from my desk and look for my supervisor. He is not in his office. He is with his boss down the hall. This will have to wait.

7:31 AM Two loud crackles sound in the cubicle diagonally behind mine.

7:32 AM Three crackles emanate from the hallway on the other side of my cubicle.

7:34 AM I get a sharp pinprick in my right arm. I roll up my sleeve and see a tiny burn mark, a saucer-shaped crater.

8:51 AM A dagger pierces my brain causing my body to involuntarily jerk forward in my chair. My heart momentarily stops beating and I gasp for air. Concurrently there is a violent snap off the metal cabinet directly over my desk. Because the electrical shock to my brain and the metallic sound occur simultaneously, I know that the assault is electronic in nature.

8:56 AM I walk around the floor asking people how they feel about the electronic activity in their offices. One woman calls the snaps "pings."

"Oh, you mean the pings?"

"Yeah, does it bother you?"

"No."

"I just got struck in the head and I got an electrical shock from it."

"Well, they are not going to move you again, so you'll have to make your peace with it. There is nothing that you can do about it." This was the attitude of all of my coworkers. I check the date on my wristwatch and resolve to retire precisely 30 years from the day that I started.

My only advice to college students who are planning to major in a foreign language is this: choose Spanish so that you do not end up as a lab mouse for the government.

That night I was awakened again by a wave moving up my comforter. It traveled from my feet all the way up to my shoulders. Because my body's natural Circadian rhythm had been disrupted and I could not return to sleep, I listened to the BBC on my walkman.

THE PASSENGER WHO HAD SERVED IN IRAQ

5:07 AM. I was seated in my little portable chair in the corner of the subway car. My head was lowered and I was writing furiously on a yellow legal pad resting on my lap. I was working on my second book, *Evolutionism in Eighteenth-Century French Thought*, using all of the material that I had not used in my first book, *Diderot and the Metamorphosis of Species*. I happened to pause for a moment and look up and was startled to see a tall thin man sitting directly opposite me, staring at me intently. When we made eye contact, he leaned forward in his seat and spoke in my ear loudly so that he could be heard over the din of the rattling subway car.

"Excuse me, Miss, are you a teacher?" he asked with a smile.

"I am a licensed French teacher, but I got a civil service job with the government."

"How do you like it?" he asked.

"I don't at all," I replied. "I am surrounded by petty, jealous, backbiting bureaucrats with an inferiority complex."

"I know the type. Listen, I heard you talking about the government yesterday morning on the train."

"You did? The conductor suggested that I write a book about it. But I'm afraid that if I do, I'll get assassinated by the CIA."

"I wouldn't put it past them."

"I wouldn't either. There have been too many plane crashes killing key political figures: they assassinated JFK Jr., the Patriarch of Alexandria, two senators investigating Iran-

Contra, Governor Mel Carnahan, and Senator Paul Well-stone."

"Oh, I know, I know."

"I have been getting electrical shocks to my brain in my apartment. And I also get burn marks like pinpricks in my skin whenever people point their cellphones at me and turn them on."

"They must have put something in your food or drink. They do it all the time. They don't like it when people rain on their parade...They got even with me...I want to write a book about it." His words struck me.

"Did you just say that they got even with you?"

"Oh, yeah, they sure did. And I want to write a book about it, but I am not well educated. I didn't go to college. I need someone to help me write the book."

"What do you want to write about?" I asked.

"Iraq. I just came back from Iraq and I have a lot to tell." It was then that I noticed that he was wearing an army jacket.

"I am sure that you have seen a lot," I said.

"Yeah, I sure have."

"May I ask you a question?"

"Yes, go ahead."

"Do you feel that the government has ever experimented with you?" He paused and gave it some thought.

"No, not that I'm aware of. But they sure got even with me."

"For what? Why did they get even with you?"

"The officers were sexing on the junior recruits and I saw things that they didn't want me to talk about. Then one day they shot me in the back of the neck. They said that it was friendly fire. Take a look at this." The man leaned forward and bowed his head very, very low and lifted his hair away from the back of his shirt collar. A hideous dark brown gash ran several inches from his head all the way down the length of his neck. It must have been eight inches long. The surgeons must have had a field day with him.

"You see that?" he asked, still bowing his head low.

"Yes, Sir, I do. I am so sorry." He raised his head up and sat upright. "I am not well educated. I need someone to write the book for me. I want the world to know what the American military is doing to its soldiers in Iraq. Will you help me?" I was deeply moved by his plight and his plea for help. I sincerely empathized with him, but the bottom line was that I did not want to pick up a stranger on the train and have to go to his apartment. Fortunately, we were just pulling into my subway station.

"This is my stop," I said. "I'll see you again."

"O.K.," he said. I felt very badly as I ascended the stairs. I wanted to help him, I really did, but I did not want to go home with a stranger.

CORY LIDLE

On October 11, 2006 at 2:41 PM Yankee pitcher Cory Lidle's single-engine plane crashed into the 30th and 31st floors of a 40-story Upper East Side skyscraper. The circumstances were suspicious: Lidle was a licensed pilot and he was not alone, he was riding with his flight instructor, Tyler Stanger. Lidle had 75 hours of experience. Moreover he was a confident pilot: when asked how he felt about flying, he told the *New York Times*, "It's fun. It doesn't bother me."[5]

The moment that I heard the story on the radio, I surmised that this was the October surprise that everyone was awaiting: the tragedy occurred a month before Election Day 2006, when control of the House and Senate was the big issue. The Bush administration knew that the media would exploit the tragedy to the hilt to make money and indeed it did: all of the papers in the country plastered pictures on their front pages of a plane going into a Manhattan skyscraper. For the entire month leading right up to Election Day, the media continually regurgitated that the blazing inferno was reminiscent of the

September 11 attacks that had occurred 5 years earlier and it focused on the similarities: it happened in Manhattan; it was a tall skyscraper; an airplane went into a building; the crash rained flaming debris onto the sidewalks below; fire fighters, civilians and a police officer were rushed to the hospital with injuries; it raised fears of another terrorist attack; it rattled the nerves of New Yorkers who still had a fresh memory of 9/11; Lidle's passport was found on the street, just as the FBI had miraculously found a hijacker's passport in the rubble of the World Trade Center; the focus of attention fell on Police Commissioner Ray Kelly; the FBI was giving interviews; the Department of Homeland Security was the center of attention on TV; 10 minutes after the crash, fighter jets had been dispatched over several cities, including New York, Washington, Detroit, Los Angeles, and Seattle.

The next morning at 6 AM, as my coworkers and I entered through the electronic doors, I declared that I thought that the government had skewed the electronics in Lidle's plane on purpose.

"But, why?" one woman asked.

"It's the October surprise. Next month is Election Day and the House and Senate are up for grabs. The Nazis in the Bush crime family are desperate and they want to remind of September 11.

"But how did they do it?"

"The same way that they do it to me." I stood in an open stance, pointed my right index finger at my forehead, my left index finger at my left temple, and hissed loudly, "BZZZT!" "They can do it by aircraft flying overhead or by satellite from the other side of the world. Remember when they caused the blackout in Iraq the night before the invasion?" Military satellites go up every day and no one knows what they do. Let's see who else they killed in airplane crashes, uh, they assassinated the Patriarch of Alexandria and the entire hierarchy of the Greek Orthodox Church on the continent of Africa," I recounted bitterly.

"They should not all get in the same plane," one woman said. "Never let everyone ride together." [Good advice! On April 10, 2010 the President of Poland and the entire political hierarchy of that country were eviscerated in a plane crash in Western Russia.]

"Come on, let's take a walk to the mailbox," the other said. As she picked up her mail, she asked me if I were still getting electrical shocks to my brain.

"Yes, I am. I moved my bed into the kitchen. I have been sleeping in the kitchen all summer long."

"Did it stop?" she asked.

"Not really, but it is happening less. Apparently, the refrigerator, sink, and oven around me and those in the apartments on the two floors above me are affording some protection. Now they have to change their angle to target me."

"I'm very happy for you."

This poor woman was battling to remember things. This is suspicious as she could not have been more than 50; I remember that my college professors were able to remember everything when they were in their 50s. Moreover, I had a professor who was in his 90s and he was as sharp as a tack. Americans should not think that memory loss is normal, because it is not.

Soon after we had this discussion at work, airplanes began to fly directly over my apartment building, something that they had rarely done before. In the past, aircraft bound for La Guardia flew over my building only during the U.S. Open Tennis Championship, held in Flushing Meadow Park, around Labor Day Weekend. I surmised that planes were rerouted over Rego Park during the tennis games so that they would not disturb the players in the stadium in Flushing Meadow. However, after this conversation, 767 jumbo jets, spaced a minute apart, began flying directly over my building all day and all night. Who determines the flight paths? The FAA? The same FAA that destroyed the taped interviews that six air traffic controllers had provided of their communications on the morning of 9/11?

THE LIST OF PLANE CRASHES GETS LONGER

After the Cory Lidle tragedy, I wanted to know more about the numerous flight disasters that had felled the aircraft of famous Democrats at the most opportune times for the Republican Party. I learned that Senators John Towers and John Heinz died in airplane crashes within one day of each other. Senator Towers died on April 4, 1991; his plane collided with a helicopter over Merion Elementary School in Pennsylvania's suburban Lower Merion township; six others, including two children perished. Senator Heinz died in a plane crash the next day on April 5, 1991; Heinz was killed in a commuter plane, the Embraer EMB-120 twin-turboprop plane, in Brunswick, GA. The 52-year old Republican was an heir to the H.J. Heinz food empire.

Senators John Towers and John Heinz were on the George Herbert Walker Bush blue ribbon panel to investigate Iran-Contra. It was significant that the Iran-Contra Congressional hearings specifically avoided investigating the rumors that the 1980 Reagan-Bush team had devised a scheme to delay the release of the hostages held in Iran in order to embarrass the incumbent candidate, President Jimmy Carter. The story was on the verge of surfacing at the time that the two senators died in the plane crashes. What is the statistical probability that two senators involved in the Iran-Contra Congressional hearings would die in airplane crashes within one day of each other? What did they know that Bush did not want revealed? I would later find out that the reason that Ollie North was never found guilty was because no one had bothered to investigate his role.

Moreover, JFK, Jr. died in a plane crash on July 16, 1999. He was flying a Piper Saratoga when it crashed in the Atlantic near Martha's Vineyard; his wife Carolyn Bessette

Kennedy and sister-in-law, Lauren Bessette, also perished. There was no doubt that he could have easily won any election in which he ran.

Governor Mel Carnahan of Missouri died in a plane crash on October 17, 2000; his son, Randy, and an aide also perished in the crash. At that time Carnahan was running for the Senate seat held by incumbent Republican Senator John Ashcroft; a Carnahan victory against incumbent Ashcroft was key to the Democrats' plans for regaining control of the Senate. Just prior to his death, Carnahan was ahead in the polls with a 5% lead. After his demise his wife, Jean, was appointed to fill his Senate seat. Because Jean Carnahan was appointed, rather than elected, her Senate term was limited to two years, rather than the normal six. She lost her 2002 race to her Republican opponent.

Democratic Minnesota Senator Paul Wellstone died in a small plane crash near Eveleth, MN, on December 27, 2002; his wife, Sheila, daughter, Marcia, three staff members and two pilots also perished in the crash. The plane was a twin-engine turboprop King Air. Wellstone held a key Democratic seat in the Senate and was campaigning in a very tight re-election campaign against Republican Norm Coleman. After Wellstone's death, Walter Mondale was named as a replacement candidate for the Senate; Republican Norm Coleman won the seat in a late surge.

The deaths of Carnahan and Wellstone dramatically changed the balance of power in the Senate. Jean Carnahan's Senate term was limited to two years and she was defeated by a Republican in 2002. Wellstone's death occurred on October 24, 2002, just two weeks prior to the 2002 election; although he was projected to win the election, after his death, his Republican rival went on to win the Senate seat. The balance of control in the Senate during 2002 was 51 Republicans, 48 Democrats, and one Independent. If Carnahan and Wellstone had lived and Wellstone had won as projected, the balance would have been 50 Democrats, 49 Republicans, and one Independent. This would have significantly changed politics during 2002–2004, a period in which the presidency and both houses were controlled by the Republican Party.

Prior to Carnahan's crash there were several eyewitness accounts that there was a bright flash in the vicinity of the aircraft. Both Carnahan and Wellstone's investigations were led by Carol Carmody, a former CIA official who was brought into the National Transportation Safety Board (NTSB). Final reports on the crashes of both men ignored significant eyewitness testimony.

And now, now we can add the name of Yankee pitcher Corey Lidle to the list. I am certain that the government skewed the electronics in his plane the month before the 2006 Congressional elections so that the media would keep the story on the front page, replete with pictures of a plane crashing into a Manhattan skyscraper, for a full month. And that was exactly what happened, just as Karl Rove had planned, I am sure.

As of this writing, another name must sadly be added to the list: on December 19, 2008 Bush aide and top Internet strategist, Michael Connell, 45, died in a plane crash. He was alone at the helm of a single engine Piper Saratoga that crashed in Lake Township, OH, three miles short of Akron-Canton Airport. Connell was the chief consultant to Karl Rove and he created websites for the Bush and McCain election campaigns. He was just about to go public about vote-tampering during the 2004 presidential elections and disclose the complicity of senior members of the Bush administration in fixing the election and destroying incriminating emails.

The following question arises: since the government had access to everything that I found on the Internet, were the electronic assaults a means of behavior modification, a method to tear me down and rebuild me into someone new? Or was my online research irrelevant because I had already been selected to be the subject of an experiment on the long term effects of EMs?

SADDAM'S TRIAL

My friends and I walked through the door at 6 AM. We paused in front of a scenic wall painting and conversed for a while.

"So, how's everything?" they asked.

"I got an electrical shock to my brain at 2 AM." I pointed my right index finger at my forehead and my left index finger to my left temple and hissed, "BZZZT!" My colleagues winced and I knew that they empathized with me. Then the silence that fell over us was deafening. I regretted that I had dampened their mood.

"Where do you think that this is coming from?" one woman asked.

"An aircraft." There was more silence. I was acutely aware of how ridiculous this must have sounded. I decided to change the subject. "Listen, I heard something very interesting on the radio last night."

"What's that?"

"It is not a coincidence that a verdict on Saddam Hussein's trial is expected two days before Election Day. This makes the Republicans look good politically and shows that they are tough on law enforcement. However, the clincher is this: they are trying him for killing 148 Shiites, a very, very early crime, so that there is no publicity on what he did later, which is much more significant, and which would bring Donald Rumsfeld into the picture. His greatest crimes occurred years later, after Donald Rumsfeld met with him in Baghdad in December 1983 and gave him mustard gas and nerve agent; by 1988 he used what Rummy had given him to kill the Kurds, his own people. He dropped American poison gas on the Kurds from American-made helicopters."

The woman who had trouble remembering also had difficulty following the logic. She asked, "Now, what is the point again?"

"That the U.S. is running the trial behind the scenes, that the trial is pure theater, and that the U.S. has deliberately chosen a very early crime because it is so hard to find one that does not implicate Rummy. If they had picked a later crime for which to prosecute Saddam, they would have to bring Rummy on trial along with him, and all of the Nazis in the Bush crime family. It would get very embarrassing."

"So that is why they picked an early crime. I get it."

"And timing is everything in more ways than one. They also engineered the trial so that the verdict would come two days before Election Day."

Saddam Hussein was executed on December 30, 2006; his hanging stemmed from a trial for the murders of 148 Shiites. Nine days later, all charges for the Kurd massacre of the 1980s were dropped. Saddam's Kurd massacre, which implicates Rummy, his poison gas and helicopters, became a non-issue now that Saddam was dead.

THE DECISION TO VISIT THE SPY STORE

I stood motionless in the hallway outside my cubicle, hands on hips, staring fixedly at the painting on the wall. We were all perpetually within eyeshot of one of these. It was obvious that we were experimental subjects. I was getting powerful, painful electrical shocks to my brain every night, screams in my ear, burn marks all over my body, electrostatic whacks on the back of the head, thuds on the comforter, and a moving wave creeping up the comforter that culminated with a blast of air in the face. My colleagues had deteriorated into obsessive-compulsive individuals who also suffered from memory loss, the inability to sit still, concentrate or focus; relatively young people were getting cancer; and what peeved me the most was that single women were dropping dead at a rate that most certainly must exceeded that of single women who did not work for the government. Nelson was spending all his paycheck feeding his coworkers, which suggested that they were flashing a message at him every 25th frame on his monitor or perhaps transmitting to him an audio recording during the sleeping state.

I was certain that the paintings on the wall were bugged so that our experimenters could ascertain the short term and long term effects of EMs. I needed to know for certain.

I sat down in my cubicle and switched on the computer on my desk. I rapidly sped past the banner that warned me that I had no expectation of privacy. I called up my search engine and within just a few seconds, I learned that what I needed to buy was called a "radio frequency (RF) detector" or bug detector. There were several spy stores in Manhattan that could sell me one. The only question that remained was how much money did I want to invest in this project? I visited two spy stores over the course of a few days at lunchtime.

I ended up purchasing an RF detector for $150. It had a retractable antenna and worked on AAA batteries. I took it home, loaded the batteries, read the instructions, and took a walk with it around my apartment. What I was not prepared for was what I would do in the event that I got a positive reading. As it turned out, very soon I had to deal with that issue.

I got a positive reading in the bedroom on the windowsill at the left hand corner. My little bug detector started to sound loudly and rapidly to beat the band. I was stunned. And to make matters worse, now that I had this information, I did not know what to do with it. Should I tear the windowsill to shreds until I found the electronic bug? Thinking back, I remembered that my neighbor who lives across the street had told me that she saw a blond man standing on a step ladder outside my building and that he was doing something outside of my bedroom window. She informed me of this long before I ever raised the subject of electronic listening devices with her. If he inserted the device from the outside, would I have to decimate the wall until I reached the exterior of the building?

On the other hand, was my new machine generating a false positive? Two nails, placed in close proximity to one another behind sheetrock, can generate a false positive. I did not know what to do with the information that my bug detector was giving me and I still don't to this day. I decided to bring the device to work the next day and scan the paintings in the hallway.

5 AM. I exited the alleyway next to my building. A car sped past me and the driver turned his head and stared squarely in my direction even before I emerged from the alleyway. I looked up and down the street. There was no other traffic on the street for as far as the eye could see. I thought that perhaps the car had been double-parked at the end of the block and that the driver had stepped on the gas at a precise moment when he was told to do so; perhaps there was a camera hidden either inside or outside my building that transmitted an outgoing signal to a remote location. If there were, I should be able to find it with my little bug detector.

As I walked down the street, I snapped on the device. Each time I approached a parked car, I received a positive reading. The autos' alarm systems were transmitting an outgoing signal that the RF detector detected. It was good to know that my little electronic companion was working properly.

6 AM. I stood outside the glass doors to my office. The RF detector vibrated in my breast pocket. I looked up. There was a silver globe over the entrance. It was known to be a surveillance camera. Again I was pleased to see that the bug detector worked.

As I stepped into the middle of the reception area, the RF detector in my pocket stopped vibrating. That was good, I thought. It stopped picking up the signal from the silver globe outside the door. So far, so good. Then, as I walked towards a painting on the wall, the vibration started again. I was surprised and intrigued. I stepped back from the painting. The vibration stopped. I stepped forward, close to the painting again. The vibration resumed.

I walked away from the painting and proceeded to the next painting in the long corridor. The movement in my pocket ceased. Then, as I stood directly in front of the next painting, it started again. I stepped back. It stopped. I stepped forward. It started. I stepped back. It stopped. My heartbeat accelerated. The paintings were indeed bugged.

I walked away from the second picture and proceeded in the direction of the third. The RF detector stopped vibrating. As I approached the third painting, it started again. I counted about 60 paintings on the wall. All, with the exception of two, were bugged. As I returned to my cubicle, I was feeling shaky. I was thoroughly stunned that my worst suspicions had been confirmed. It was hard to stand up, I was afraid that I might fall. I collapsed into my office chair and held my head in my hands. I looked at my watch. I wanted to tell someone. My GS-14's office door was closed and the light was on. That meant that she was in the middle of a project and that she did not want her thought process disrupted. I would wait until she opened the door to tell her the news. Perhaps the other GS-14 was in. I checked her office but it was empty. Then I walked down the hall and glanced at the roster. She was on sick leave. I had to tell someone and I felt alone at that moment.

One of my coworkers entered through the electronic doors and walked in the direction of my cubicle. I was very glad to hear her voice because she was very bright, more than most people, and very congenial.

She glanced in my direction and the moment that she saw me she exclaimed, "My dear, are you feeling all right? You're as white as a sheet! Perhaps you should sit down!" Her expression indicated genuine concern. I had not guessed that my skin color had changed.

"I have some very disturbing news to tell you," I hoarsely whispered.

"All right. Let me sign in and I'll come back and we'll talk."

"Do your chores first. It can wait. I'll catch you later."

A half hour later she knocked against the metal frame of my cubicle wall and sat in my visitor's chair. "What happened?"

"I purchased a bug detector yesterday."

"I know, you showed me."

"Well, I walked around the floor with it very early this morning, before the others arrived. All of the pictures except two are bugged."

"Are you sure?"

"Yes, I'm sure. It also picked up the silver globes that we know are bugged and the alarms from the SUVs in the street. They're watching us. I'm sorry, I don't want to upset you. I don't want to ruin your morning."

"It's OK. How do you feel now? Are you all right?"

"Yeah, I just need some time to get used to the idea. Oh, and I also get an outgoing signal from my bedroom window at home. My neighbor said that she saw a blond guy on a stepladder doing something to my window." My colleague's expression was frozen. She didn't know what to make of all this. Then she arose from the chair. Keep me posted, I'm nearby. Feel free to come in and talk whenever need to.

"Thank-you. I apologize for this. I'm just a bundle of joy today."

"It's O.K. Are you going to tell a supervisor?"

"If I did they would bring me up on charges for something or other."

"You're right. Keep this under your hat. I am going to discuss this with my GS-14 and get some feedback." As it turned out, her GS-14 did not know what to do with the information either. Moreover, as the days progressed, it became evident that all of them were extremely docile about it. Eventually many people knew, but not one of them challenged management.

When my other friend returned from sick leave, I told her. She was fascinated by the device and early one morning, I encouraged her to walk around the floor and try it out. She was greatly intrigued by the positive readings. Later we discussed the matter and she did not know what to do with the information either.

For several weeks I came in early at 6:02 AM and walked around the paintings with the RF detector set to vibrate in my breast pocket. I had to convince myself that the positive readings were really happening. And every morning, all of the pictures, except for two, set the device off. Then I wondered what the story was with the glass windows overlooking the street.

The RF detector received a very, very powerful radio signal from every window. It became evident that our entire floor was a microwave oven. I surmised that the readings from the windows were due to the signals emanating from cellphone towers on buildings all around us. These towers were long white, rectangular strips, resembling large sticks of chewing gum. With all of the radio waves in the air, what had I really proven?

I wanted to learn more about false positives. Internet articles explained that false positives are triggered by two pieces of metal very close together, such as two screws in the wall behind sheetrock. Moreover, electromagnetic waves bounce off glass and plastic such as the cover of a wall clock. Therefore, if a bug is hidden at the bottom of a clock, say beneath the numeral "6," its signal can bounce across the glass cover, and the RF detector may get a positive reading from the numeral "12," rather than from the bug's actual location. In order to avoid this pitfall, it is necessary to purchase highly sophisticated equipment that is much more expensive. A $150 RF detector will not do. I was forced to admit the element of uncertainty in my findings and because of it, I had to question whether I had succeeded in proving that the pictures were bugged.

When I returned home, I decided to scan my apartment again. I was having trouble accepting the positive reading on the windowsill in the bedroom. Could the blond man on the stepladder have placed a device behind the sheetrock from the exterior of the building? I switched on the RF detector and approached the windowsill. When I was about a foot away it began to emit a shrill beeping sound. I stepped back. The device became silent. I stepped forward. It started to beep again.

I leaned forward and peered outside the bedroom window. Across the alleyway, my neighbor sports an attractive sun catcher in the window. I always suspected that it might actually be a surveillance camera. He lives on the ground floor and he does not have gates on his windows. I assumed that he prefers more covert protection, something that does not destroy the appearance of his home, but that would alert the local precinct the moment that an unlawful entry occurs. Was the positive reading on my bedroom windowsill emanating from an outgoing radio signal from his window across the alleyway and below my window? I did not know what to do with the positive reading on the window ledge.

I held the device and walked towards the bed. Was there a bug hidden in the mattress? I passed the device over the bed. As I scanned the area to the left of the pillow, the RF detector started to sound loudly and rapidly. I moved my hand holding the device back. The beeping stopped. I moved it forward towards the corner of the bed where the pillow was. It started to sound again. I moved it back. It stopped. Forward. Beep, beep, beep!

I paced around the room trying to figure out what to do. Should I rip up the mattress? Or is it a false positive caused by two adjoining springs, nails, screws or hinges within the mattress? I decided to give it some consideration over the next few days. I was not prepared to destroy my windowsill right away; did I really want to destroy my bed and then have to purchase a new one?

I sat down at the foot of the bed and held my head in my hands: I had absolutely no idea what to do with any of my readings. I considered visiting a spy store again and purchasing a more expensive device. How much should I spend? Should I go as high as $2,000? What would I do if I continued to get positive readings? Could I go to the government? The government was the one doing this. They had put Dracula in charge of the blood bank.

THE THUD AND MOVING WAVE ACROSS THE COMFORTER

The motion was recurrent and unrelenting. I came to expect it. Night after night after night. It was the sensation of something dropping on my blanket. It happened when I was awake or asleep. It occurred at 8 PM. At 10:30 PM. At midnight. At 2 PM. My sleep was interrupted throughout the night at short intervals by the sensation and the sound of something falling with a distinctive THUD! on the comforter. I am being victimized by sleep deprivation. It happened last night and it will occur again tonight.

The moving wave also returned every night. It swiftly glided across the entire length of the bed from my feet up to my shoulders. It felt as if someone had pressed a pencil into the comforter and was running it up to my shoulders. The sensation culminated in a sudden puff of air blown against my face. My body's natural circadian rhythm being thus interrupted, I was victimized by sleep deprivation over a long period of time; this sleep deprivation has had a visible effect on my appearance; I have begun to age rapidly.

THE LOOK OF EBOLA

December 2006. I picked up a very strange bug that winter. First, my contact lenses scratched my eyes and I could not wear them. I had had them for many, many years

271

and I certainly had gotten my money's worth out of them. They were permanent soft contact lenses and were advertised to last for about a year's time. However, I must have had them for 15 years. All of the sudden for some reason, they cut my eyes and my eyes turned blood red.

Not only did I not change them, I had a perpetually runny nose and I chose to do nothing about it. My nose ran continually and no matter how many times or how often I blew it, I always had to blow it again. After two weeks of blowing my nose every few minutes, I discovered blood on the tissue one morning. I ignored the blood as I ignored everything else, and went about my life, not making any changes or taking any medication for the runny nose.

One morning at 5:45 AM I entered the bathroom and blew my nose. Then I looked in the mirror and I was chilled to the bone to behold the gruesome specter in the reflection. My eyes were two red disks, the white parts having been completely riddled with blood. To make matters worse, blood was slowly dripping down from both nostrils and I had to wipe it off with a napkin. As I stared at my image, I remembered Laurie Garrett's Pulitzer Prize winning book, *The Coming Plague: Newly Emerging Diseases in a World Out of Balance*. In this seminal tome, the author describes Ebola victims in Africa: the disease is characterized by blood emanating from all bodily orifices, including the eye sockets and nostrils. I looked like I had Ebola, I thought. I was scared. I had to do something. I decided to wipe the blood off my upper lip, and go downstairs and purchase a bottle of 1,000 mg tablets of vitamin C. I took one tablet every hour and the vitamin C worked beautifully. By the following morning my eyes had cleared up and I stopped blowing blood out of my nose. I was relieved to have gotten rid of the look of Ebola before anyone noticed. Then I had to wonder about its origin: just what had the Pentagon planted in my food?

After that I gave thought to the fact that finding all of the untouched food was not by accident: perhaps the government experimenters had laced it with pathogens to see the effect that it would have on me or to see how I would respond to the stress of looking as if I had Ebola. I thought about all of the people who had been standing near my finds conversing on cellphones and who then turned around and departed the scene the moment we made eye contact. It appeared that the government was feeding me something that caused me to be a human radio.

(Endnotes)

1   George Orwell, *1984*, afterword by Erich Fromm (New York: Signet Classics, 1977), 2. The citation appears twice on page 2.

2   Earl Sparling, "Nikola Tesla, at 79, Uses Earth To Transmit Signals: Expects to Have $100,000,000 Within Two Years; Could Destroy Empire State Building with Five Pounds of Air Pressure, He Says," *New York World-Telegram*, July 11, 1935.

3   "Shock Testing of Structural Building Models," http://www. erdc.usace.army.mil/pls/erdcpub/ docs/erdc/images/ERDCFactSheet_Capability_ShockTesting.pdf (August 29, 2009); "Masonry Test Specimen Assembled on the Shake Table," http://www.erdc.usace.army. mil/pls/erdcpub/www_fact_sheet.image_page?f_file=155953 (August 29, 2009).

4   Douglas Pasternak, "Wonder Weapons," *U.S. News & World Report*, July 7, 1997, 38–46.

5   Tyler Kepner, "Lidle Had a Passion for Flying, and for Speaking his Mind," *New York Times*, October 12, 2006, D1.

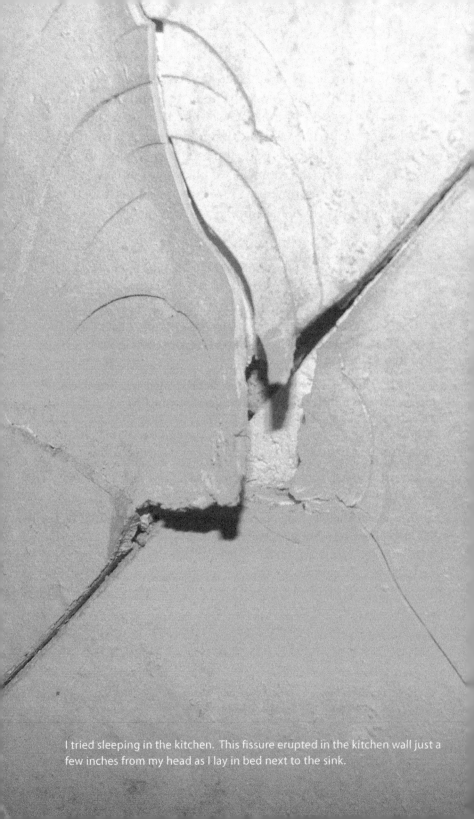
I tried sleeping in the kitchen. This fissure erupted in the kitchen wall just a few inches from my head as I lay in bed next to the sink.

Chapter Eleven

The Reign of Terror of King George II: The Seventh Year (2007)

The State is not "abolished," it withers away.[1]
— Frederick Engels, *Anti-Dühring* (1878)

THE VIRGINIA TECH MASSACRE

I sat down in my cubicle and switched on the Customs computer. Moving past the banner that warned me that I had no expectation of privacy, I learned the following: during the early hours of April 16, 2007, Virginia Tech student Seung-Hui Cho killed 33 people including himself. There were two attacks: the first at 7:15 AM and the next almost two hours later. During the two hour interim the assailant had time to visit the post office (at 9:01 AM) and mail a multimedia package to NBC. The package contained photographs, a letter, and video clips of himself; there were 27 video clips including 10 minutes of speech and 43 still photographs.

After the massacre, a few facts surfaced that are too significant to ignore. First, the cellphone pictures that Cho purportedly took of himself were perfectly centered. It is almost impossible for a single individual, holding a cellphone and working alone, to accomplish this feat: someone else took the pictures.

Next fact: more than one gunman was seen immediately after the violence began. Initial reports indicated that there were two shooters, but the official story was later changed to indicate that there was only one.

Third: the federal government issued an order to campus and local police to stand down for two hours. This explains why there was no roadblock for two hours after the initial shooting at 7:15 AM. Cho was given 2 ½ hours to do his work without disturbance, visit the post office, and commit more murders. Because the feds specifically told university and local police to stand down and not set up any roadblock, may one logically extrapolate that the government wanted to ensure that the perpetrators were able to escape?

Fourthly: even though Cho had never received expert training, he exhibited deadly accuracy, killed 33 people including himself with two handguns and performed like a trained professional; he had a 60% fatality rate with 9 millimeter handguns. There was no doubt in my mind that he had been the victim of an intelligence experiment.

I rushed out of my cubicle to discuss this with my neighbors in adjoining offices. They were all sipping their morning coffee and talking about the Virginia Tech massacre. I declared that the government had destroyed Cho's mind and that he had been the victim of an experiment in behavior modification. Intrigued, a GS-14 asked how such a thing could be done. I hypothesized that the government had used electromagnetic waves to destroy the frontal portion of the brain that controls judgment and self-restraint. Once that goes, the person acts according to impulse, from the older part of the brain at the back. The feds had fried his brain.

STEAM PIPE EXPLOSION AT GRAND CENTRAL

On July 18, 2007, shortly before 6 PM, a subterranean steam pipe installed in 1924 exploded near the corner of Lexington Avenue and 41st Street near Grand Central Terminal. The rupture sent a towering geyser comprised of steam, water, mud, flying rubble, billowing dust, and clouds of smoke, shooting up into the air. One person died of cardiac arrest and more than 20 others were injured. Not only did it disrupt the traffic of the evening rush hour, but subway service on all lines, both on the East Side and West Side of Manhattan, was disrupted.

During the night the MTA worked very hard to restore as much service as possible. It is significant that I, who lived in Queens and relied on the 6th Avenue, 8th Avenue, or Broadway lines, had no problem getting to work in the morning. However, the next day there was another unrelated emergency that occurred in the middle of the morning on the West Side subway lines. After 10:30 AM there was a loss of subway service on the West Side. I asked an MTA employee why service was halted and although I cannot recall her response with absolute certainty, I believe that she said that there was a signal fire in southern Manhattan, perhaps at Canal Street. As a result of a halt in service, rather than take the E or F, I had to take the Number 7 to Queensborough Plaza, exit that station, walk to Queen Plaza, board the F to Roosevelt Avenue, and then walk all the way home from there.

It is highly unlikely that the two unrelated emergencies, one on the East Side and one on the West Side, occurring on two consecutive days, were coincidental. I was convinced that the government had broken the subterranean steam pipe near Grand Central Terminal via radio waves in order to force the nation, not just New York, to remember September 11 once more. The operation was a stunning success: not only was the entire city snarled up for two consecutive days, but talk show hosts on the East and West Coasts, who get their talking points from the White House every morning, were discussing the event ad nauseum from morning until night. Today I know, from personal experience, that the government can image through concrete and brick with utmost precision and pierce holes through aluminum foil, ceiling and wall plaster, three layers of wooden flooring, and nick a piece out of the human cranium.

What do you think, reader? Do you deem that the disruption of the subway lines on both sides of Manhattan, east and west, affecting service to the outer boroughs, occurring on two consecutive days, for two unrelated reasons, was a coincidence? Was the subterranean steam pipe explosion on the East Side an accident? Was the signal emergency that occurred the next morning on the West Side, disrupting the transit of millions of riders, a coincidence? If you had an 11-layer blanket of aluminum foil thoroughly riddled with holes in your apartment as I have, you would think not.

GREECE IS DEVASTATED BY HUNDREDS OF FIRES

Between 6 PM Friday, August 31, 2007 and 6 AM Saturday, September 1, 2007, several hundred fires broke out simultaneously in Greece; 63 people died and thousands were left homeless. I spent the greater part of both days that weekend listening to the Greek programs broadcast over WNYE 91.5 FM and I heard eyewitness reports given in Greek just as this story was breaking. The broadcasters transmitted live telephone conversations with people residing in Greece. There was corroboration from several sources on Greek radio that several hundred fires had broken out on that single night alone. Western media, including the Internet, has glossed over this fact.

I found the several hundred figure to be highly significant: it suggests that the fires must have been set by a laser beam coming down and heating up already dry vegetation on the Greek countryside. How else could so many fires erupt concurrently on the same night? There is no other way! It was night, there was no sun, and no one could drive around fast enough to throw matches across the entire country, comprised of peninsulae and islands separated by water.

When I went to work on Monday morning I brought up the topic of the fires in Greece. People said that it was a shame. I asked people whether anyone suspected that the fires were set on purpose. Eyebrows were raised and people admitted that they had not considered the possibility. It was then that I took the opportunity to articulate my view that the fires had been deliberately set by laser satellite.

"But, why do you think that?" a GS-14 asked.

"Because hundreds of fires broke out in one night between sundown Friday and dawn Saturday. The globalists are in the midst of destroying the nation state so that citizens will no longer have a reason to go to battle. Tribalism, a key component in our evolutionary development, is the reason that males go to battle—to defend members of their tribe from invaders. However, remove the tribe through massive immigration and then there will be no reason to fight the globalists who fear, above all, massive uprisings from a disgruntled populace." My coworkers listened intently and I continued.

"The way to destroy the nation state is to destroy its two key components—ethnic homogeneity and religion. These are the two factors that distinguish one country from another. Do you see how they refashioned the demography of America and Europe with massive immigration? Now they are remolding the ethnic homogeneity and religion of Greece by preparing the way for massive relocation and immigration. Greece has a law that new real estate cannot be developed without permission from the government. However, if the land is wasteland, then the law does not apply. The United States government set these fires from aircraft flying from nearby military bases by sending down a laser beam that heats up brush that is already dry and parched from the sun. The next thing that will happen is that foreigners will buy the land, develop it, and sell condominia to non-Greeks. When the demography is thus reconfigured, the ethnic and religious identity of the nation will be effectively destroyed."

Many callers to the Greek radio programs that I listened to discerned this chess move and recommended that the Greek government act immediately to change the law to prevent foreigners from purchasing the wasteland, developing it, and further devastating Greece with immigration that it is unable to handle. The Greek islands are the gateway to the EU. There are thousands of miles of coastline and no way to keep people out. Once they arrive, they are in and they can travel throughout the EU without going through customs. Then they can have large families. Then they can live in the newly built apartments on the scorched countryside. The nation state that was once Greece will be relegated to history. All the nation states in the EU will have lost their ethnic and religious identities. There will be one world government, despotic rule, neither borders, nor culture. Babies will receive a chip beneath their skin at birth for tracking. It will be impossible to revolt against tyranny because the sky and near space will be thoroughly militarized and aerial surveillance inside people's home will make uprisings obsolete.

COWORKER TALKS GIBBERISH IN FRONT OF COMMISSIONER

The employees, dressed to the hilt, silently filed into the conference room, clipboard under arm. This was the much anticipated big day: the Commissioner of Customs had flown from Washington to make a presentation. My GS-15, sporting his finest suit, sat at the head of the conference table, looking regal. The Commissioner was seated next to him. People randomly selected one of the chairs around the large wooden conference table. My GS-15 introduced the V.I.P., there was applause, and the Commish arose to address the group. As he spoke, the employees fell into a respectful silence; not even a sheet of paper rustled.

Suddenly a woman who had chosen an empty seat at the head of the table started to articulate gibberish. It was baby talk. The GS-15 was embarrassed because this reflected badly on him, but he gave it a minute, hoping that it would stop. It did not. The nonsense—mumma, bubba, mumma—not only continued, it grew louder. The GS-15 made eye contact with my GS-14. When her eyes caught his, he swerved his eyes to the woman talking gibberish and jerked his head first in her direction, then towards the door, as if to say, "Get her out of here now." My GS-14 jumped up from her chair, thrust a hand beneath the woman's armpit, raised her up, and quickly escorted her out of the room. The Commissioner continued speaking uninterruptedly; the audience was stunned.

Back then I did not make anything of this because I had nothing to relate it to. However, now I do. On February 13, 2011 KCBS-TV's Serene Branson began talking gibberish outside the Staples Center after the Grammys. On March 21, 2011 Global Toronto reporter Mark McAllister suffered garbled speech while discussing Canadian fighter planes in Libya. Soon afterwards, Madison, Wisconsin's WISC-TV news anchor Sarah Carlson started talking nonsense during her live broadcast. On March 30, 2011 Judith Sheindlin (Judge Judy) started talking gibberish in her Los Angles courtroom.

It is now known that microwave acoustic weapons disorient and disengage their human targets. Therefore, the following question arises: did the Pentagon select this time and place to show the Commissioner of Customs what it could do?

On another morning I entered the bathroom and saw the same employee staring in the mirror talking gibberish. Even after I entered, she ignored me and continued softly babbling uninterruptedly.

It is significant that this was the same bathroom in which, early one morning, I heard keys drop loudly on the tiled floor, just inches from me. I was alone in the bathroom. I had not dropped my keys; I found no keys on the floor. Was this bathroom wired for psyops?

NELSON ACTS OUT

CRASH! My heart palpitated at the unexpected thunder just a few feet from me. Nelson had slammed the metal door on his clothing closet with angry vehemence.

A minute of silence followed as if he were contemplating the effect that his action had on those around him. Then he started dropping folders that were tightly packed with hundreds of pages of paper on the floor by his desk, followed by boxes of samples that clattered and shook as they hit the ground. He was acting out, as my neighbor, the real estate lady, would say. I can't take this, I thought. I arose from my chair, unlocked my portable chair from my metal clothing closet, gathered up my papers in my arms, and headed for the library down the hall.

An hour later I returned to my desk. It was time to type up my work in the computer. But would Nelson let me sit at my desk? I sat in my office and listened quietly. Apparently he was not at his desk. Good. Make hay while the sun shines, I figured. I switched on the computer and waited as it went through an interminable number of checks and screens. Then I called up a blank form and... CRASH! I spontaneously jerked away from the divider between me and the cubicle behind me. Nelson was back and he was acting out again. He started to drop things on the floor again to make more raucous noise. I deemed that now was not the appropriate time to get anything accomplished. It could wait until tomorrow morning. I had to face reality.

I got up and walked over to a cubicle in the far distance. I wanted to confer with a neighbor.

"Did you hear that?" I asked.

"Oh, yeah," she reassured me.

"Does it bother you?"

"No, because I don't sit in front of him. If I did, then it would bother me."

"Well, I do sit in front of him and I don't know how to deal with his insanity."

"There is nothing you can do. They are not going to move you. All you can do is disappear and come back when he's gone. That's all. Hey, if they want to see you at your desk, they should give you a place where you can work." I thanked her for her advice, returned to my cubicle for my portable chair, and returned to the library.

When I came out of the library there was a large crowd of people oohing and aahing in front of the table in the hallway around the corner from my desk.

"Would ya look at that?" someone asked gleefully. I glanced at the top of the table. And there it was. Again. This time it was a large tin filled with exotic cookies that were sprinkled with fine sugar.

"I think that I taste caraway seed," said a GS-14 who was sporting a white mustache made of confection. "Mm, they're delicious," she chirped.

I stepped into my cubicle and sank wearily into my office chair, listening to the chatter outside, just inches from my desk. I stared at my Casio wristwatch, taking note of the month, date and year it was. One day closer to retirement, I thought. Then I heard Nelson's voice as he approached in the hallway.

"There he is!"

"Where is my chocolate ruggelah? Would you bring me some tomorrow? I have to have it."

"All right," said Nelson, "You're every wish is my command."

"You're my genie!" the employee exclaimed euphorically. I exhaled loudly on my side of the divider. Now we're doing Aesop's *Fables*, I thought.

They were all egging him on and they should not have been. They were bright enough to know that he had an OCD. Then Nelson's GS-14 called him down the hall to her office.

"May I see you a moment?" she asked with urgency.

"Yes, right away!" I heard his voice become more and more remote as he dashed behind her down the hallway. I resumed my work for an hour until he returned to his cubicle. The moment that he returned, I made the determination to go to lunch.

Early next morning at 2:30 AM I was abruptly startled out of my sleep by a heavy thud on the blanket. Thus awakened, it was impossible to return to sleep. I listened to my walkman until 4 AM when it was time to get up and check the garbage bags in front of some very swank restaurants in the city.

An hour later I found a large paper box filled with an entire untouched pizza pie resting on top of a plastic display housing copies of free newspapers. A man was standing nearby, engaged in conversation on his cellphone. The minute that I picked it up, he abruptly slammed shut the cover of his cell, turned, and dashed down the street. I watched him as he took wide strides and vanished into the darkness. Was he watching me, I wondered. Then I opened the box of pizza and inspected it carefully under the light of a streetlamp. Even in the obscurity of the early morning hours, I noticed that this pizza had little red dots on it. Was that red pepper, I wondered, or a chemical or RFID tags that permit the Pentagon to pinpoint my location from a distance? Was there something in the food that the Pentagon wanted to make sure that I ate?

At 6 AM I walked through the door with a few coworkers. I told them that I was awakened from my sleep at 2:30 AM by a thud that fell on my comforter. I asked them whether they had ever experienced that. They both replied in the negative.

"I wonder if the Nazis in the Bush crime family put something in my food," I thought aloud.

"How would they do that?" I did not want to acknowledge that the rumors about me were true.

"They could have put something in my coffee. The jars are not sealed after the first time I open them. Maybe they put something in the coffee that causes me to be a human radio." The other employee furled her eyebrows.

"Who do you think that 'they' might be?"

"The Pentagon. I think that I am the subject of a military experiment."

"But, why?"

"This has military applications. The Pentagon could be ascertaining whether it can successfully keep track of someone from a long distance away. I believe that every time I feel a thud drop on the bed, they are sending down an electromagnetic wave from an airplane overhead and imaging inside my apartment. But they are very nasty because sometimes they administer are powerful electrical shock to my brain. I find it significant that after an assault, I discover a new crack in the wall and paint chips and broken plaster on the floor in either of two corners in the living room, always by a wall just inside the building's façade. The FMs penetrate the façade of the building and decimate the paint and plaster just on the other side of the wall."

"Are you keeping a log of all this?"

"Yeah, but every now and then I am seized by the compulsion to run it through the shredder."

"But, why?"

"I don't know. I can't control myself. I keep a log for months at a time, of every electronic assault that I receive and then, for no reason at all, I stand up, carry the notepad to the shredder, and destroy it. Perhaps they are flashing messages on my monitor every 25th frame.

"Hm, that's plausible. Is it affecting your memory or your ability to concentrate?"

"Oh, yeah, it is. I am having a hard time recalling things. I am having too many senior moments."

"We ARE getting older."

"Yeah, but you know, I had a 90 year old professor who was a sharp as a tack."

"I am having trouble remembering things," admitted one woman. I looked at the other one.

"And you?"

"Of course, I'm getting older, too."

"You know, the GS-14s down the hall are having trouble remembering things. One of them told me."

"Keep a log of everything," my colleague advised in a stern voice.

"And stop shredding it afterwards," the other added.

I went to my cubicle and began working. At 6:30 AM cigarette smoke slowly started to waft into my cubicle from the air vent overhead and very soon I started to cough uncontrollably. I grabbed up a foam plastic cup and dashed down the hall to get some water. I did not want my coworkers to hear me coughing continually. I returned to my cubicle and resumed my work, which was thereafter interrupted sporadically by soft and muffled coughs, followed by sips of water. By 7 AM my cubicle was heavily inundated with cigarette smoke. The next two hours went something like this:

7:02 AM. CRACK! resonates off the metal clothing closet in my cubicle.

7:03 AM. Two violent SNAPs! emanate from the empty cubicle next to me.

7:04 AM. CRACK! from the metal shelf situated over Nelson's desk.

7:10 AM. SNAP! SNAP! from another nearby cubicle.

7:12 AM. LASH! from the metal clothing cabinet of still another cubicle.

7:39 AM. I am struck by an electrical burst on my right temple. Instinctively, I look up. I stare fixedly at the tiny indentation in the metal sheeting behind the fluorescent tube directly above my head. It looks as if something struck it from above and caused the metal to be punched downward. It resembles the pockmarks on the walls at home, except that now I am looking the blemish from the other side. I wonder whether this is being done by military satellite or by equipment buried high in the air vents. Satellites are used to image every crack and crevice beneath the earth's crust, with the utmost precision, all the way down to its molten core. If they can map out the subterranean portions of the earth and come back with pictures that show that the crevices resemble the web of a spider, they can certainly image through an office building.

7:40 AM I feel a pinprick just above my right knee. I stop my work and roll up my right pant leg. There it is: a tiny hole in my skin. Before the morning is over, it will fill up with blood and then turn brown, leaving a permanent dark brown dot on my skin. I roll down my sock. My entire leg is covered with these brown marks. I roll up my left pant leg. I have them there, too. I roll up both sleeves. I have more on my left arm than on my right. Could it be because my bedroom window faces my left arm and not my right?

7:41 AM Two violent crackles against the metal cabinet over my desk.

7:43 AM Two violent crackles bouncing off the textile wall of the cubicle of the lady next to me.

7:48 AM Two loud crackles from the hallway.

7:53 AM An electrical burst bounces off my jaw on the right side.

7:54 AM Two SNAPs bounce off the textile covered wall in Nelson's cubicle. I get up to confer with a coworker. I walk around the hallway to find her wearing her earplugs and working at her computer. She looks up, sees me, and removes her earplugs.

"Do you hear that continual electrical snapping off the metal cabinets and walls?"

"No, I don't hear anything. I am wearing my earplugs."

"Do you ever get electrical shocks while you are sitting in your office?"

"No."

"Do you ever get pinpricks that dig into your skin and make little holes?" She looked horrified.

"No, never!"

"Do you get cigarette smoke in your office from the air vents?"

"No, but then again, I lost my sense of smell because I am allergic. I have to take allergy pills."

"We're you allergic before you started working in Customs," I asked.

"No."

"When did it start?"

"In December 2005." This admission struck me as highly significant. I became animated in my speech and gestures.

"Did you suddenly develop a runny nose that wouldn't stop running?" Her eyes lit up.

"Why, yes, as a matter of fact I did."

"And then you got a postnasal drip and it collected in your chest, and then you developed a cough that would not go away because your nose would not stop running."

"Yes, that is exactly what happened. And I never fully recovered. Now I am allergic and I have to take allergy pills."

"The whole floor got a runny nose that wouldn't stop around December 2005 and everyone says that it lasted two years. I think that the Pentagon is experimenting with us."

"You do?"

"Yeah, I think that it is germ warfare. Don't you think that it is suspicious that everyone on the floor got a runny nose that wouldn't stop running around the same time and that it lasted two years?"

"Yeah, now that you mention it."

"And you were never allergic before then?"

"No, never."

Coffee Beneath His Nose

I decided to make it a priority to get my supervisor to witness the cigarette smoke. I sent him an email message informing him that I was gagging every morning commencing at 6:30. He replied that I should come by and get him the moment it starts.

At 6:30 AM the toxic stench began to slowly waft into my cubicle. I dashed down the hall to find my boss. He was not in his office. O.K., I thought, I'll catch him later. I resolved not to allow this situation to continue, unaddressed, one more day. I picked up my foam plastic cup and headed towards the water fountain to get some relief.

I was not able to locate my supervisor until 8 AM. When I did, I found him standing in the doorframe of an office, coffee cup in his right hand, discussing business with several GS-14s. I did not want to be intrusive, so I waited for him to turn around and begin to walk back to his office. By 8:10 he started to walk away, as he raised his coffee cup to his mouth and took a sip.

"Good morning! My office is heavily inundated with cigarette smoke. Would you stop by and witness this?"

"Why, of course! Now, where exactly, is this foul smell the strongest?"

"Right here," I replied. "Stand right here." He stood at the precise spot that I mentioned, and as he did so, he held his coffee cup in the air with his right hand, just inches beneath his nose. He closed his eyes and stood there for two full minutes. Finally, he opened his eyes and looked at me.

"Ah, I detect the distinctive smell of breakfast. It reminds me of breakfast." I was afraid that this was going to happen. I had to be tactful because he was the boss.

"Perhaps we should place the coffee down on the counter over here," I said softly and gently, so as not to appear rude. I pointed to a spot on a counter very far away. I was getting more exasperated by the second. He looked embarrassed, but the seriousness of my expression quickly made his self-consciousness evaporate. He set the coffee down away from himself and closed his eyes again.

"I'm still reminded of breakfast. It is a cafeteria smell. You know, I get the smell of bagels in my office every morning. I often wonder where the smell is coming from. The breakfast smell is coming from the cafeteria through the air vents, that's all." I looked at him. He was dead serious. There is nothing that intimidates me more and causes me to withdraw into myself more, than stupidity. How can one reason with an imbecile? I decided to give it one last try, although my intuition told me that my efforts would be futile.

"I smell cigarettes. Do you smell cigarettes?"

"No, I don't."

"O.K., thank-you very much."

"Right," he said, and returned to his office.

THE DECISION TO RETIRE

Friday, November 9, 2007. I felt the squeeze between a rock and a hard place and therefore, I gave serious thought to retirement. I had four reasons for getting out on the exact day of my thirtieth year in Alcatraz. The reasons were, in order of importance:

Focus groups. I did not want to sit in conference rooms, picking up the lice from chairs, listening to obnoxious humor, and getting insulted under the guise of folksy conversation.

Nelson was out of control and he intimidated me. I was afraid to sit in my office after he came to work in the morning.

I could not breathe in my cubicle after 6:30 AM because of what my supervisor thought was the smell of breakfast.

Commuting in a New York City subway was hell, the passengers were animals, and the trains were delayed on a daily basis, either because of a police investigation or signal problems.

Monday was Veteran's Day and so I had a three day weekend to think about it. Because I was aware of how much I dreaded going back to work Tuesday morning, I knew that it would be best to hand in my papers and cut the umbilical cord as quickly as possible.

On Tuesday, November 13, 2007, I mailed my papers to Washington, DC in time for the afternoon pickup by the post office. I did not tell my supervisor that I was retiring. I did not want to talk to him and I figured that the managers in Washington would tell him. I figured wrong.

Everything was somewhat surreal after that. It was hard to believe that after 30 years I would have a new life and I would be out from under the bus. By mid-December I started to panic about the fact that my apartment was not livable: I needed a telephone so that I could purchase my Treasury bills from the Federal Reserve Bank and fine tune my federal tax withholding with OPM; I needed a computer so that I could write books, and along with it, peripherals and supplies, such as a printer, ink cartridges, printer paper, writing pads, pens, mailing envelopes, and blank CDs so that I could mail my manuscripts to publishers on CD. I needed to reopen my account with Con Ed because I needed electricity to run my computer and printer. I needed a refrigerator because I was ready to live like a human being and stop going on safaris.

I arrived at work at 6 AM and called Con Ed. The representative reopened my account for me. The second thing that I did was to call my landlord and leave a message on his answering machine: I requested a refrigerator, one that was used, so that he would not increase my rent. When I came home that afternoon, my midget super was waiting for me in the driveway.

"Maria," he said with an Egyptian accent, "I have your refrigerator."

"Oh, thank-you," I replied, "Send it right up."

When the handyman delivered the refrigerator, he discovered that the outlet did not work by the hole in the wall that was specially shaped to hold a refrigerator.

"You don't have electricity?" he asked.

"I do, but I had water coming down from the ceiling last year and it probably knocked out the power. See? The kitchen light does not work, either. However, the outlets by the sink work just fine." So far, so good, I thought.

The handyman attempted to insert the plug into the outlet by the kitchen sink, but discovered that it did not penetrate the holes. He glanced down at the plug in his hand, raised his head, and gaped fixedly at the outlet. Then he realized that the outlet had two holes, but the plug had three prongs. The wall had no third hole to accommodate the grounding prong. He narrowed his eyes, pursed his lips, and nodded vigorously as if to say that he knew exactly what to do.

"What here, don't move," he instructed and vanished out the front door. I thought that he was going to bring back an adaptor. I figured wrong.

Minutes later he reappeared bearing a wide smile and a pair of pliers. He grabbed the third prong with the pliers and forcefully twisted it until it became disengaged from the plastic plug. Then he picked it off the tip of the pliers and cast it down the hallway where it snapped loudly off the bathtub. He thrust the plug into the wall and the refrigerator started to purr. Laughing, he disappeared out of the door. He's a one minute manager, I thought. Is that legal? Who knows?

The following morning at 6 AM I decided that I would take care of the next chore: I needed a telephone and telephone service. At lunch time I purchased a beautiful white telephone with very large buttons that are easy to see. I returned to my office with my new treasure and looked around for someone with whom to share my joy.

I walked around the hallway and found one of my friends sitting at her desk.

"Guess what!"

"What!" she asked with great enthusiasm. She was just opening the plastic clamshell that was holding a Caesar's salad

"I bought a new phone. Wanna see?"

"Sure!" she exclaimed cheerfully as she lifted a piece of tomato to her mouth. I opened the box and set it on her desk.

"I think that white is very pretty and it has large numbers that are easy to see." My colleague was very bright and suspected that something had changed or was just about to change in my life.

"Why did you buy this all of the sudden? Are you retiring?"

"Uh, well, I don't know what I am going to do from one minute to the next." That certainly was the truth.

"Well, in case you decide to do it, you are prepared. Enjoy your new phone in good health!"

"Thank-you." I realized then that if I were to walk around the floor and show this around, people would start to get suspicious and ask questions. I really wanted to just disappear out of the door one day.

I returned to my cubicle and looked at the phone. Then I thought of my GS-14. I really had to tell her that I was retiring. If I didn't, she might take it personally and I didn't want to hurt her feelings.

I stood in the doorframe as she worked at the computer until she looked up.

"Yes?" she asked.

"Uh, well, I don't know how to articulate the words..." She waited patiently. "I have given it a lot of thought, and I may retire at the end of the year for four good reasons. First, I don't want to be in a Focus group; secondly, I can't stand Nelson and he scares me when he slams shut his metal clothing closet; thirdly, I can't breathe in my office after 6:30 AM because I have poison gas coming through the air vents; and fourthly, commuting is hell and the subways are not fit for a herd of swine." She nodded her head affirmatively.

"Well, you don't have to make up your mind right away, but thank-you for giving me a heads up."

"I just bought a new telephone. Wanna see?"

"Sure." She moved her work aside and created an open space on the desk. I opened the box and removed the new phone. She raised the receiver and then returned it to its cradle. The she pressed the large buttons.

"This is great because it is easy to see the buttons. I like this very much. How much did it cost?" I told her and included the tax. "That is very reasonable. I especially like the size of the buttons. I think that this is a very wise purchase. And it will last a long time. Just do me a favor, will you? Let me know when you have made up your mind about retiring." I fell silent. I thought that she had understood. I surmised that I should make myself a little more clear.

"Well, while an argument can be made that I don't know what I am going to do from one moment to the next, I think that it is safe to say that my life is a living hell because of the four reasons that I listed, the Focus group, Nelson, the cigarette smoke that asphyxiates me, and the subways. I believe that I am going to retire at the end of the year."

"O.K., well, you still have time to change your mind. Let me know what you decide." I walked out of her office, new phone in hand, with the uncomfortable feeling that she did not believe for one moment that I would actually go through with it.

I sat in my cubicle and called the telephone company to open a new account. The representative told me that I would have to be home the next day to let the telephone man into the apartment. I used eight hours annual leave and got my new phone service. The telephone man replaced the rusty jack on the wall and I had a dial tone.

My final week in Customs was positively surreal. I was all set to retire on Thursday, January 3, 2008. By Monday, December 31, 2007, reality was beginning to set in: my life would radically change after 30 years of abject misery, sorrow, and continual aggravation. Well, I thought, I had taken care of business: I had electricity, a refrigerator, and a telephone. I needed to purchase a computer and printer next. Then I heard a tap, tap, tap! Startled, I looked up. It was my GS-14. She looked serious. But then again, she usually did.

"May I see you in my office for a moment?"

"Sure," I replied reflexively. I wondered what I had done now.

She closed the door behind me and asked, "Did you tell the supervisor?"

"Ah...no, not yet. I believe that the managers must have told him in Washington either on the phone or by email..."

"Would you mention it to him because I am going to need a replacement as soon as possible."

"O.K., I'll tell him right now." She looked relieved. Ten seconds later I was knocking on his door. I told him. He looked surprised.

"I had no idea!" he cried.

"I thought that the managers told you from Washington."

"No, they are not allowed to do that." There was a big silence. It appeared that I had to draw the reason out of him.

"Is it because people change their minds all the time and take their papers back?" He nodded in the affirmative. "And that after they do, their managers hold it against them that they want to get out? Is that why it is the employee's responsibility to tell his supervisor?" Again, he nodded in the affirmative.

"Yes, that's right. I did not get a sheet from you about your retirement present."

"That is because I sent an email to the personnel office in Washington and told them that I do not want a retirement present, that I just want to leave quietly. They said that I am not required to submit the form. I don't have to get a present if I don't want one."

"O.K., I just have a few forms that I need for you to fill out. I need them as soon as possible."

"I'll fill them out right now."

I returned to my office and completed the paperwork. I glanced at my Casio watch. It was December 31. I couldn't wait until New Year's was over and then the two days after that. I wanted it to be Friday morning, January 4, so that I would not have to get out of bed in the morning and come into the city to face these people ever again.

(Endnotes)

1 Frederick Engels, *Anti-Dühring*, Part 3, Chapter 2 (Peking: Foreign Languages Press, 1976), 363. In this work, Engels ridicules the positivist philosophy of Eugen Karl Dühring (1833–1921), German economist, socialist, and university professor.

They riddled all of the aluminum foil in my home with thousands of pinholes as an aircraft hovered noisily overhead, even as I lay underneath it. Imagine all of the radiation that they administered to my body. I have since noticed that in the early morning hours, long streaks of white chemtrails appear over Rego Park; then they rapidly dissipate into cloud covering over which military planes, with their distinctive whistle, fly all day and all night; the electromagnetic harassment never ceases; occasionally we see a black helicopter.

Chapter Twelve

The Reign of Terror of King George II: The Eighth Year (2008)

DOWN WITH BIG BROTHER
DOWN WITH BIG BROTHER
DOWN WITH BIG BROTHER
DOWN WITH BIG BROTHER
DOWN WITH BIG BROTHER[1]
—George Orwell, *1984* (1949)

On Thursday, January 3, 2008, my last day of work, at exactly 1 PM I knocked on my supervisor's door. He was sitting at his desk with an employee who had a cleaning compulsion and whose rolled up shirt sleeves revealed arms that were red from alcohol and cleaning solution. The two were waiting to collect my little plastic cards and process a form for each one. First, I produced my photo ID and placed it squarely in the middle of the supervisor's desk; then my swipe card for the door and elevator bank; then my government credit card; and finally, my Customs badge.

My supervisor smiled warmly and asked if I would like to have my Customs badge laminated in a cube so that I could keep it as a souvenir and have a nice paperweight.

"No," I replied coldly. He felt the chill in the room.

The assistant filled out a form for each item that I was handing in. Then he wrapped each article with its form and put a rubber band around it. Thus he made four packets. The procedure took five minutes.

One of the GS-14s was walking through the hallway and I asked her if I could speak to her for a moment because I had something to tell her. She said, "Sure," and we entered her office. In a very low voice I apologized for not telling her sooner, but I was retiring, and I came to say goodbye. She opened her eyes wide in surprise. At that moment her GS-12 walked past the doorframe and I waved to her to come inside and close the door. I spoke to them both briefly for about five minutes.

"How does it feel?" the GS-14 asked with wonder.

"Yeah, what's it like?" asked the GS-12 with great curiosity. The answer was automatic.

"I feel like my attorney just sprung me on a plea deal." They laughed. That was a good one, they said. But I was not kidding. Then I walked out through the glass doors one last time, never to return for a visit or call on the phone again.

(Endnotes)
1   George Orwell, *1984*, afterword by Erich Fromm (New York: Signet Classics, 1977), 18.

Conclusion

According to the capabilities of the reader, books have their destinies.[1]

      —Terentanius Maurus, *On Letters, Syllables, Feet, and Meters* (2nd century AD)

During World War II Germany attacked its own citizens and blamed it on Poland. The false flag operation was used as propaganda to justify crossing its border and attacking its neighbor. This tactic was exposed during the Nuremburg trials. On August 22, 1939, Hitler stated, "I will provide a propagandistic *casus belli* [opportunity for war]. Its credibility doesn't matter. The victor will not be asked whether he told the truth."[2] Subsequently, Germany selected victims from a concentration camp, dressed them up as Polish soldiers, killed them with poison, placed their bodies near the Polish border, shot them, and then took credit for preempting an invasion. Roger Manvell and Heinrich Fraenkel, in *Heinrich Himmler: The Sinister Life of the Head of the SS and Gestapo*, advise:

> The general plan to stage faked incidents along the Polish frontier in order to provide suitable provocation for the invading forces had already been in Himmler's mind...It was part of the plan that a number of prisoners from concentration camps should be dressed in Polish uniforms, given fatal injections by a doctor and at the right moment shot at...Their bodies were to be photographed for publication and show to press representatives..."[3]

Moreover, this was one staged attack among several: similar false flag operations were conducted at the German radio station Sender Gleiwitz, a German customs station at Hochlinden, a forest service station in Pitschen, and Kreuzberg.

In the same vein, the evidence is overwhelming that 9/11 was also a false flag operation, a key chess move in the globalists' quest for world empire. 9/11 had far reaching consequences and succeeded in fulfilling its purpose: the Constitution was destroyed; the government got the right to enter our homes when we are away; read our snail mail and e-mail; sift telephone conversations through the DARPA computer looking for key words and then recall specific communications at a later date; listen to conversations on the street from one of the 60,000 white box trucks that came north after 9/11; image inside our homes and vehicles from aircraft flying at a distance, discern us from our furniture by the motion of our heartbeats and breathing, and then strike us with forceful blows; monitor us from driverless cars; subject us to sleep deprivation by assaulting us with EMs intermittently throughout the night; experiment with unsuspecting, non-consenting federal employees and soldiers. What is the next major chess move? It is all outlined in Brzezinski's seminal playbook of 1970, *Between Two Ages: America's Role in the Technetronic Era*:

- "...technology and especially electronics—hence my neologism "technetronic"—are increasingly becoming the principal determinants of social change, altering the mores, the social structure, the values, and the global outlook of society."[4]
- "Gordon J.F. MacDonald, a geophysicist specializing in problems of warfare, has written that accurately timed, artificially excited electronic strokes "could lead to a pattern of oscil-

lations that produce relatively high power levels over certain regions of the earth...In this way, one could develop a system that would seriously impair the brain performance of very large populations in selected regions over an extended period...the technology permitting such use will very probably develop within the next few decades."[5]

• "Today we are...witnessing the emergence of transnational elites, but now they are composed of international businessmen, scholars, professional men, and public officials."[6]

• "Persisting social crisis, the emergence of a charismatic personality, and the exploitation of mass media to obtain public confidence would be the steppingstones in the piecemeal transformation of the United States into a highly controlled society..."[7]

Brzezinski predicted these events back in 1970; they have all materialized. Now what are we going to do? If anyone is going to fight the control of the masses via electronics, it will be those who refuse to purchase cellphones and hold them next to their brains all day: someone must retain the healthy functioning of his mind.

Next, it is imperative that adults and children spend their time reading books, rather than staring at text on a computer's monitor: the brain processes information very differently when one is reading text in a book, rather than on a computer screen. My dentist mentioned this fact to me. It is true: I have been staring at a monitor since Customs put a dumb terminal in my office in the 1980s, and I find it difficult these days to read books and process the information on pages. When I switch from the computer to a printed book, I need time to become acclimated to absorb information from the written page again. This is very scary: all we have is our brain; if we lose the ability to read a book, we lose control over ourselves; someone else will control us. Next:

Taxpayers Must Stop Funding Intelligence Agencies

Your money is being spent on black ops projects in which Nazis are experimenting with the bodies and minds of unwary American citizens. Do you see now what a chance you take when you land a federal civil service job? If you are a person living alone, you would do well to stay away from public service. Have you counted all of the deaths, sicknesses, and mental disorders in this book? I have: 71.4% of the 56 people who died or got sick fall into one or more of the following categories: single, Jewish, or handicapped. These demographics are reminiscent of Nazi Germany. And this is just Customs in New York. I have a neighbor who works for another agency in 26 Federal Plaza in Manhattan and when I raised the subject, she enumerated a wide gamut of mysterious deaths and psychiatric disorders that have been manifested at her worksite. My experiences getting shocked in my home every night, my neighbors' experiences with similar harassment, and the deaths and illnesses in Customs and in agencies in 26 Federal Plaza, all cry out for a Congressional investigation!

Both the log that I kept and the testimony of my neighbors reveal several crucial points:

- The assaults originate from military aircraft because they continue, unabated, during snowstorms, rain, and thunderstorms when commercial flights are grounded.
- One of the twin brothers that I met in the Rego Park Library mentioned that "a lot of old women get it" in his building and that they have gashes in their walls from the ceiling to the floor. This indicates that the Pentagon is targeting people who live alone.

- One of these twin brothers demonstrated how his body involuntary jerks when he is targeted with a radio wave. Other Queens residents corroborate this. It is always accompanied or preceded by the sound of aircraft.
- The victims are single men and women, senior citizens, Jews, handicapped, and twins. Is this reminiscent of Nazi Germany?

Do you see that the Pentagon is using technology that was made for Iraq and Afghanistan on domestic soil? In August 2008 a Pentagon website offered a huge contract to any firm that could produce planes equipped with high-powered microwave and laser pulse weaponry within six months. The posting emphasized that the planes had to be delivered in 6 months. When I showed the ad to one of my neighbors, he drew the conclusion that the U.S. was going to invade Iran in February 2009. Wrong! February came and went and we did not invade Iran. The Pentagon is using these planes here! In Queens! It is imaging inside our homes and delivering electrical shocks and forceful blows from unmanned drones, via a network, from a remote location, made in real time. Read *Air Force 2025*, available on the Internet, and find out what the Air Force had predicted back in 1996! Retrieve some of the documents listed in our endnotes from the Internet. Take a look at David A. Fulghum's articles in *Aviation Week & Space Technology* and learn about what an aircraft, flying at a distance, can see and do through barriers! Read the second and third books of this *Microwave* trilogy, *Microwave War: The Government's Preparation for the Police State and Extension of Empire* and *The Science behind Microwave War*. The second volume reveals the discoveries that I made in Queens after I retired: my neighbors are experiencing electronic harassment; the technology is being used to identify gangs such as MS-13, undocumented workers, and illegal activities being conducted behind brick walls. Senior citizens are subjected to a moving wave over the lymph nodes night after night and subsequently they get cancer of the lymph nodes! The third tome documents aviation and military articles, available online, in which the Pentagon actually brags about what it can do.

Don't you think that the time has come to totally defund black ops and the 24 intelligence agencies? Isn't it time to stop financing the Nazis in the NSA who bugged the Vodaphones in Greece and hung the Greek software engineer who made the discovery from the ceiling? His body was discovered on March 9, 2005. Sixteen months later an Italian head of security at a telecommunications firm was also found dead, his body thrown over a freeway overpass. He had discovered extensive spyware at his firm in Italy. This is what happens when a country has 24 intelligence agencies with unlimited resources and no oversight.

And what is to become of me? I just moved my bed from the floor in the hallway back onto the box spring in the bedroom. Last night my entire body suddenly involuntarily jerked for one second as an aircraft hovered continually over my building. I wrote this book to warn people. Books have their destinies.

(Endnotes)

1   "Pro captu lectoris habent sua fata libelli." Terentianvs Mavrvs, *De litteris syllabis pedibvs et metris e recensione et cvm notis Lavrentii Santenii*, verse 1286 (Utrecht, Netherlands: Traiechti ad Rhenvm e typographia I. Altheer; London: Apud H. Bohm, 1825), 57.

2   Bradley Lightbody, *The Second World War: Ambitions to Nemesis* (New York and London: Routledge, 2004), 39.

3   Roger Manvell and Heinrich Fraenkel, *Heinrich Himmler: The Sinister Life of the Head of the SS and Gestapo* (London: Greenhill Books/ Lionel Leventhal Ltd, 2007), 76.

4   Zbigniew Brzezinski, *Between Two Ages: America's Role in the Technetronic Era* (New York: The Viking Press, 1970), 5.

5   Ibid., 28. Brzezinski cites Gordon J.F. MacDonald, "How to

Wreck the Environment," in Nigel Calder, ed., *Unless Peace Comes; A Scientific Forecast of New Weapons* (New York: The Viking Press, 1968), 181.

6   Ibid., 29.

7   Ibid., 97.

I tried sleeping in the hallway with aluminum foil first on one side, then on both sides, then with an aluminum tarp over the blanket. They perforated all of it and delivered an electrical shock to my brain and heart, even during snowstorms when commercial traffic was cancelled; that is how I know that it was done by military aircraft.

Timeline

- 1887 – Nikola Tesla creates earthquake in NYC with resonance device.

- 1940 – Resonance causes collapse of Tacoma Narrows Bridge.

- 1943 – Tesla is found dead in Hotel New Yorker; little black book marked "Government" and technical papers are missing.

- 1949 – Guy Obelensky replicates a Nazi acoustic device that delivers a blow with a sonic wave.

- 1951 – Andrei Sakharov discovers way to generate EMP without a nuclear detonation.

- 1958 – G. Patrick Flanagan invents the Neurophone®, a device that permits humans to hear without the benefit of the ear; this brain entrainment device moves the brain into any state desired.

- 1960–1978 – USSR bombards US embassy in Moscow with electromagnetic waves to ascertain physiological effects.

- 1962 – Pandora Project: US discovers incoming RF waves at the Moscow embassy; CIA allows experiment to continue to profit from it. 3 American ambassadors will die of radiation-related illnesses.
  - Starfish Prime: US creates a new radiation belt 750 miles in depth with nu-clear detonation in near space. K Project: USSR conducts 3 tests that generate EMP.

- 1965 – Victor Sedletsky tests new weapon directing RF at the body.
  - My father and I hear a monosyllabic human sound, "Aaargh," erupt in midair over the kitchen table in the Bronx; I hear it again on another occasion.

- 1966–1972 – Operation Popeye: weather control is used in Vietnam war to extend monsoon season, increase mud on the Ho Chi Minh Trail, and restrict enemy movement.

- 1968 – Gordon J.F. MacDonald advises that extremely low frequency (ELF) waves impair brain performance, that this has military applications and that in covert situations, entire populations could be attacked and not know it.

- 1970 – Pentagon discloses interest in developing ethnic weapons designed to kill certain races.

- 1971 – Biaxial Shock Test Machine (BSTM) is installed for US Army Construction Engineering Research Laboratory (USAC-ERL): it is a shake table that uses resonance to biaxially shake and test the tolerance of equipment in Anti-Ballistic Missile System.

- 1972 – Former Ambassador to USSR, Llewellyn Thompson, dies of cancer at age 67.

- 1973 – William Ross Adey, who had worked on CIA's Pandora Project, conditions cats to behave a certain way by bombarding their brains with EMs; the learned behavior continues for months after EMs stop.
    - R. Wever alters natural sleep cycles in humans by bombarding them with EMs.

- 1974 – Henry Kissinger orders the assassination of Archbishop Makarios in 3 documents.
    - The CIA stages a false flag coup in Cyprus over two waves, ethnically cleansing 160,000 Greek Cypriots from 37% of the island; 50,000 Turks move into the homes of Greek Cypriots, who are forced to abandon them. I lose the house and property that I inherited from my father; the Turks force my elderly uncle to sleep out in the cold and he dies.
    - Former Ambassador to USSR, Charles Bohlen, dies of cancer at age 69.

- 1976 – US Ambassador to USSR, Walter Stoessel, develops rare blood disease similar to leukemia, headaches, and bleeding of the eyes.

  - The UN condemns weather control for hostile purposes.

- 1978 – I am hired as a Customs Aide at JFK; I transfer to the World Trade Center. It was just prior to my hiring that an employee had been dismissed because he pretended to shoot people with an imaginary gun and then cry real tears.

  - Deafening crackles snap against metal cabinets in empty rooms both at JFK and WTC adjacent to where I was sitting on a daily basis. Lights are found turned on in offices upon arrival in the morning.

  - At WTC several employees compulsively talk to themselves and smoke. Their compulsivity makes them excellent employees, as they scour the minutiae of documents, looking to collect every last dollar in duty; they arrive and depart with clockwork precision. They can be relied up to be the perfect employee.

- 1979 – Adey advises that the brain tissue irradiated with EMs releases calcium ions that interfere with brain function; EMs cause confusion and disorientation in humans and animals. Adey warns of dangers of radiation from mobile phones.

  - I am promoted. I set out to save my money.

- 1980 – Secretary contracts lupus and is forced to retire.

  - Several Customs employees are arrested for graft and demanding kickbacks from importers and brokers.
  - Psyops: lights are discovered turned on in offices upon arrival; cigarette ashes are strewn across rugs; cabinets are left open; Customs samples are in disarray.
  - Cleverest psyop: heavy desk is pulled behind locked door and perpetrator exits from ceiling.
  - I meet an employee, single, who will suddenly drop dead after 9/11/01.

- 1981 – I meet 2 clerks, both handicapped and single, who will drop dead in a few years. One will die after his mother dies; the other will die of a heart attack, alone, with a hot iron on her chest to stop the pain.

- 1982 – I meet a clerk, handicapped and single, who talks to herself incessantly; she will sudden drop dead after 9/11/01.

- 1983 – Microwave bombardment of US embassy in Moscow begins again.
  - I meet a clerk, single, who in a few years will go home and drop dead over the bed with her coat still on.

- 1985 – Bernard J. Eastlund applies for a patent for an ionospheric heater; he says that it can generate the power of a nuclear detonation, its purpose is "weather modification," and "a moving plume could also serve as a means for...focusing vast amount of sunlight on selected portions of the earth"; as source material he cites 3 articles on Nikola Tesla.
  - A tornado devastates Rego Park and Forest Hills. NYC is not in a tornado belt.
  - I meet a clerk who will drop dead after 9/11/01.

- 1986 – Former Ambassador to USSR, Walter J. Stoessel Jr., dies of leukemia at age 66.

- 1987 – USSR uses RF weapon to kill a goat 1 km away.
  - The lights are discovered on in offices when employees arrive in the morning.
  - Everyone on the floor contracts a nasty virus in April; people become obsessed with losing weight.
  - Subsequently I develop an OCD with saving money and I save $1 million by eating from garbage and cutting electricity, telephone and gas.
  - Water pipes burst and boiler breaks on the average of 3 times per week in my apartment building; pipe gushes water from ceiling of basement.
  - Steam pipes crack in my bathroom, bedroom, and living room. Powerful sound and orange light burst forth from them when boiler kicks on every 4 hours. I cover bathroom pipe with metal and wood to protect myself; have super remove bedroom radiator and seal pipe with cap; leave living room radiator turned off. Apartment fills with carbon monoxide from bathroom pipe and I must open windows.

- I go on crash diet and reduce to 118 lb in a few months. My coworkers go on diet and form a Weight Watchers® club. Suddenly we all become obsessed with the way we look.

- 1988 – Montreal earthquake; my apartment shakes; radio reports that chandeliers are swinging back and forth in Forest Hills.
    - I start looking for food in garbage to save money. I purchase phone to get one less bill in the mail. Then I terminate phone account.

- 1989   ELF waves detected immediately prior to earthquakes in Japan and California.
    - I collect soda cans and make $6 per day.

- 1990 – DARPA's HAARP project is built; it regularly shoots EM waves into the ionosphere.

- 1991 – Senators John Towers and John Heinz die in airplane crashes one day of each other. They were on a blue ribbon panel investigating Iran-Contra. The reason Ollie North was never found guilty was because no one had investigated his role.
    - Navy generates nonnuclear EMP bombs in Gulf War.
    - Dr. Martin L. Lenhardt publishes a paper explaining how Flanagan's Neurophone® works: humans detect ultrasonic sound through the skin, bones, and body liquids; the saccule in the inner ear, associated with balance, also detects ultrasonic sound.
    - Customs employee dies of ovarian cancer at age 41. She is replaced by a woman who contracts pancreatic cancer; another in that room is transferred to San Francisco and dies.
    - I get a detail on another floor. The top executive there will contract cancer and die after 9/11/01; a youthful-looking man will age rapidly; a bright woman will have trouble remembering.
    - Psyops: money disappears from the safe.

- 1992 – I terminate account with electric company to save money.
    - My coworker compulsively opens and slams the metal cabinets in office; runs around the room; collects garbage and stacks it high; talks without ceasing.

311

- Psyops: I discover a trail of semen on the floor behind my desk. A few months later I find swastikas and smile faces etched in dust all around my desk; a sticker of an American flag appears on the side of my desk.

- 1993 – Vista Hotel (3 WTC) is bombed by blind sheik who gets his dynamite from the FBI.
  - FBI plane ignites fire in Koresh compound in Waco, TX, via microwave pulse: FBI infrared aerial surveillance video shows rapid flashes of light coming from plane moments before the interior of the compound bursts into flames.
  - During the 1990s 4 people die on the same floor around the same time: 2 drop dead over the weekend; 2 get cancer and die. The boss tests vents for Legionnaire's Disease, but the lab report is negative. Another man becomes morbidly obese, although he was slim when I worked with him in 1978.

- 1994 – Earthquake in Bolivia originates 600 km beneath earth's surface, 24 times deeper than normal.

- 1995 – The annual meeting of 4-star Air Force generals approves a project called, "Put the Enemy to Sleep/Keep the Enemy from Sleeping," in which acoustics, microwave, and brain wave manipulation are used to alter sleep patterns.
  - US Army Corps of Engineers builds the Triaxial Earthquake and Shock Simulator (TESS), a shake table upgraded to triaxial capability: it uses resonance to produce earthquake simulations to test survivability of military equipment, structures and large payloads.
  - Scientific paper shows that EMs break up single strands of DNA in brains of rats.
  - I meet a secretary, a single woman, who will contract cancer and die as soon as she retires.
  - I move into a new office: snaps and crackles course across the synthetic woven modular walls, indicating a highly charged electronic environment. The employee on the other side obsessively rips paper from morning until night.

- 1996 – Air Force 2025 discloses that heating the ionosphere holds great potential for weather modification; it contains pictures of towers, identical to HAARP ; the heaters bring ions together to do more than enhance or disrupt communication: they create torrential rains or extreme drought, wiping out entire populations.

- Scientific paper shows that EMs break up single- and double DNA strands in brains of rats.
- I move into new office space: bursts of electrical energy snap violently across the acrylic fabric on walls. A lot of disease develops in this area: a man contracts colon cancer and requires a colostomy; a woman begins eating obsessively and cannot stop, she cannot remain awake at her desk, and ultimately dies of obesity; a woman develops progressive supranuclear palsy (PSP), a brain disorder, and dies in a nursing home. PSP has come to be related to disturbances in calcium homeostasis in the brain; in 1973 Adey found that cats subjected to EM bombardment suffered changes in the binding of calcium in their brains.
- I move into another office in which I hear snaps against the metal bookcases; the 2 people in their have suffered severe personality changes since I met them in 1978: they are hostile, talk to themselves, and one is violent.

- 1997 – Pentagon discloses newest bio-weapons: "confusion weaponry" that focuses EMs on the target, incapacitates the nervous system remotely, knocks people down at a distance.
  - Secretary of Defense William Cohen warns that terrorists could alter weather, set off earthquakes and volcanoes remotely with EM waves.

- 1998 – The US treks to the Arctic Tundra to dig up corpses of people who died from the 1918 Spanish flu (H1N1) and harvest DNA. Subsequently, scientists sequence the 8 viral gene segments and reverse engineer the flu.

- 1999 – I move into another office. The electronic phenomena in there are the most severe to date: thunderous lashes crash into metal cabinets.
  - Psyops: one morning I discover that the wall is slashed behind my chair where my head would be if I were sitting there. Xs are dabbed in dirty liquid all around my walls; dirty liquid poured on rug.

- 2000 – Governor Mel Carnahan of Missouri dies in an airplane crash. He was running for Senate as a Democrat and was ahead in the polls. His death contributes to Republican control of the Senate.

- 2001 – Psyops at home: the man who lives next door plays loud music all night long; stampedes into the living room every time I enter the bathroom as if racing to view a monitor; climbs my fire escape and tries to enter my apartment, but I scream at the window and he runs back down the fire escape; thereafter, he climbs his own fire escape every weekend and vigorously shakes the gates back and forth; he stands on the sidewalk with all of his car doors open; the landlord evicts him; he leaves a 27" TV in the living room when he moves.

  - 9/11: Several hijackers have addresses and diplomas from US military bases, i.e., Mohammed Atta and Abdulaziz Alomari graduated from US International Officers School at Maxwell Air Force Base.
  - I run out of the Customhouse (6 WTC) at 8:46 AM; discover that the CIA moved its cabinets out of 7 WTC at 6 AM!
  - Passenger aboard Flight 93 on cellphone reports bright flash of light outside window seconds before aircraft crashes, providing evidence that plane was felled by an EMP attack.
  - I walk across the 59th Street Bridge. When I get home I practice speaking French with my CDs for 3 hours before I turn on the radio. I have become very disciplined and focused, dutifully practicing my lessons even though the WTC just collapsed!
  - We move to a new site in October. I start getting pinpricks and burn marks in my arms and legs as I sit at my new desk. This is something new: I did not get pinpricks in the WTC.
  - Loud crackles reverberate from cabinetry in empty cubicles at 6 AM.
  - 60,000 white box trucks come to the northeast after 9/11.

- 2002 – Senator Paul Wellstone dies in an airplane crash. His death and that of Mel Carnahan change the balance of power in the Senate.

- DARPA announces Grand Challenge for auto teams that can get a driverless car to navigate southwestern US.
- Planes change their descent path to LaGuardia and begin flying directly over my building for the first time. This is the first indication that Rego Park has become a DARPA test site.
- I start getting pinpricks to the skin as I sit in my apartment.
- Employee about 39 years of age has aged rapidly and looks and dodders like an 80-year old.

- 2003 – Earthquake in Bam, Iran kills 26,271 people and injures 30,000.
    - Prince Charles visits Serbian Orthodox Chilandar Monastery on Mount Athos in Greece. In 6 months this monastery will be devastated by fire.
    - The Air Force spends more than $100 million to investigate bio-weapons or beams that can disrupt the electrochemical balance and electrical impulses of the nervous system and thus alter behavior and body functions.
    - Scientific paper shows that mobile phone radiation breaks up the DNA in brains of rats.
    - We move into second temporary office while permanent office is built. There I hear loud snaps off of metal cabinetry in unoccupied offices at 6 AM.
    - I get burn marks to my skin at work and at home. Then it starts happening on the street, in the subway, in stores.
    - A soft spoken coworker metamorphoses into raving lunatic who forcefully throws chairs across the room, pulls open doors as if to break the wall behind them, and utters strange, low gurgling sounds.
    - Psyops: $5 is stolen from desk drawer in next cubicle. A report binder is stolen from me. Employees discover objects in strange places, i.e., underneath desk, upside down and stuffed in pencil box.
    - We move into permanent offices, but my section remains unlit for several weeks. Work is being done in the ceiling.
    - I notice the proliferation of wall hangings and tell management that the paintings are sold on the Internet as surveillance tools. The boss denies that we are being watched. I tell all my friends that the pictures are bugged and I point out a tiny glass fisheye protruding from one particular

painting at the exit. I explain that we make ideal lab mice because they can watch us for 30 years and we do not quit.

- Then I start getting pummeled with electrical shocks all over my body at work. I talk to people in the elevators and learn that none of this is happening on other floors occupied by private industry.

- Then there are more psyops: I hear keys drop in the bathroom when I am alone there. An employee informs me that he has heard high heels shoes outside shower stall, even though he was the only one there.

- A thud starts to drop on my comforter every night and wakes me up. It disrupts my sleep cycle and energizes me. I listen to the BBC and suffer from sleep deprivation.

- I am awakened by the sensation of a powerful wind blowing across my face and hair.

- 2004 – A fire erupts in Serbian Orthodox monastery on Mount Athos in Greece. Prince Charles sends his condolences to the Serbian Embassy in Great Britain. The fire must have been caused by laser to send the Serbs a message not to interfere with Kosovar sovereignty or the establishment of the New World Order in Eastern Europe.

  - The school massacre in Beslan, Russia, occurs during the week of the Republican National Convention. The ratings of candidate Bush temporarily go up, as is the case when Americans are scared. This rise is helpful to the RNC, as the race is close. Putin consolidates power.

  - On September 11, 2004 the Patriarch of Alexandria dies in a helicopter crash in the Aegean. He had written George Bush a letter pleading with him not to invade Iraq because it would disturb the fragile peace between Christians and Muslims. There are many prominent clerics in the helicopter and the entire Orthodox hierarchy in Africa is eviscerated that morning.

  - DoD offers $1 million prize to first team that can get a driverless car to travel 142 miles from Barstow, CA to Primm, NV. No one wins the prize.

  - Roof collapses at airport in Paris; the roof was new; Jacques Chirac had blocked Rumsfeld's plan to send AWAC surveillance aircraft and Patriot missiles to Turkey.

  - Scientific paper shows that exposure to mobile phone radiation for more than 10 years increases risk of brain cancer.

- I move to an office down the hall. The morning I move in, the lights are turned off every morning for 2 weeks, as work is performed in the ceiling. They worked just fine before I moved in.

- I occupy the cubicle of a Customs employee who has just died at age 54 of liver cancer that has metastasized from his pancreas. The supervisors attend 3 funerals: his, that of a woman who dies of obesity, and that of a man who dies of kidney failure at age 52. This last person was doing fine for a while and returned to work, but suddenly his body rejected the kidney—perhaps from all the radiation he was getting at work. Another man, single and handicapped, develops intestinal cancer and has to have a portion of his intestine removed. Another woman, handicapped with cerebral palsy, falls out of her chair one day for no apparent reason and hurts herself; she retires on disability.

- An employee compulsively feeds his coworkers.

- Cigarette smoke comes from the air vent directly over my head; the people in the other cubicles do not get it. My supervisor is disinterested.

- I find a cat and give it to a senior citizen who lives across the street. She informs me of the electronic phenomena that she is experiencing in her top floor apartment. That is when I learn that others in Rego Park are experiencing what I am getting.

- Crackling sounds materialize in midair over my bed. A few days later little bursts of energy strike my arms and legs as I walk around my apartment.

- The senior tells me that someone removed the doorknob from her apartment and left it on the floor in the hallway; a metal bar that she had placed in the window to keep it open was knocked out and sent flying across the room; objects roll off high shelves, tables and dressers by themselves and she finds them on the floor in the morning; her cat jumps in the air and tries to grasp something that is not there.

- 2005 – 7/7: London Underground bombings occur at stations where Visor Consultants, a firm that trains the FBI at Quantico, is staging mock drills. Visor's Managing Director Peter Power is on the BBC that morning and says he is surprised that a real terroristic attack has occurred at the same stations where he is having a drill.

- Helios Flight HCY 522 crashes on the 31st anniversary of CIA-sponsored coup in Cyprus; all 121 people on board are killed.
- The NSA bugs the phones in Greece and hangs the man who made the discovery from the ceiling.
- Wall collapses on the Henry Hudson Parkway.
- DoD increases Grand Challenge prize to $2 million. Five teams win the prize.
- Pentagon concedes that it can project a plasma (high-powered microwave or HPM) and see through barriers into buildings and vehicles; this is being fit onto manned and unmanned aircraft; it can stage nonlethal attacks, shut down TV and radio stations, stop cars; it can destroy the electronics components and circuitry in any machine from a distance.
- Scientific paper shows that cellphones increase risk of brain tumor in rural areas where towers are spaced further apart and signals are stronger.
- I learn that Customs had once opened the diplomatic mailbags at JFK Mail Branch and discovered monetary certificates with swastikas at the top, underwritten by a major financial institution.
- I start screaming, "George Bush is a Nazi," in the streets of Rego Park as I walk to the subway in the morning, and make announcements about the Nazi certificates on subway platforms and inside trains.
- I see several driverless cars in the streets of Rego Park each day. A pedestrian is killed on Queens Boulevard and when the cops open the car, they discover that there is no one inside.
- Employee continues to bring food to work each day and lay out a big spread.
- Nurse is fired from VA hospital for writing a letter to an editor about ending the war in Iraq.
- I change my password in the Customs computer to "1nazi."
- I am followed by a helicopter across the long blocks between avenues in Manhattan. White box trucks stand at every corner around major transportation hubs.
- Electronic doors at work are perpetually jammed, permitting unauthorized entry at night without a swipe card.
- My neighbor sees a blond guy on a stepladder install something in my bedroom window.

- I am awakened every night by a tap at the foot of the bed, then a moving wave traveling from my feet to my neck, and then a strong puff of air against my face. Thereafter, my sleep cycle is altered and I cannot sleep. I listen to the BBC and learn that Chancellor Wolfgang Schüssel of Austria formally opposes the Turkish accession to the EU that Bush is pushing; Germany also recommends "privileged partnership" or less than full membership.

- Everyone on the floor gets a runny nose this winter; the congestion lasts for 2 years; people's doctors tell them that they must have developed allergies. They start spending a fortune on over the counter medications.

- 2006 – There are roofs collapses in Germany and Austria after these countries oppose Turkish admission to EU. Roof collapses in Poland. Explosion severs gas supplies in Georgia. Roof collapses in Moscow. These events occur in a space of 2 months.

  - October surprise: Cory Lidle's plane crashes in a Manhattan high-rise a month before Election Day. The media shows photos and continually reiterates the similarities with 9/11 for a full month.

  - Saddam Hussein is tried in court 2 days before Election Day; his crime is an early one, committed long before Rummy gave him mustard gas, nerve agent, and helicopters. He is executed on December 30, charges for the Kurd massacre are dropped because he is dead, and hence, Rummy is not implicated.

  - The Air Force discloses that it is building small aircraft whose hulls, called "smart skins," take on 3 new functions: sensor, antenna that receives and transmits, and weapon that delivers a stunning blow from a distance. This smart skin permits the unmanned drone to be as small as a missile, fly undetected and invisible to radar, and fire high-power spikes of energy. These drones can fly at altitudes of 65,000–70,000 feet. Britain, Australia, and Italy express interest in directed energy weapons produced with software modification to F-35's electronically scanned array radar.

  - Ohio State University announces radar that can image through walls and identify everything on the other side; it distinguishes humans from inanimate objects by the motion of the heartbeat or breathing; this new radar cannot be detected because unlike its predecessors, it simulates random noise.

- The Pentagon tests its newest aerial weapon in the descent path to LaGuardia: I am sitting at the foot of my bed and the government chips my cranium as a jumbo jet roars overhead; subsequently, a sharp piece of cranium juts up like a toothpick.
- I start getting shocks to my cranium and needle marks to my arms and legs as I sit in my office at work.
- My neighbor hears a powerful strike against her metal roof as an aircraft passes overhead, presumably in its descent path to LaGuardia.
- The radiator breaks in the unoccupied apartment above mine and the water falls through my living room ceiling. My landlord does nothing about it and I live with it for 3 months; then I decide to let the water fall on the floor so that my downstairs neighbors would complain and it would get fixed. Observation: I am become incredibly docile, since I live with the aggravation for 3 months before making a change.
- Early one morning I feel wind against my face and then I receive a violent electrical shock to the brain that causes my head to involuntarily move from left to right.
- I move the bed into the living room, but I get electrobolts to the brain there.
- I move the bed into the kitchen. I get shocks there.
- A coworker obsessively brings food to work and makes noise, making it impossible to concentrate. I sit in the Customs library a lot.
- Customs sends me an email message wanting to know whether I have a cellphone.
- A woman takes a seat right next to me in an otherwise empty subway car, stares at me, and asks me if I have a cellphone.
- I get a sharp pinprick to my back as someone walks behind me on the subway platform with a device in hand.
- I get pinpricks to the arms and legs as white box trucks circle the block.
- I notice that every time I approach a street corner in Rego Park, a white box truck appears in front of me and turns the corner.
- Psyop: I sit down in a folding chair on a corner in Rego Park and talk to a pedestrian. Four cars approach the intersection, stop and remain there for several minutes until the

pedestrian crosses the street. Then the drivers salute each other and step on the gas.

- One night I hear repetitive ping, ping ping, in my sleep. When I awaken it stops. Another night I hear tap, tap, tap against the window; it stops when I awaken.
- Taps and moving waves across the blanket continue nightly, subjecting me to sleep deprivation.
- A cashier in Duane Reade tells me that she started getting pinpricks to her arms recently.
- I am awakened by a deafening burst of sound that explodes in midair next to my ear. Later I learn that this is also happening to a young woman who lives alone across the street.
- A subway passenger tells me that he is awakened by a blast of air in the face when the windows are shut.
- I develop the compulsion to scream "George Bush is a Nazi" to passing cars whose windows are open.
- A pedestrian tells me that he began experiencing the sensation of a bug clawing to his back after he had a cellphone conversation in which his friend told him that he would like to kill George Bush.
- Smoke wafts into my cubicle all morning, forcing me to work elsewhere.
- I start getting daggers into my crown at work, similar to the one I received at home in 2006.
- I get electrobolts to the heart that leave me gasping for air. I always discover broken paint and plaster on the floor behind my bed, indicating an EMP directed at the wall.
- I see 8 or 10 men in overalls walking around the floor at work at 5:45 AM. When I report them to security, the guard is surprised, as he authorized only 2 men to go upstairs.
- Printers start and stop by themselves as I walk down an empty corridor at 6 AM.
- A passenger on the subway, just back from Iraq, shows me an 8" gash on the back of his neck: he was hit with friendly fire after he commented on officers having sex with recruits.
- I purchase a bug detector and discover that all but 2 of the 60 FEMA paintings on the wall are bugged.
- The moving wave across the blanket starts the minute I get in bed and continues until I get up in the morning.

- My eyes turn blood red and blood comes out of my nose. I appear to be bleeding from my bodily orifices like an Ebola victim.

- 2007 – Several hundred fires break out simultaneously in Greece between 6 PM Friday, August 31 and 6 AM Saturday, September 1. The only way that hundreds of fires could erupt overnight is if a laser beam is directed down on vegetation that has been already parched in the daytime sun.
  - Sandstorm in Bam, Iran kills 5, injures 14.
  - Virginia Tech massacre: originally 2 gunmen are seen; the cellphone photos that Cho sends to the press are perfectly centered, indicating that he did not take them himself; there are no road blocks for 2 hours because feds order campus and local police to stand down; he was an excellent marksman even though he had not received training.
  - An underground steam pipe explodes at Grand Central snarling the subway line on the East Side of Manhattan; the next day a signal fire erupts, snarling subway traffic on the West Side. People have to walk home as the entire system is in chaos, reminiscent of 9/11.
  - DARPA holds Urban Challenge, a timed 60-mile race in which driverless cars must negotiate congested urban traffic as they perform military missions. Stanford team's car can navigate city blocks, negotiate 4-way intersections, stop at intersections and wait for other vehicles before proceeding, and pass a stationary car immediately after an intersection.
  - 7 macaque monkeys are injected with the reverse engineered 1918 Spanish flu virus because the government wants to assess its effects on primates. The virus triggers an immune response, the animals' lungs fill with liquid, and they must be euthanized.
  - Employee begins talking gibberish during a big meeting in front of the Commissioner of Customs. On another day the same person is found in the bathroom, staring in the mirror, talking nonsense.
  - Upon arrival in the morning, a coworker violently slams his metal locker and throws objects around his cubicle. People ignore him and their docility is noteworthy.
  - The EEO office shows us a movie about someone who walks around the office, holding a tray full of food, urging his coworkers to take a sample. Are they being sarcastic?

- The violent electronic lashes against metal cabinetry occur seconds apart and continue throughout the day. Employees ignore them, as they wear headphones, walkmen and ipods. No one cares.
- People are continually coughing and blowing their noses for 2 years now and they accept their condition as an allergy.
- My supervisor agrees to come to my cubicle to witness the cigarette smoke coming from my vent, but he holds a cup of coffee under his nose and says that he smells breakfast.
- I mail my retirement papers to HQ in Washington. I buy a telephone, get telephone service, electric service, get a used refrigerator, start shopping for a computer, printer, and paper shredder.
- My first book, Diderot and the Metamorphosis of Species (Routledge), is published. I am determined to earn my Ph.D.

- 2008 – Cyclone Nargis hits the breadbasket of Myanmar with surgical precision; the international banks had been trying to gain access to Myanmar, but the junta would not let them in.
  - Bush aide and Internet strategist Michael Connell dies in an airplane crash. He was just about to go public about vote-tampering in the 2004 presidential elections.
  - On October 1 the military is deployed within 100 miles of US borders. The last week of September I saw USMC license plates all over Rego Park.
- Psyop: a red pickup truck featuring a GI pointing a rifle on the back of its cab is parked in various places at various times. The neighbors notice.
- I retire from Customs.
- When the boiler kicks on and carbon monoxide seeps from the cracked steam pipe in the bathroom, I pass out. I come to on the floor in the hallway.
- My gums get infected and my dentist has to clean me up.
- Suffering from sleep deprivation via electronic shocks administered throughout the night, I have suddenly begun to age rapidly in appearance.
- Neighbors across the street says that their furniture shakes all night as if there were an earthquake; one has red pinpricks all over her body; she hears a scream next to her ear at night; they

both get a thud and moving wave on their blankets as a plane approaches.

- White box trucks repeatedly stand in a double parked position in front of my building. The men in the cab remain idle for a half hour. Then they step on the gas. Traffic enforcement never gives them a ticket.

- I start keeping a log, minute by minute, all night long, so that readers might be able to match the time with specific planes, if they know how.

- I hear musical notes in my head without the benefit of the ear.

- High pitch ringing permeates the bedroom.

- Electronic beeps wake me up.

- I wake up gasping for air.

- I hear pellets bouncing off the window glass.

- My walls crack from ceiling to floor. Adjacent walls are separating from each other. Wooden slats in the floor are spaced farther and farther apart as the floor separates.

- A woman holding a cellphone stands behind me in the Elmhurst Library, reading my monitor.

- I get struck on the back of the head as a plane emerges over the building behind me.

- A reflection of an "X" in a circle appears on the brick façade of the next building between 9–10 AM each morning.

- Graffiti that says "RUFF RIDERS" is painted in bright white paint behind my building and on the roof.

- My second and third books, Evolutionism in Eighteenth-Century French Thought (Peter Lang) and An Eastern Orthodox View of Pascal (Light & Life) are published. I format the text for Lang's book according to specifications, setting up typefaces, type sizes, block quotes, running heads, etc. Thus I remain extremely focused on the minutiae of the publisher's requirements, despite the distractions in my apartment.

- 2009   Copenhagen conference on global warming is undercut by freezing weather and 4 inches of snow just as world leaders arrive to discuss how to fund global greenhouse gas emission cuts; President Obama returns to Washington as blizzard dumps 2 feet of snow on the city; cap and trade is before Congress.

- Several aluminum tarpaulins in my apartment are thoroughly riddled with holes as an aircraft is heard hovering above the building; NORTHCOM perforates them as they rest over my blankets, recklessly exposing me to EMs. I hear a sound like that of sand falling on a ceramic plate when the metal is being rifled.

- Sleeping in the kitchen, I suffer electrobolts to the brain and heart that leave me gasping for air. They make a gash in the wall just a few inches from my head. They decimate the wall behind the appliances. I hear taps off the appliances and floor when this is happening.

- During a heavy snowstorm in which all commercial air traffic is grounded, planes continually hover over my building all night, delivering shocks. They have to be military.

- EMP weapons made from dual-use components purchased on the Internet can bring down a plane.

- A reflection of an "X" in a circle appears on the brick façade of the next building between 9–10 AM each morning.

- New phenomena: a thud drops on the blanket directly over my body and remains there for a while, feeling like a weight; I hear a fine spray against the pillow or window; my muscles start to twitch before an airplane overpass.

- Sounds materialize in midair next to my ear; a car horn explodes inches from me, waking me up.

- A neighbor notices that chemtrails crisscross the sky, followed by rain which brings a cooling trend. She says that every time she sees the chemtrails, it rains the next day.

- A tiny golden spark shoots across the bedroom creating a gash in the bathroom wall on the other side and chipping a ceramic tile.

- I meet two brothers in the library who are getting electrobolts to the brain. One of them sleeps on the floor without the metal mattress springs beneath him.

- An NYPD car follows a driverless car down the street. This indicates that NYPD is working with the DARPA.

- A blind woman who lives in the descent path to JFK says that she experiences a fine electrical spark traveling up her leg at night.

- They were in my apartment: the plug to my laptop is now scratched and bent; it fits snuggly into the wall outlet when previously it used to drop out.

- When I get shocks at night, my neighbors get up, turn on their lights, walk around their apartments, and flush the toilet. The whole building awakens at the same time.

- The government blocks my access to Alex Jones websites.

- My fourth book, Miracles of the Orthodox Church (Light & Life) is published.
- I format the text of my fifth book according to the publisher's specifications.
- 2010   The Head of SOUTHCOM conducts an emergency preparedness drill in Miami to practice for a Haitian natural disaster the day before the Haitian earthquake. The Navy is off shore the night before. The next day the earthquake devastates the most populous area of the country.
- There is an earthquake in Chile just as Hillary Clinton is concluding her tour of Latin America: she appears with 25 satellite phones in hand, in a photo-op with outgoing President Michelle Bachelet.
- Peruvian glacier melts and drops down; it provided drinking water to the people living there.
- Volcano erupts in Iceland, disrupting air traffic and costing the airline industry $1 billion. Were put options purchased the week before?
- Gang members are rounded up in Far Rockaway, Jamaica, and Newburg, NY; undocumented Russians are apprehended in Rego Park. Was terahertz imaging employed in these operations?
- I purchase a Nikon P100 camera, take 3,000 photographs, and several high def movies of military planes and black helicopters circling my roof.
- I shave my head and photograph the scarring on my crown that remains from the high-power spike of energy that the government directed at me 3 ½ years ago.
- I figured out the purpose of the chemtrails: they create cloud cover within minutes; the military flies above the cloud cover; we hear the planes, but we cannot see them; they harass the entire neighborhood all night long.
- Some chemtrails disappear in 2 minutes leaving a gray haze through which the naked eye cannot see; others create fluffy white clouds that luminesce. The Pentagon can now make all evidence of chemtrails disappear immediately.
- A line is carved across the tiles in front of the bathroom window.
- A salesman in a local electronics store gets shocks to the brain when he is sitting in his chair watching TV.
- A furniture delivery man gets a shock to his brain in his apartment.

- The people in a high-rise in Forest Hills are getting shocks to the brain; they have to have the super in every 2 months to repair the gashes in the walls.
- A super in Forest Hills gets shocks to his brain at night.
- Cars are parked here with signs in the window that read "ON OFFICIAL US MILITARY BUSINESS."
- There are cars with Air Force license plates.
- My friend gets an electrobolt to the brain as she is talking to me on the street in Forest Hills.
- I put up double sheets of aluminum tarps across every room in the apartment. They do not help: the EMs come in diagonally from outer walls and the moving waves continue all night.
- My neighbor develops a tumor in the lymph nodes of the groin. I notice that the moving waves are targeted towards my armpits and groin. She has also developed high blood sugar and elevated platelets, like the ambassadors in Russia during the Pandora Project. Her cat cries out in the middle of the night and hides behind the toilet.
- Another neighbor announces that she has gotten cancer twice.
- Two men in post office say that they have developed a rash; their skin is 3 different colors; the white part of their eyes has turned gray; they surmise that it is from aluminum-based chemicals and barium in chemtrails.
- Three dead fish appear on the asphalt outside my windows.
- Now there are multiple reflections of "X" in a circle in the brick of the next building and on the pavement around my building.
- New phenomena: electronic whacks leave black and blue discolorations on my legs; my teeth involuntarily click together as a plane approaches.
- They remove the date and time stamp from my photos. This is distressing as I need them to show that on 04-30-10 at 7 AM there was a stormy black cloud directly over my roof, but the sky was blue over the next building, 20 feet away.
- My fifth book, Freedom in French Enlightenment Thought (Peter Lang) is published.
- I complete Microwave Experiment, Microwave War and The Science behind Microwave War, remaining focused despite the fact that the government is allowing me to get only 4 hours of sleep each night.

- 2011   KCBS-TV's Serene Branson begins talking gibberish outside the Staples Center after the Grammys.
- Global Toronto reporter Mark McAllister suffers garbled speech while broadcasting.
- Madison, Wisconsin's WISC-TV news anchor Sarah Carlson begins talking nonsense during her live broadcast.
- Judge Judith Sheindlin starts talking gibberish in her Los Angeles courtroom.
- The tumor in my neighbor's groin is found to be malignant; she feels an electrical spark travel along her leg at night; her cat cries miserably.
- A 59-year old Russian immigrant feels a moving wave across the blanket at night and light pressure gently brush across his face.
- I continually get moving waves and electrical sparks all night long as there are violent snaps against the walls and paint fragments and broken plaster carpet the floor. An aircraft targets the lymph nodes in my armpits and groin.
- My sixth book, Search for Self in Other in Cicero, Ovid, Rousseau, Diderot and Sartre (Peter Lang) is published.